THE CLOSING OF THE LIBERAL MIND

# The Closing
# of the Liberal Mind

## HOW GROUPTHINK AND
## INTOLERANCE DEFINE THE LEFT

Kim R. Holmes

Encounter Books
New York · London

First American edition published in 2016 by Encounter Books, an activity of Encounter for Culture and Education, Inc., a nonprofit, tax exempt corporation.
Encounter Books website address: www.encounterbooks.com

Manufactured in the United States and printed on acid-free paper. The paper used in this publication meets the minimum requirements of ANSI/NISO Z39.48–1992 (R 1997) (*Permanence of Paper*).

FIRST AMERICAN EDITION

Design and composition by Wilsted & Taylor Publishing Services

LIBRARY OF CONGRESS CATALOGING-IN-PUBLICATION DATA
Names: Holmes, Kim R., author.
Title: The closing of the liberal mind : how groupthink and intolerance define the left / by Kim R. Holmes.
Description: New York : Encounter Books [2016] | Includes bibliographical references and index.
Identifiers: LCCN 2015037276| ISBN 9781594038518 (hardcover : alk. paper) | ISBN 9781594038525 (ebook)
Subjects: LCSH: Liberalism–United States. | Freedom of speech–United States. | Political correctness–United States. | Toleration–United States. | Right and left (Political science).
Classification: LCC JC574.2.U6 H655 2016 | DDC 320.51/30973–dc23
LC record available at http://lccn.loc.gov/2015037276

# CONTENTS

# INTRODUCTION

When most people think of intolerance, they imagine a racist taunting a black person. Or they may envision a male chauvinist hurling bigoted insults at women. It seldom occurs to them that intolerance comes in all political shapes and sizes. A protester storming a stage and refusing to let someone speak is intolerant. So, too, are campus speech codes that restrict freedom of expression. A city official threatening to fine a pastor for declining to marry a gay couple is every bit as intolerant as a right-winger wanting to punish gays with sodomy laws. Intolerance exists on the right and the left. It knows no exclusive political or ideological affiliation. It happens any time someone uses some form of coercion, either through government fiat or public shaming rituals, to restrict open debate and forcefully eliminate opponents from the playing field.

There is a word that describes this mentality. It is illiberal. For centuries we have associated the word "liberal" with open-mindedness. Liberals were people who were supposed to be tolerant and fair and who wanted to give all sides a hearing. They cared about everyone, not just their own kind. They wanted to include people in the exercise of liberty, not exclude them. They believed in pluralism. By contrast, illiberal people were hardheaded in their opinions and judgmental about others' behaviors, hoping to control what other people thought and said and to cut off debate. In extreme cases they would even use violence to maintain political power and exclude certain kinds of people from having a say in their government.

Sadly, the kind of liberalism we used to know is fast disappearing from America. All too often, people who call themselves progressive liberals are at the forefront of movements to shut down debates on college campuses and to restrict freedom of speech. They are eager to cut corners, bend the Constitution, make up laws through questionable court rulings, and generally abuse the rules and the Constitution in order to get their way. They establish "zero-tolerance" regimes in schools where young boys are suspended for nibbling breakfast pastries into the shape of a gun.[1] They claim to be unrelenting defenders of science, yet they will run scientists who deviate even slightly from climate change orthodoxy right out of the profession. They are supposedly great haters of bigotry but sometimes speak of Christians in the most bigoted manner imaginable, as if Christians were no better than fascists. They support laws and regulations that over-criminalize everyday aspects of American life, to the point that people can be fined or imprisoned for violating some environmental or other regulation they did not know existed. They can be neighborhood bullies or petty tyrants on town or county councils, launching campaigns to stop people from building houses they do not like or going after the parents of "free-range children."[2]

These are not theoretical threats, but actual incidents from recent years. Once known as the quintessential free thinkers, liberal intellectuals today are primarily keepers of a stifling ideological orthodoxy. They have become like mandarin servants of today's ruling class, presiding, for example, over academic departments teaching hopelessly incoherent subject matter ("queer studies," anyone?) while eagerly awaiting the next government grant, contract, or invitation to a White House party.

American liberals are, in short, becoming increasingly illiberal. They are surrendering to the temptations of the closed mind.

We must be careful about what this means. There are hard

(sometimes very hard) and soft forms of illiberalism that exist regardless of their ideological (left-right) variations. The hard forms are totalitarian or authoritarian. They rely on the threat of force in some measure to maintain power, and they are invariably anti-democratic and anti-liberal. Think of communism, fascism, and all the various hybrids of authoritarian regimes, from Putin's Russia to Islamist states that support terrorism. Soft forms of illiberalism, on the other hand, are *not* totalitarian or violent. Outwardly they may observe the limits constitutional democracies place on the arbitrary use of power, but there is a suspicion that liberal democracies are not fully legitimate. For example, nationalists and military regimes see them as weak and corrupt, incapable of maintaining order and protecting national security. On the other side of the political spectrum, leftists often judge liberal democracies as economically and socially unjust because they are capitalist. Since most liberal democracies still allow conservatives to have a voice in the democratic process, leftists find them wanting, and in some cases condemn them outright as inherently oppressive (of racial and sexual minorities, for example), precisely because conservatives still have a voice.

Hard forms of illiberalism certainly exist in America today. On the right they are manifest in the form of hard-core racists and nativists, and on the left as communists, anarchists, or any radical who openly threatens violence. But soft illiberalism is present as well, and in America today it is pervasive. Much of its growth and energy is a left-wing phenomenon.

This brings me to the subject of definitions. Historically, a progressive liberal was viewed as someone who imbibed the intellectual nectars of both progressivism and classical liberalism. The progressive tradition is easily recognizable. It is the legacy of such prominent progressives from the turn of the 20th century as Herbert Croly, John Dewey, Teddy Roosevelt, Woodrow Wilson, and others. The classical liberal tradition is less well known, and as a result our understanding of it is murkier. Classical liberalism is a set of ideas about individual liberty and constitutional government inherited from the moderate Enlightenment.[3] In America those ideas influenced the Revolution and the founding of the Republic. In Europe they were taken up in the 19th century by such liberals as Benjamin Constant, David Ricardo, Alexis de Tocqueville, François Guizot, and John Stuart Mill.

Although originally swimming in the same intellectual stream, American progressives and classical liberals started parting company in the late 19th century. Progressives initially clung to freedom of expression and the right to dissent from the original liberalism, but under the influence of socialism and social democracy they gradually moved leftward. Today they largely hold classic liberalism—especially as manifested in small-government conservatism and libertarianism—in contempt. Thus, what we call a "liberal" today is not historically a liberal at all but a progressive *social democrat*, someone who clings to the old liberal notion of individual liberty when it is convenient (as in supporting abortion or decrying the "national security" state), but who more often finds individual liberties and freedom of conscience to be barriers to building the progressive welfare state.

To untangle this confusing web of intellectual history, we need a more accurate historical rendering of what "progressive liberals" actually are. If they are not really liberals, then what are they? As this volume will explore in more depth, they are *postmodern leftists*. A postmodernist is someone who believes that ethics are completely and utterly relative, and that human knowledge is, quite simply, whatever the individual, society, or political powers say it is. When mixed with radical egalitarianism, postmodernism produces the agenda of the radical cultural left—namely, sexual and identity politics and radical multiculturalism. These causes have largely taken over the progressive liberal agenda and given the Democratic Party most of its energy and ideas. The illiberal values inherent in these causes have been imported from such movements as neo-Marxism. Combined with the dreams of the old social democratic–socialist left, of either dismantling or radically containing capitalism, the culture of the postmodern left today is a very potent force in politics.

Many books discuss the intolerance of the left. Allan Bloom's *The Closing of the American Mind* (1987), which inspired the title of this book, focused on the American academy. Other recent books lament the liberal groupthink of the U.S. media.[4] I intend to paint a much broader picture. I will show that the decline of liberalism has been long in the making, and that the illiberalism in the media and academic worlds described in these books is now widespread in the political system and rapidly gaining ground in society. Illiberalism is not only the defining feature of what we call progressive liberalism today; it is, in fact, the predominant worldview of Barack Obama's Democratic Party. The focus of this discussion, however, will not be on that party, since political parties have often changed their platforms and priorities to win elections. The focus instead will be on how deeply this progressive illiberalism infects many aspects of our society today—so much so that our very identity as the nation that championed liberty in the 20th century is threatened, and we may not keep that title for long in the 21st.

I would not wish to leave the readers of this book entirely without hope. Despite the rather gloomy prognosis I offer for the future of American liberalism, it may still be possible to save it from the ravages of the postmodern left. Moderate liberals and conservatives have one thing in common: neither has an interest in the triumph of illiberal values in America. Both should like to see a country in which freedom of expression, open intellectual inquiry, constitutional democracy, and the rule of law prevail. If not a unified front, at least a tacit alliance against illiberalism and extremism may be possible. However, in order for this to happen, liberals have some very deep soul-searching to do. Frankly, it should not be left up to a conservative to point out the vulnerabilities that threaten to destroy their movement. Liberals themselves should be concerned and stepping in to save liberalism from itself.

A word about the purpose of the book: It is ultimately about ideas. It is about how they have evolved and are shaping today's politics and culture. Mixing intellectual history with an analysis of contemporary politics is tricky. People always wonder whether the ideas developed by intellectuals lead or merely follow the broader evolution of historical events. In reality they do both, but I do believe that ideas developed by serious thinkers, once they are digested by the popular political culture, are more influential than many people think. It is not about everyone being mini-philosophers, but about people looking for reasons and justifications to do what they do. This does not happen in a historical vacuum. Historical ideas, and ideas in general, are like lighthouses helping people to navigate in the darkness. Captains of ships fighting the offshore currents that take them this way or that will latch on to known sources of light to find their way home. For a culture such as ours, ideas are these known sources of light, and we underestimate them at our peril.

Not everything done in the name of progressive liberalism today can be traced back to its intellectual roots. But much of it can be. That, at least, is the slice of the matter that I explore and hope to add to the current debate about the nature of contemporary American liberalism.

THE CLOSING OF THE LIBERAL MIND

# ONE

# The Decline of American Liberalism

Americans think we know what the word "liberal" means. A liberal is a "progressive," or someone who is "liberal-minded." It is a person who supports gay marriage, higher taxes on the rich, and bans on "hate speech." It is a politician, activist, or scholar who believes that a vast swath of the American people—like American history itself—is infected with unconscious racial and class prejudices, and that the Constitution is outdated and, more often than not, a barrier to equality and civil rights. It is someone who believes strongly in using the power of government to redistribute income and to force people to adhere to a liberal notion of social justice. Today, a liberal can be a moderate Democrat like Bill Clinton, a self-described socialist like Bernie Sanders, or even the protester who jumped the stage at a progressive conference to shout Sanders down.[1] "Liberal" is a fairly elastic word, and it is used broadly to mean anyone who is on the left of the political spectrum.

Whatever a liberal is today, it is not the same as the liberals of the 18th century or the progressives of the 19th century. It is not even the same as those of the New Deal or Lyndon Johnson's Great Society in the 20th. To understand the difference and the huge extent of the change in American liberalism, we need a historical reference point. We must understand what liberalism was in order to grasp how far it has declined as a viable American idea. Unfortunately for the liberties of Americans tomorrow, the change has been as dramatic as Darth Vader's devolution to the Dark Side in *Star Wars*.

## WHAT IS LIBERALISM?

Historically, liberalism evolved largely from the ideas of the moderate Enlightenment, particularly its British and Scottish variants. The most famous classical liberal theorists were John Locke, the Baron de Montesquieu, Adam Smith, Immanuel Kant, and James Madison. The ideas they developed helped shape the American Founding; but they also spread across Europe after the Napoleonic era to establish the liberal tradition there, which was largely a negative reaction to the excesses of the French Revolution. Although dormant today, the liberal tradition in Europe was quite vibrant in the 19th century. Such luminary liberal figures as Alexander von Humboldt in Prussia; Benjamin Constant, François Guizot, and Alexis de Tocqueville in France; and Jeremy Bentham, Herbert Spencer, and John Stuart Mill in Britain developed sophisticated theories of liberalism that are studied to this day.

Whether of the American or European variety, liberalism is a set of shared principles. As British political journalist Edmund Fawcett explains in *Liberalism: The Life of an Idea* (2014),[2] these principles are:

- Conflicts of interest and beliefs are inevitable, and it is foolish and even dangerous to try to eliminate them.

- Superior power of some people over others is not to be trusted.

- The meaning of history and human aspirations are open to change and thus should never be assumed to be static or unchangeable.

- There should be moral limits on how superior people should treat other people, and limits on what the state, in the name of the people, can do to obstruct a person's chosen enterprise or belief.

◆ Harking back to John Locke and Thomas Jefferson, there is the assumption that one person's rights extend only until they infringe on the rights of someone else.

From these principles arise a set of core practices of the liberal political order. Among the most important are religious toleration, freedom of expression and discussion, and restrictions on police behavior. They also include the practice of free elections, establishment of a constitutional government based on the separation of powers, respect for private property, and belief in the sanctity and freedom of personal contracts. These practices are joined by what New York University political science professor Stephen Holmes calls "core norms or values," which mirror in practice the principles outlined above.[3] One is personal security, whereby the monopoly of violence enjoyed by the state is monitored and regulated by law. Another is individual liberty, whereby the person is given a sphere for the exercise of freedom of conscience, which includes the right to be different and to believe or think something even if one's neighbors or the majority disagree. Also vital is the freedom to travel and emigrate. Although it was not always the case in classical liberal theory, liberalism today assumes respect for democracy—namely, that all citizens have the right to participate in self-government regardless of race, class, creed, or gender.

These principles and practices revolve around efforts to solve a particular set of problems. One is how to preserve the freedom of the individual. Thomas Jefferson and the American Founders tended to take Locke's view that rights were possessed by individuals originally living in a state of nature, and that the purpose of government was to protect those rights. Rights were natural rights, bequeathed by God or nature, and they were, as Jefferson described them in the Declaration of Independence, "unalienable." The French liberal Benjamin Constant, writing many years after Jefferson, took the sovereignty of the individual even further, stating in *Principles of Politics Applicable to All Representative Governments* (1815) that "There is a part of human existence that remains of necessity individual and independent, and which lies by right utterly beyond the range of society."[4]

Today, many social scientists believe the liberal conception of the individual is a fiction.[5] Individuals are either socially constructed, to the point of disappearing as individuals, or they have acquired a new kind of individuality, often called dignity, that comports more easily with contemporary norms of social justice. Most philosophers, under the spell of what we will shortly describe as postmodernism, dismiss the notion of universal justice—the idea that a single ethical reference point exists for all people and all times. Under natural law, universalism had been a cornerstone of classical liberalism, but it is now largely rejected by modern philosophy. Some liberal theorists such as John Rawls resisted this trend, holding on to a newly constructed universalism that could survive the critiques of neo-Marxism and postmodernism. But they have been overtaken by events. Most of philosophy today is totally at odds with classic liberalism.

One of the most important differences between liberalism and socialism concerns the issue of equality. It is a well-known story, but one that is often misunderstood. Stephen Holmes describes the liberal approach to equality this way:

> Concerning equality, the liberal attitude is traditionalism turned upside down. In traditional societies, as liberals understood them, inherited inequalities were accepted, while new economic inequalities were unwelcome. Liberals wanted to reverse this pattern, banning aristocracy while considering new inequalities of wealth as perfectly legitimate. The liberal societies they helped construct reject all claims to inherited monopoly, especially the authority of a

few "great" families owning large tracts of land. But classical liberals were not militantly egalitarian because they thought that *poverty and dependency* were more pressing problems than economic inequality itself.[6]

Holmes's explanation dispenses with one of the hoariest myths about classical liberalism. For centuries, socialists have been accusing classical liberals of only wanting to protect the rich. They forget that the original impulse of the liberal idea was to overturn the power of the rich of their time, namely, the aristocracy and the monarchy. Liberals objected to inherited wealth and to the static legal order of the *ancien régime* that froze the social classes in place. They believed poverty and dependency existed because people did not have opportunities to rise and improve their station in life. Inequality would either go away or at least be ameliorated if the ability of the government to freeze the social order were abolished.

Later in history, when liberals were locked in battle with socialists, this liberal principle remained. By then, it was no longer aristocrats and kings who wanted to establish a new static order enforced by the state, but socialists and communists. Given the fact that communist societies did end up in such dire poverty, perhaps socialists should have been more attentive. It turns out there is a relationship between dependency and poverty after all, one that exists apart from the particular forms a statist regime may take. Whether the state is communist or feudal, it creates conditions by which large numbers of people are forced into and then kept in poverty.

Another liberal principle involves the question of power. Following in the footsteps of Montesquieu, James Madison and the other framers of the U.S. Constitution believed power must be divided among the branches of government: allowing power to be concentrated in a single sovereign monarch was a recipe for tyranny. Distrust of centralized power got a boost from the negative reactions to the abuses of the French Revolution. The liberal François Guizot, Prime Minister of France in 1847 and 1848, maintained that restraining power was the first task of all politics. What he and other post-Revolutionary French liberals such as Constant and Tocqueville feared most was the "radical illegitimacy of all absolute power."[7] As Fawcett puts it, power had to be "talked back to,"[8] lest it become a beast of domination. The mistrust of power was present not only in the American Constitution's separation of powers but also in the near-constant American suspicion, present even in populist politics, of any kind of untouchable concentrated authority, whether manifested in government, economic monopoly, or the status pretentions of an elite social class.

Related to the mistrust of power in the liberal tradition was an abiding faith in freedom of speech and expression. So powerful was this principle in America that it was enshrined in the First Amendment to the Constitution. Madison, its author, thought freedom of the press would be a check on the power of government. Largely reflecting Locke's notion of religious tolerance, freedom of expression was directly linked to freedom of religion, which is also guaranteed by the First Amendment. In Europe the element of religious freedom was largely missing, but liberals there had an equally strong belief in freedom of expression. Guizot thought allowing unorthodox opinions was the only way to prevent the abuse of power, and British liberal philosopher John Stuart Mill made freedom of expression a central tenet of his thought. In the 20th century, liberals such as the Briton Isaiah Berlin and the Austrian Karl Popper argued that allowing for freedom of thought was the best way to combat the scourge of mass democracy gone mad—namely, totalitarianism. Freedom of expression was a fragile liberal principle, often honored only in the breach even by liberal governments. But it was an unassailable principle that practically all liberals believed in one way or another.

Finally, there is the principle of economic freedom. Normally associated with the great founding theorists of modern capital-ism—Locke, Adam Smith, Jean-Baptiste Say, and David Ri-cardo—the idea that people were entitled to their property always has been a key liberal idea. It is important in this respect to realize that Smith and other early theorists were not considered econo-mists per se, but rather moral philosophers. They were trying to discover the laws of economy that suited the interests of every-one, regardless of class or personal fortune. They believed these laws governed economics, but they also assumed they mirrored the natural laws of morals for all mankind. Discovering what these economic laws were was just another way of getting at the funda-mentals of natural law.

In the 19th century the altruistic motive of economic liberal-ism often got lost, particularly in Europe, as moral philosophy gave way to the cold new discipline of economics. In Britain liberalism came to be widely perceived to mean defending the wealth of the propertied classes, thus inadvertently becoming a prop for the old class system. Not so in America. Here, economic freedom and democracy worked hand in hand. The poor aspired to be rich, and there was enough freedom for everyone (provided you were not a slave in the antebellum South) to realize their dreams. Put simply, in America, freedom plus democracy equals equality of opportunity and equality before the law. The light hand of government over commerce, and the existence of the rule of law to buttress business and contracts, made the growth of the American economy a liberating instrument of peaceful social revolution.

The principle of economic freedom applied also to free trade. Both in America and in Europe it was a key liberal economic principle. The British Empire put it into practice after the repeal of the Corn Laws in 1846. In antebellum America, the planter class in the South favored free trade while the manufacturing North tended to be protectionist. Whether in America or Eu-rope, protecting free trade and property rights are two sides of the same coin. To this day they remain central features of classical liberalism, explored theoretically by economists and philosophers such as Milton Friedman and Richard Epstein, and largely extant in the political platforms of the Republican Party in the United States and the liberal political parties of continental Europe.

Behind all these principles is an assumption, as Jefferson once paraphrased: "The earth belongs in usufruct to the living" generation.[9] Put another way it is the belief that every generation must find its own way of practicing the enduring principles of liberty without encumbering future generations. Although somewhat controversial when Jefferson uttered it, this dictum contains the seedling of the liberal progressive idea that societies must always change, with the hope that it will be for the better. It is, frankly, a double-edged principle, always containing the seeds of its own destruction: after all, if each new generation gets to decide what liberty is, it is perfectly free to do away with liberty altogether. Nevertheless, the more enduring consequence is the notion that society and the political system must remain forever open to new ideas. Any new idea that emerges may be considered and tried, but only insofar as it does not impede the openness of the system itself. The view that progress is open-ended and requires never settling on any "end-of-history ideology" is a fundamental principle of liberalism. It can be seen not only in Jefferson but in the great early European liberals such as von Humboldt and Constant. It lived on in the 20th century in the ideas of Berlin and Popper, who incorporated it into their notions of pluralism and the open society.

### THE PRACTICE OF LIBERALISM

We have reviewed the history of liberalism, but what about liberalism in practice? It is one thing to have fanciful ideas and principles, but what do they look like in action?

Edmund Fawcett has developed a useful taxonomy. He has

drawn up a list of instrumental principles that capture those of liberalism in action. In keeping with its original defensive posture against tyranny, these principles are largely negative, that is, they identify things that should not be done or that could keep bad things from being done. They are: 1) nonintrusion; 2) nonexclusion; 3) nonobstruction; and 4) balance.[10]

Fawcett defines nonintrusion as being "about not compromising people's security. Primarily legal, it enjoins a cluster of restraints on state, market, and society."[11] Examples include carving out a private sphere of freedom where no state or social majority can interfere and not infringing on freedom of speech. Liberals have different takes on how this principle works. Laissez-faire economists believed nonintrusion protected commerce from state interference, while American progressives at the turn of the 20th century applied it against corporate monopolies. Radical liberals (otherwise known as libertarians) believe it is the central idea of liberty. Despite these different interpretations, nonintrusion is an enduring instrumental principle that no philosophy calling itself liberal can ignore.

Nonexclusion is more complicated, mainly because it has been understood in different ways throughout history. Early on it was simply an effort to apply Jefferson's dictum that "all men are created equal," as prescribed by liberal interpretations of natural law. If every person was equal in the eyes of God or nature, then in theory at least no one should be excluded from the polity. Of course, the principle did not always apply to everyone in practice, not least of all in the case of slavery. And indeed, for most of the past two hundred years the story of nonexclusionism was about breaking down social barriers and adding formerly excluded minorities to the new liberal democratic order. By the end of the 20th century, however, nonexclusion had more or less evolved into its more positive twin, inclusiveness. It was a subtle shift but a profoundly powerful one politically. It was the main agent for transforming political liberalism into social liberalism, that is, making liberalism a political program aiming for social equality.

As for the principle of nonobstructionism, Fawcett defines it this way: "Nonobstruction, socially, included equality of opportunity, the borderless ideal of removing barriers to social advance. Economically, nonobstruction found expression in volumes of mid-nineteenth-century legislation that broke down old commercial barriers."[12] Thus, government should not interfere too much in the private economy, not only because it is economically inefficient to do so but also because it blocks people from having equal opportunity to get ahead. It was assumed that any action by the government would be arbitrary and benefit some special interest. The emerging socialist notion that the government represented social justice for all was dismissed as injurious to individual freedom. Notwithstanding the growing legitimacy of democratic politics, which dramatically "socialized" liberalism, the liberal idea remained fixed on the assumption that there are limits to what the state and society can do to obstruct persons from reaching their full potential. The principle applied not only to equality of opportunity in the economy, but also to the freedom of people to hold their own views about politics and religion.

Finally there is the instrumental principle of balance. One of the secrets of liberalism's success over the centuries has been that it was flexible and open to change. There were always two opposing poles in liberalism—individualism and the needs of society—that had to be in balance in order for it to work. In the early days there was an emphasis on individual rights and the fear of collective action by government. But as the 19th century wore on, those fears diminished as liberalism became democratized and made more compatible with the value of social equality. Regardless of the different ways liberals executed the balance, one thing that always distinguished liberalism from socialism was its refusal to give up entirely on the core liberal principles surrounding liberty and individual rights.

## WHAT IS CLASSIC AMERICAN LIBERALISM?

Before we consider what classic American liberalism is, we should define what is meant by *classic*. Classical liberalism most often refers to liberalism before the 20th century. It is the individualistic and laissez-faire liberalism of Constant, Ricardo, and Mill in Europe and the small-government constitutional liberalism of the American Founders. It is distinguished from the social liberalism that emerged in the 20th century and is today a central feature of American progressive liberalism. Some libertarians call themselves classic liberals. There is some truth in this claim. Yet there are also significant historical differences, having to do with the U.S. Constitution and a unique political culture that separate America's classic style of liberalism from the more theoretical and sometimes doctrinaire ideas of libertarianism. Conservatives, on the other hand, often refer to classic liberalism as shorthand for their beliefs in limited government and the primacy of individual rights, particularly with respect to property and freedom of expression.

Scholars have from time to time tried to offer grand theories about liberalism's meaning to the American nation. Harvard professor Louis Hartz argued in *The Liberal Tradition in America* (1955) that Americans are quintessential liberals.[13] Lacking a feudal heritage and born essentially middle class, Americans did not develop a strong conservative or socialist outlook in their politics and governmental institutions. Instead liberalism is a national consensus. More recently, Richard A. Epstein, a legal theorist with libertarian leanings, has argued in *The Classical Liberal Constitution* (2014) that the U.S. Constitution embodies the classical liberal tradition both in spirit and in law.[14] There have been many other attempts to explain the American historical experience as fundamentally liberal, and they have often been met with strong disagreement from scholars. But suffice it to say that most agree that what we call the classical liberal tradition, if not actually explaining everything about America in some grand theory, has nonetheless been quite influential in shaping American history.

As a reference point, then, for understanding the meaning of classic American liberalism, it is best to start with the Founders. Rather than offer them up as though they were mere mouthpieces for John Locke's philosophy, it would be more useful to relate what they actually said and believed. Unsurprisingly, we discover that although they do sound a lot like Locke and Montesquieu, they have their own take on their ideas.

There are two aspects of the classical liberalism of the Founders to consider. One involves how they understood philosophical concepts such as liberty, rights, the individual, and natural law. The second can be called constitutional liberalism, having to do with how they translated their concepts into the governing rules of the U.S. Constitution, covered in detail in *The Federalist Papers*.[15]

Let's start with liberty. The Founders clearly understood it mainly as freedom from government tyranny. They essentially took the liberal tradition of Locke and others, with its belief in natural rights and the consent of the governed, and combined it with the English common law tradition. So long as the Crown respected their rights as Englishmen, they had no quarrel with Britain. But once Parliament breached that trust, thereby breaking the social contract, their right to revolt fell back on the natural rights—rights that Locke and others believed existed in the state of nature. Thus liberty and the right to revolt were grounded in natural law. Since governments were supposedly instituted to protect citizens' rights (indeed that was their sole purpose), any government that failed in that duty was illegitimate. Implicit in this right to revolt was the notion that government, and only government, was the source of tyranny. It established the quintessential American idea that freedom for the individual and for society rested solely on the question of how government treated people's rights.

Jefferson's unique spin on Locke notwithstanding, his rendering of Americans' rights in the Declaration of Independence is pretty standard fare. Rights are understood to belong to individuals. Moral law restricts what individuals should be allowed to do not only to themselves but to others. In fact, it was always understood that the restraining civil influence of moral law is absolutely necessary for liberty to succeed. Indeed, John Adams in 1798 said, "Our Constitution was made only for a moral and religious people. It is wholly inadequate to the government of any other." Thus liberty was political and extended only to the point that it began to infringe on the liberties of others. Individuals should have the freedom to decide what they believe in political and religious affairs, to assemble with whom they wish, and to petition the government. However, this did not give them the right to take other people's property or to infringe on the political rights of others. Liberty was not license.

America's constitutional liberalism was certainly informed by the ideas of Locke and other theorists of natural rights, but the U.S. Constitution is much more than a reification of Lockean liberalism. Its primary author, James Madison, studied far and wide as he prepared the rough draft of the Constitution, and clearly many influences even beyond Montesquieu and the republican tradition are at play. Once Alexander Hamilton's perspective is thrown into the mix of *The Federalist Papers*, the new American balance of constitutional liberalism emerges. It is a pragmatic result far more complex than pure liberal theory might suggest, and in some ways even a bit different.

For one thing, the Founders' view of human nature is bifurcated. It is both positive and negative at the same time. On the one hand there is the pure liberal position, perhaps represented best by Jefferson, that man is by nature good. Otherwise, if he is not, why trust him with self-government? Madison and Hamilton were less trustful.[16] Madison feared the tyranny of the majority while Hamilton dreaded anarchy. Despite their rather low opinion of human nature, Madison and Hamilton differed fundamentally over how to deal with it. Hamilton believed a strong government was necessary, while Madison (and of course Jefferson behind him) feared that very government could, in the hands of ambitious, low-minded men, become tyrannical. Madison's solution was to establish checks and balances in government. For Hamilton the solution was checks and balances plus a strong executive. Neither man was a democrat. Indeed, they were republicans opposed to both monarchy and the direct democracy of the people. Distrustful of human nature, Madison and Hamilton's views were closer to Thomas Hobbes's than to Locke's or Jean-Jacques Rousseau's.

Why is this understanding of human nature important? It reveals one reason why political liberalism in America would be largely insulated from social radicalism. Democracy would grow in America without the utopian expectations of radical egalitarianism implicit in the ideas of Rousseau and other devotees of the radical Enlightenment. It would grow slowly and organically in a constitutional liberal order that valued the natural rights of individuals over the collective passions of society. Indeed, democracy in America, as Tocqueville would point out some fifty years after the Founding, would be achieved not by top-down government action but through the bottom-up actions of civil society. This is significant for understanding classic American liberalism, because otherwise the persistent belief in the virtues of governmental restraint, which remained even as America democratized, would make no sense.

These distinctions are important for another reason. Americans have been, for most of their history, uncomfortable with the radicalism of the European revolutionary tradition. Natural law and natural rights, even as they were being repudiated by progressives, pragmatists, and other liberals, persisted in the public mind as a kind of archaic heritage. That is why in America, unlike in Europe, it was not so hard to explain the moral imperative of governmental restraint. Our revolution had been founded on this very idea, unlike in France, where revolution had been aimed at overthrowing feudal society. Religion in America reinforced the sense of universal justice originally developed by natural law. Even as historicists and progressives killed off natural law philosophy, that sense of universal justice survived as a religiously inspired idea in civil society. This meant there was an external moral point of reference that could not be changed or tampered with, even by the social contract or by the government. Mankind might be free to discover the different ways rights can be protected, but it had no right to use new social contracts, or changing attitudes about government, as an excuse to violate basic rights.

Put simply, rights were unalienable. According to the framers, the only way to protect them was to ensure a multiplicity of interests. As Madison said in Federalist No. 51, "Ambition must be made to counteract ambition,"[17] and,

> In a free government the security for civil rights must be the same as that for religious rights. It consists in the one case in the multiplicity of interests, and in the other in the multiplicity of sects. The degree of security in both cases will depend on the number of interests and sects; and this may be presumed to depend on the extent of country and number of people comprehended under the same government.[18]

The diversity of interests in all cases is necessary to protect the rights of everyone. The purpose of the government is not to produce absolute harmony between all competing interests, or for that matter between everyone's rights. Rather it is to establish an equilibrium of competing rights that can keep the social peace. A war of all against all would be anarchy. Absolute social peace would mean tyranny. Madison sought a middle way. Competition would serve the same purpose as the strong hand of the state to keep order, only it would be done without tyranny and oppression. As Madison explains:

> In a society under the forms of which the stronger faction can readily unite and oppress the weaker, anarchy may

as truly be said to reign as in a state of nature, where the weaker individual is not secured against the violence of the stronger; and as, in the latter state, even the stronger individuals are prompted by the uncertainty of their condition, to submit to a government which may protect the weak as well as themselves; so, in the former state, will the more powerful factions or parties be gradually induced, by a like motive, to wish for a government which will protect all parties, the weaker as well as the more powerful.[19]

Natural rights theory came on hard times in the 19th century. First it was democracy that challenged the primacy of individual rights. Then it was the historicism of German philosopher Georg Wilhelm Friedrich Hegel and others, which helped to create the relativism of the Progressive Era. Even science and positivism undermined it. Only truths empirically verified as facts are said to be true. Marxism attacked the liberal idea in a devastating pincer movement, hitting natural law's flanks on one side with historicism and on the other with science. American pragmatism undermined it as well, though without Marxism's dogma about history and scientific materialism. By the end of the 19th century, little natural law theory was being taught in academia. It had been largely consigned to a backwater of history and political studies in small colleges and schools.

It was not only science, historicism, and pragmatism that killed off natural rights and natural law. Its abuse by defenders of slavery also played an important role. John Calhoun was one of the worst offenders. He had once studied under a student of Hegel, and as a result he cynically believed in the primacy of self-interest in establishing a political order. This view enabled him to argue that slavery was part of the natural order.[20] Jefferson, Madison, John Adams, and other founding liberals never believed this to be true. But they did agree to the political compromise that saved slavery from immediate constitutional abolition.[21] It was a concession that mocked the solemn promises of natural rights, as

Abraham Lincoln and the abolitionists would argue years later. But it was also one that greatly weakened the moral authority of natural law theory.

In the end, what saved the universal ethical position of natural law in American history—the idea that there was one single reference point for justice and truth—was not philosophy. It was religion. As the 19th century slipped into secular progressivism, American liberalism was being lured away from its ancient roots by modernization and by new ideas of social freedom. And yet through it all, religion—mainly Christianity—kept the principle of natural law alive. Religion confirmed the natural law universalism of classical liberalism even as it rejected the secular assumptions that gave rise to it. The power of religion in civil society kept the substrates of American political culture firmly grounded in a sense of right and wrong, so much so that even modern progressives often approached politics as if it were a religious calling. That was how the progressive believers in the "social gospel" saw it. Try as they may, they could not entirely shake off America's religiosity.

Why is this important? Unlike in Europe, religion in America was an ally of classical liberalism, even its conscience. Without the religious outrage of the abolitionists, slavery might never have been abolished. Liberalism alone was not up to the job of getting rid of slavery as an entrenched economic interest. Religious conscience was necessary too. But religion alone did not undermine slavery. An abiding faith in the principles of the American Founding was also at work. As Lincoln argued time and time again, the original promise for abolishing slavery had been made in the Declaration of Independence, a promise that had been broken in the making of the original Constitution. Liberating the slaves would fix that mistake by making good on the promise. When the liberation of the slaves finally did come, it was done not by a rational liberal like Jefferson or a religious zealot like John Brown, but by a leader, Abraham Lincoln, who believed in both the Declaration and in God—in both classical liberalism and the Bible.

Conservative thinkers such as Russell Kirk and M. Stanton

Evans are therefore correct that the liberal tradition alone cannot explain the American Founding and the American system.[22] Other factors including religion, English common law, and medieval notions of contract, which Americans inherited from the British system, were important as well. However, it is not true, as Evans contends, that the Enlightenment played little or no role in the American Founding. The spirits of Montesquieu, Locke, and in Jefferson's case the French *philosophes,* were very much alive in the Founders' thinking.

The American tradition is not just one thing. It is not merely a set of philosophical ideas. It is definitely not an ideology. It is rather a coherent worldview that can rightly be said to encompass a political culture: a belief in limited government, respect for natural rights, the assumption that all people are equal before the law, and a faith in a higher power (above even government) that provides a moral compass for the country and its people. That culture changed as America democratized, but it would never completely disappear. Like the undertow of an ocean's wave, it would always tug at the forward motion of history, reminding Americans that what they became depended on what they had been.

## FROM PROGRESSIVISM TO NATIONAL LIBERALISM

The classical liberal tradition remained a vibrant political force in American history for most of the 19th century. But soon enough it came under direct assault. The aggressors were none other than the progressives who came to define American politics at the turn of the 20th century.

Progressivism was a full-frontal attack on every major principle of the Founding. Scholars like the young Woodrow Wilson believed the Constitution was outdated and needed to be revised to suit the needs of a modern industrial society. Thinkers such as Herbert Croly of *The New Republic* railed against the individualism of John Locke and its influence on American political culture. The philosopher John Dewey, like many of his progressive contemporaries, were critics of capitalism and longed for a political reform program that could ease the social disruptions it was causing. Politicians who advocated social reforms and direct democracy included Robert M. La Follette of Wisconsin. Nearly all progressives favored a strong central government to push through reforms. Such new social movements as the agrarian populists and urban-based union movements mobilized the lower classes into a force demanding more government action to solve social problems. Teddy Roosevelt, the arch-progressive, eagerly embraced big government not only domestically but internationally, to make America into a new imperial power.

It was a long way from Jefferson's agrarian republic and his fussing over the rights of yeoman farmers. Starting with Andrew Jackson, America had begun its slow march toward the democratic republic it is today. A bloody civil war wrenched the country from its early roots, empowering the federal government in ways Jefferson and Madison could scarcely have imagined. Population growth, industrialization, and mass immigration changed the face of America, creating huge teeming cities by the end of the 19th century. The expansion westward created a wholly different country with new social norms and seemingly endless economic and business opportunities. Responding to these changes, the two major political trends of the century—government expansion under the Whigs and the Republicans and the democratization of the masses, largely by Democrats—laid the foundations for the rise of the progressives at the end of the 19th century.

American progressivism was mainly a political project to create a new American style of social democracy. It wanted to do nothing less than completely transform the political constitution of the United States. As for its social values, they were a mixed bag and sometimes not as progressive as one might think. On the one hand, progressives championed women's suffrage, supported birth control, and in some cases campaigned for rights for black people. On the other hand some, such as Croly and Wilson, were known to harbor racist views.[23] Oddly enough, progressives tended to view eugenics as scientifically progressive. Planned Parenthood's founder Margaret Sanger, for example, was an outspoken proponent of eugenics as a method to rid the human race of the "unfit."[24] Some progressives were champions of a free press, but not all were. Teddy Roosevelt was a severe critic of unscrupulous journalists, whom he called "muckrakers." During World War I, President Wilson restricted free speech and freedom of assembly, which he believed undermined the war effort.

For all their famed liberality, progressives were not the wild-eyed radicals some have made them out to be. There were socialists like union leader Eugene V. Debs, but they were a minority. They believed women should have the vote, but they did not believe in absolute equality for women, and they did not share the anarchist's disregard for the value of the nuclear family in society. They were social democrats, but not in an internationalist sense of the word. Croly, Dewey, and Teddy Roosevelt were actually nationalists. Roosevelt was an imperialist.

During and after World War I, a second generation of progressives rose up to challenge the moderation of the old guard. America did have brushes with radical populism and anarchism in the 19th century, but those movements had been limited and restricted to certain parts of the country. The radicalism of this era was more widespread and hard-core. Suddenly America was facing Bolsheviks, anarchists, radical socialists, pacifists, and cultural radicals, among them Randolph Bourne, who chafed at Croly's nationalism and Wilson's cultural conservatism. Union movements joined up with antiwar protesters to launch campaigns in favor of free speech and freedom of association. The American Civil Liberties Union (ACLU) was established in 1920 by pacifist Roger Nash Baldwin, who was critical of the Wilson administration's clampdown on antiwar speech. Writers such as Upton Sinclair, Sinclair Lewis, John Dos Passos, and Sherwood Anderson turned literature into a weapon of radical politics.

It was in these years that freedom of speech—and the right to dissent—became associated with American progressivism. Antiwar protesters and unions championed the freedom of assembly and freedom of expression. Radical writers joined in to popularize their causes. During World War I public opinion had not been sympathetic to the radicals. Even the progressive Oliver Wendell Holmes, Jr., had believed a "clear and present danger" could be used as grounds for restricting speech. But shortly after the war the tide of opinion began to change. In the Supreme Court case *Abrams v. United States* (1919), Holmes shifted gears, coming out in favor of free speech. "The best test of truth," he argued, "is the power of the thought to get itself accepted in the competition of the market, and that truth is the only ground upon which their wishes safely can be carried out."[25] Freedom of speech was now indelibly a progressive cause, which was a bit ironic insofar as it had been the Founders' cause too.

Progressivism had a good run, but by the 1930s it was an intellectually spent force. Among intellectuals the old progressivism looked stale and out of date. Communism was the fresh new idea. Liberal intellectuals like I. F. Stone became involved in the communist Popular Front, and Whittaker Chambers volunteered to spy for the Soviet Union. In the wake of the Depression, there was a palpable sense of crisis among America's intellectuals. In the fall of 1932 many prominent writers and scientists in America signed a manifesto entitled "Culture and the Crisis" that rejected capitalism, supported the Communist Party, and called for an overthrow of the existing system through "the conquest of political power and the establishment of a workers' and farmers' government, which will usher in the Socialist commonwealth."[26] It was signed by Sherwood Anderson, Edmund Wilson, Waldo Frank, Sidney Hook, Malcolm Cowley, and Granville Hicks. Its sympathy for communism was anything but subtle, and it shows just how far the old progressivism had sunk in the estimation of America's intellectuals.

Eventually the funk of the Depression gave way to the "happy days" of the New Deal. At about the same time America's radical intellectuals were forsaking their country, most Americans were falling in love with an updated kind of progressivism. Franklin D. Roosevelt's New Deal was hyper-progressivism. Combined with Roosevelt's leadership in World War II, it solidified a powerful new liberalism that became the linchpin of American politics in the 20th century. Once joined to America's war effort in World War II, liberalism outgrew its old nationalist pants and stepped onto the world stage as a brassy, new kind of liberal international-ism. The world would be made safe not only for democracy in general, but American democracy in particular and the "Ameri-can Way of Life." Patriotism was back in style. So, too, was the old American can-do attitude that had been badly battered by the Depression. In this respect, the New Deal changed America for good. It not only helped bury the Depression, it also killed off the radical politics of the communist writers, making their gloomy pessimism superfluous.

Roosevelt jumpstarted American liberalism, but it was up to Harry Truman to seal the deal. Domestically Truman struggled to extend and maintain Roosevelt's programs, but internationally he succeeded even beyond Roosevelt's wildest dreams. As president, Truman basically created the post–World War II order. He in-ternationalized the liberalism Roosevelt had reinvented at home, essentially laying the groundwork for what we now call liberal democracy. Although often forgotten in the haze of recent his-torical revisionism, America's original Cold War posture against Soviet expansionism was in part progressively liberal. Liberal de-mocracy as we know it today—the belief in democratic elections, human rights, and the rule of law—was predicated on the belief that it was, as a form of liberalism, an alternative to communist totalitarianism. This idea was carried over into the quintessential

Cold War liberal presidency of John F. Kennedy, who along with his "best and brightest" intellectual advisors embodied the muscular international liberalism of that era.

Liberalism in the Cold War era basically had two camps. On one side were the radicals, many of whom had flirted with communism in the 1930s. Although no longer communist, they could not abide Truman or Dwight Eisenhower's Cold War policies. They included such intellectuals as Edmund Wilson, C. Wright Mills, and Dwight Macdonald. On the other side were the intellectuals sometimes known as national liberals. They were writers and thinkers like Seymour Martin Lipset, Daniel J. Boorstin, and Daniel Bell. Horrified by the dangers of totalitarianism but also unnerved by the failure of intellectuals in the 1930s to foresee the horrors of communism, these liberals rediscovered the value of America's original liberal tradition. Like Alexis de Tocqueville, they feared unfettered democracy and believed totalitarianism was the natural consequence of mass democracy run amok. They found a renewed faith in the American system, with its liberal checks and balances as barriers to the barbaric insanities of utopian politics. America, they said, stood above it all, representing an "end of ideologies," a new synthesis of practical equality and democracy.

By the onset of the Sixties, America's future looked bright. The country was in an optimistic mood. There was an attractive new liberal in the White House by the name of John F. Kennedy. Intellectuals were behind him. The popular culture was enthralled. It looked as if the new synthesis of liberalism and progressivism was here to stay.

Alas, it was not to be.

## THE NEW LEFT'S WAR ON LIBERALISM

The rise of the New Left in the 1960s represents a great divide in the history of progressive liberalism. After it, nothing was ever the same. The liberal optimism of a Lipset and even the socialist dreams of the *Partisan Review* were cast aside in a wave of apocalyptic warnings about the flaws and sins of America itself. Liberalism had been in decline for decades, but its revival during the New Deal, and the new prestige it enjoyed intellectually in the 1950s, came to an abrupt halt in the mid–1960s. Student radicals and neo-Marxist intellectuals ridiculed liberalism's most cherished values—individualism, pluralism, and tolerance—as capitalist instruments of oppression. Whereas turn-of-the-century progressives had been mere critics of America's liberal tradition, the New Left declared war on the whole lot—not only the classical liberalism of the Founders but also the progressive liberalism of Roosevelt, Truman, Lipset, Bell, and the New Frontier liberal intellectuals surrounding Kennedy. To the extent that America was, as Hartz had argued a few years earlier, a quintessentially liberal country, the New Left's beef with America was just that: America was evil precisely because it was liberal. To reach the new promised land of social justice, that tradition had to be expunged, or as President Obama would put it decades later, America's historical DNA had to be "cured."[27]

Allen J. Matusow explains the difference between the New Left and the old liberals:

> New leftists . . . were not liberals. Liberals, for example, saw politics as a means to resolve conflicts; early new leftists, as a way to achieve a moral society. Liberals had unlimited faith in the electoral process; new leftists were moving beyond elections to direct action, both as a tactic to achieve justice and as a way to testify to principle. Liberals still believed in America's anti-Communist world mission; most new leftists were trying to detach themselves from the Cold War, and a few were moving with the leadership of the Student Peace Union into a third camp that blamed both great powers for current tensions. And, beyond, issues, the early protestors shared a vague

feeling, entirely lacking in contemporary liberalism, that somehow the form of existing institutions discouraged authentic personal relations.[28]

Progressives had their radicals in Debs and Bourne, but they faced nothing like what the national liberals of the 1950s encountered in the New Left. Its surfeit of moral outrage was predicated on the very charge that liberalism had failed to live up to its promises. Tom Hayden of the Students for a Democratic Society (SDS) likened America's failures to a spiritual crisis. Its hierarchical, bureaucratic institutions supposedly deprived people of emotionally satisfying lives.[29] Hayden and his friends saw America as a cultural wasteland of isolated individuals living among a sea of hypocritical bureaucrats. America was bereft of real community because people lacked direct control over their lives. The New Left promised to give people new, authentic lives by liberating them from the tentacles of the "machine."

The civil war inside progressive liberalism in these years was partly generational. It was a fight between the spoiled Baby Boomers raised in the ease of the 1950s and the hard-bitten old liberal bulls like Lyndon Johnson who had been traumatized by depression and war. But there was more to it than that. This was also a profoundly ideological conflict. Unlike in earlier times when Marxist orthodoxies and even communism had failed to capture the liberal imagination, this time around the demands of the New Left grabbed the headlines and sent hundreds of thousands of people into the streets. Participatory or direct democracy, a very old dream of America's anarchists, came to be seen as more authentic than elections.[30] Philosophies of cultural Marxism fused with Freudianism to drive a new wave of politics aimed at sexual liberation. Not only did the New Left invent identity politics, giving the world the now popular doctrine of "white privilege"; it also spawned radical feminism, black separatism, and the transformation of environmentalism into an overt war on capitalism.

Instead of liberal evolution there must now be revolution, which toward the end of the Sixties found violent expression in the Weathermen, Black Panthers, and other movements.

To get an idea of how radical the New Left was, consider this: it was even too radical for the socialists at Irving Howe's *Partisan Review*.[31] The turn to neo-conservatism by former radicals such as Irving Kristol and Norman Podhoretz was in no small part the result of a confrontation with the radicalism of the New Left. There was something about the New Left that traditional socialists found unsettling. Despite their differences over doctrine, both national liberals and socialists distrusted fanaticism. When SDS members burned American flags or threw blood on police, they saw not a glorious Marianne waving the flag of the Revolution but the black jackboots of the brownshirts. To national liberals and old socialists alike, identity politics was not only incomprehensible but dangerous. For liberals it destroyed any hope for a just and liberal society, whereas for socialists it was a distraction from the underlying economic class problems of capitalism.

The New Left was like a solar superstorm. It flared up, emitting huge amounts of energy, but eventually burned itself out. By the early 1970s it was already a fading movement. On its own stated terms, the New Left was a huge failure. None of its ideas about direct democracy or the overthrow of bureaucratic institutions came to pass. If anything, its excesses helped give rise to the counterreaction of the Reagan era. Despite its immediate failures, however, it did sow the seeds for greater things to come. The New Left's intellectual storms broke down the lines of communication between the old and new progressivism. It severed links with traditions that would never be repaired. The radicals of the New Left bided their time. They marched through the institutions of society and worked on their radical theories quietly in their studies and workshops. It was only a matter of time before they—more accurately, their offspring—would get another chance at transforming America.

### THE LIBERTARIAN DISSENT

No story of American liberalism is complete that does not include the libertarians. They are sometimes referred to as classic liberals. That is true, but only partially. Some self-described libertarians such as Friedrich Hayek and Milton Friedman fit that description. But most libertarians are too radical philosophically to be described as classical liberals. In searching for a single word to describe them, historian Brian Doherty believes that

> the most significant thing about libertarianism, the element that distinguishes its unique place in modern American thought, is that it is *radical*. It takes insights about justice and order and the fight between liberty and power farther and deeper than most standard American liberals, patriots, or Jeffersonians.[32]

Libertarianism, therefore, is a species of liberalism, but it would be misleading to call it classical liberalism. Most doctrinaire libertarianism is actually radical liberalism; it is closer to the anarchistic spirit of the New Left than to the staid moderation of John Locke.

Brian Doherty calls libertarians "radicals for capitalism."[33] They may have roots in the ideas of classical liberalism, but they are overshadowed in their original intent by a tendency to push their logic to extremes. Driving the radical spirit is a penchant for utopian thinking not unlike that found in extreme ideologies on the far right or far left. Most libertarians care far more about the purity of their ideas than whether they are accepted by the political system. Libertarianism shares with classic liberalism a love of liberty and a mistrust of the state, but that is about all.

The differences between classic liberalism and libertarianism have a lot to do with different historical pedigrees. Classical liberalism was born in the 18th century and adjusted to the demands of democracy and industrialization in the 19th century. Libertarianism by contrast was a radical movement of dissent that formed mainly in the 20th century. It is not an old movement at all, but a very modern one.

Let's look at its historical roots. There are several: 1) the Austrian School of economics represented by Ludwig von Mises and Friedrich Hayek, who in turn drew on the influences of Austrian economists Carl Menger and Eugen Böhm von Bawerk; 2) the American tradition of anarchism developed by Benjamin R. Tucker, Lysander Spooner, Josiah Warren, and Alexander Berkman in the 19th century and taken up by radical libertarian Murray Rothbard in the 20th;[34] 3) the tradition of radical freedom, which had various permutations ranging from the super Americanism of novelists Rose Wilder Lane and Isabel Paterson, who influenced Ayn Rand, to the radical heroic individualism and moral relativism of late 19th-century German philosophers Max Stirner and Friedrich Nietzsche;[35] and 4) a strong penchant for anti-militarism, which existed on both the far right and far left at the turn of the 20th century. A powerful influence in this regard was the always difficult to categorize Albert Jay Nock, the anarchist co-editor of the early 1920s journal *Freeman* and author of the revisionist book on German war guilt, *The Myth of a Guilty Nation* (1922).[36] Also critically important was the thinking of Randolph Bourne, who gave libertarians their motto: "War is the health of the state."[37]

Free market economics and classic liberal theory figure most prominently in the international libertarian movement, represented by the Mont Pelerin Society founded by Hayek, von Mises, Friedman, and others in 1947. But the American strain of libertarianism is different. It possesses a strong streak of anarchism. One of the well-known examples is Murray Rothbard, known in the 1970s and 1980s as "Mr. Libertarian."[38] Rothbard saw himself above all as a revolutionary. He was an admirer of the French Revolution, and he was not shy about taking lessons from Vladimir Lenin concerning the importance of building revolutionary cadres.[39] In the 1960s Rothbard made common cause with the New Left, starting a journal with Leonard Liggio called *Left and Right*, which was known to publish pieces singing the praises of the Black Panthers and Che Guevara.[40] The only real constant in Rothbard's politics is radicalism. He changed sides with head-spinning inconsistency, at one time being an Old Right hater of Franklin Roosevelt and at other times supporting Adlai Stevenson and even the Maoist Progressive Labor Party. Rothbard was the quintessential radical libertarian—restless, eccentrically doctrinaire, and always escaping into extreme and often contradictory positions as surrounding circumstances changed.[41]

Given their different historical pedigrees, it should be no surprise that there are significant intellectual differences between classical liberalism and libertarianism. Whereas classical liberals are mistrustful of the state and thus see a need to remain vigilant toward it, libertarians believe the state *is* more often than not illegitimate. The hatred of the state, inherited from anarchism, trumps the give-and-take of liberal social contract theory, whereby one naturally gives up certain freedoms in return for protections from the state.

Another difference involves the notion of the individual. The liberal may believe that the individual is the natural repository of rights, but he or she is also a social animal who accepts some restrictions on those rights in order to achieve social stability. The libertarian by contrast claims to be radically free, completely sovereign unto himself, and nothing is permitted by way of coercion without the individual's express permission. Whereas the classical liberal lives with all sorts of social compromises, the libertarian bridles at them. Capitalism—or the free market—is the most comfortable economic system for both, but for the libertarian capitalism is an article of faith in which the radical freedom of the individual is to be discovered and cultivated as a grand moral gesture. For the classical liberal, its significance is more modest.

Capitalism is merely the best system to maximize economic freedom for all.

Most libertarians see themselves as champions of natural rights. Nock rightly criticized the modern state as being the heir of the German idealist tradition in which rights were (mistakenly, in his view) created and granted by the state to the people. But mainly because of the strains of anarchism pulsing through their ideological veins, radical libertarians like Nock did not buy into the social constraints implied by natural law theory. Rights were more about what a person was free to do than what he was obligated to do in exchange for those rights. The moral constraints implied by natural law theory were largely missing from the rights theories of radical libertarians. This belief in absolute freedom is one of the reasons why Rand, Rothbard, and others were open to that other byproduct of German idealism, the heroic radical individualism of Stirner and Nietzsche, which in Ayn Rand's philosophy was called "the virtue of selfishness."

Another crucial difference between libertarianism and classical liberalism involves war and peace. It is true that the classic liberal principle imagines an ideal international order of peace based on free commerce. This was the dream not only of Adam Smith but of Immanuel Kant. But libertarianism's revulsion to war is not mainly inspired by classical liberalism. It has other origins. One was the Old Right's fight with Woodrow Wilson and Franklin Roosevelt, which opened the door to "war revisionism"—blaming Wilson for getting the U.S. into World War I and emphasizing the negative role played by the Versailles Treaty, rather than Hitler's aggressiveness, for causing World War II. Another source was that old standby, anarchism. Once someone concludes, as Lysander Spooner and Rothbard did, that the state is nothing more than a gang of bandits, it is not a great leap in logic to conclude that all wars are con jobs foisted on the world by statism run amok.[42]

Radical libertarians developed a theory of war that was not all that different from Lenin's. They believed that the state—in Lenin's lexicon, the *bourgeois* state—was imperialistic. Lenin believed war represented the highest state of imperialism, which was not all that different from how Bourne viewed it. The antiwar connection could end up creating some strange bedfellows for libertarians. It was a major driving force behind Rothbard's flirtation with the antiwar New Left in the 1960s, and it also figures very prominently in the thinking of leftist libertarians like Noam Chomsky, who often end up sounding like apologists for America's enemies.

This view of war may indeed be libertarian, but it is not liberal. Notwithstanding what some of its theorists may say, in practice liberalism is quite comfortable with the making of war. The American Revolution was made through war, and throughout the early American republic military force was used to spread Jefferson's "Empire of liberty." Liberalism developed in both America and Europe to reflect the new interests of a democratic society, and one of those was to ensure the constitutional protections and securities provided by the new liberal nation-state. National liberalism in Europe was, in fact, an actual driver of wars in the 19th century. While liberal theorists in Europe and America would occasionally complain about the waste of war, they never indulged in the anarchist fantasy of abolishing war by abolishing the state. Progressives like Wilson and FDR were war leaders, and although they irritated the Old Right and the anarchists alike, their leadership in war was not a break with some pristine American past free of war. By the 1950s America's national liberals were completely in sync not only with America's role in World War II but also with its policies in the Cold War. There was dissent on the left, to be sure; but it was not liberal dissent. It was the far left sometimes meeting in common cause with the libertarian left to go after their common enemy—progressive liberalism.

It is commonly understood that libertarians despise progressives, but what is poorly understood is that they really do not like classical liberals either. Rothbard explains:

> [W]e are *libertarians* because we believe in individual liberty. I used to think that we were "true liberals," but I have recently come to the conclusion that it is better not to be identified with the old liberals of the 19th century. Despite their merits they were (a) great advocates of democracy and majority rule, and (b) adherents of the public school system, and (c) anti-clerical to the extent of banishing Jesuits, etc. Best to start afresh with the "libertarian" appellation, which, for once, we have seized from the leftists instead of *vice versa*.[43]

Although American libertarianism today is often associated with the far right, historically it is more accurate to view it as a hybrid—a radical leftist position on war and social policy fused with the defense of small government and individual rights normally associated with classic liberalism and the right. Libertarians and social leftists have different reasons for holding traditional progressivism and classical liberalism in disdain, but that does not change the fact that they are against both. This disposition more than anything else explains the strange "the enemy of my enemy is my friend" alliances between libertarians and leftists not only on foreign policy but sometimes on social policy such as gay marriage. These alliances can be found in most policy areas, in fact, except for economics, where their feud over capitalism still trumps everything else.

### THE RAWLS-CLINTON SYNTHESIS

Liberal theory had fallen on hard times by the 1970s. The New Left had no use for it. Decades of theoretical hammering from socialists on the left and positivists and traditionalists on the right had reduced liberal theory to a rather thin gruel. Liberalism often came across as a shallow political compromise between social-ism and conservatism. The actual practice of welfare state liber-alism in the 1970s was outpacing its theoretical foundations. So much critical work had been done to undermine the theoreti-cal foundations of the old liberal notion of universal justice—by utilitarianism, Marxism, and positivism, and most recently by the postmodernists—that the time seemed ripe for liberal thinkers to grapple with the fundamentals of liberalism.

Into this messy and confused world stepped philosopher John Rawls. A former student at Oxford University, where he was heavily influenced by Isaiah Berlin and legal theorist H. L. A. Hart, Rawls was a Harvard University professor of moral philoso-phy. He published his most influential work, *A Theory of Justice*, in 1971.[44] It was nothing less than an attempt to revive liberal theory after decades of theoretical doldrums. Rejecting the rela-tivism of the age, he developed a theory he called "justice as fair-ness." There was, Rawls insisted, an "original position" in moral philosophy roughly understood as a sense of fairness. Other lib-eral philosophers were involved in this revival as well, including Richard Rorty at Princeton and Ronald Dworkin, who taught at Yale, Oxford, and New York University. But it was Rawls who best captured the spirit of the neoliberal age. He wanted to offer a sound moral rationale not only for the modern welfare state but for maintaining some semblance of balance between the old veri-ties of liberty and the new demands for social justice.

About the same time Rawls was trying to revive the fortunes of liberal theory, Democrats were rethinking their love affair with the New Deal. In the wake of Reagan's presidency, a new, more moderate, Democrat emerged in the person of Bill Clinton. He made the politics of the "third way"—meaning an alternative to conservatism and progressive liberalism—popular in America. Like Rawls, President Clinton believed that there were limits on what the government could do to establish social equality. When Clinton said the "age of big government is over" or when he complained that America's welfare system had "trapped" people in poverty, he was not channeling the standard progressive or even New Left values of the past. He was seeking a new synthesis. Like Rawls, Clinton was trying to find a balance between liberty and the welfare state. How well he and Rawls succeeded is contested, but the point is that, for whatever reason, they were trying.

In fact, Bill Clinton so admired Rawls that he honored him posthumously with the National Humanities Medal in 1999. As he said of Rawls:

> John Rawls is perhaps the greatest political philosopher of the 20th century. In 1971, when Hillary and I were in law school, we were among the millions moved by a remarkable books [sic] he wrote, "A Theory of Justice," that placed our rights to liberty and justice upon a strong and brilliant new foundation of reason.
>
> Almost singlehandedly, John Rawls revived the disciplines of political and ethical philosophy with his argument that a society in which the most fortunate helped the least fortunate is not only a moral society, but a logical one. Just as impressively, he has helped a whole generation of learned Americans revive their faith in democracy itself.[45]

It is important that Clinton mentioned an interest in reviving Americans' faith in democracy. Coming on the heels of the Sixties' chaos, not to mention the stagnation of the 1970s, liberalism needed a new theoretical foundation. Clinton believed Rawls provided it. Even more importantly, Rawls helped establish the legitimacy of the welfare state as a liberal, as opposed to socialist, undertaking. This was important at the time because Clinton was interested in welfare reform. He wanted to prove that welfare was not simply socialism light, but something in tune with the traditions of America. By reforming it, Clinton felt he could put the welfare state on a much firmer footing.

While Clinton wanted to save welfare by firming up its political foundations, Rawls wanted to provide the welfare state with a new rationale. He called it the "difference principle." It was an adaptation of the notion, familiar in game theory, that everyone should cooperate to ensure that the worst outcome for all would be as good as possible. The presumption is that everyone should want to kick in to support the welfare state because it is in their self-interest. Since anyone could find themselves in trouble, they all would benefit from a system that established a safety net for everyone.

Rawls was a liberal, not a socialist, and this limited the lengths to which he would go to establish an egalitarian society. He was willing to endorse an extensive welfare state so long as it did not violate the principle of liberty. British historian Alan Ryan explains that Rawls's first priority was to make the rules "governing the distribution of our fundamental freedoms take absolute priority over all other social rules."[46] In other words, liberty had priority over social equality.

At bottom Rawls was saying that if you had to choose between liberty and social welfare policies, you must always side with liberty. The implications are not very friendly to socialism. Once you assume that everyone should have the greatest freedom consistent with the like freedom of all, you cannot insist that the government forcibly redistribute income to make everyone absolutely equal.[47] To do so would inevitably end up depriving some people of their liberty. Moreover, since civil liberties were sacrosanct (they had "lexical" priority over the social obligations of the difference principle), they could not be trumped by anything else, including economic matters. Rawls's fundamental idea—the one that ultimately defines him as a true liberal—is that one should not be used as a means for the ends of others.[48] Certain individual rights (particularly civil liberties) are irreducible and should not be sacrificed for any purpose whatsoever, even for the public good, because doing so would inevitably erode the freedoms of all.

This is not to suggest that Rawls and Clinton were carbon copies of one another, or even that Rawls should be given singular responsibility for influencing Clinton's politics. Rather, they are offered as two very different examples of a singular phenomenon occurring in these years—namely, that liberalism was trying to reconnect with its roots, much as it had tried to do with the national liberals in the 1950s. Whether Clinton or Rawls succeeded on their own terms is a topic for another day. Suffice it to say that attempts to put liberalism on firmer theoretical and political ground defined the mainstream of Democratic politics until the ascent of Barack Obama.

TWO

# The Rise of the Postmodern Left

Progressive liberalism in America today is not at all like what has come before. It is not merely a logical extension of the old progressivism popular at the turn of the 20th century, or the New Deal liberalism of Franklin Roosevelt and its outgrowth, the "Great Society" liberalism of Lyndon Johnson. It is not even the same as the 1960s New Left. It is something entirely new. It has roots in these old movements, but it has acquired a new ideology all its own. It is a fusion of very old ideas from radical egalitarianism with very new notions of culture and morality. It is the postmodern left.

### WHAT IS THE POSTMODERN LEFT?

To understand the postmodern left, we first must appreciate what postmodernism is.[1] Originally inspired by French theorists Jacques Derrida, Michel Foucault, and Jean-François Lyotard, who worked primarily in the latter half of the 20th century, postmodernism is not a political philosophy but a way of seeing the world. Professors Alan Sokal and Jean Bricmont describe it this way:

> Vast sectors of the humanities and the social sciences seem to have adopted a philosophy that we shall call, for want of a better term, "postmodernism": an intellectual current characterized by the more-or-less explicit rejection of the rationalist tradition of the Enlightenment, by theoretical

discourses disconnected from any empirical test, and by a cognitive and cultural relativism that regards science as nothing more than a "narration," a "myth" or a social construction among many others.[2]

Its intellectual aspects include

a fascination with obscure discourses; an epistemic relativism linked to a generalized skepticism toward modern science; an excessive interest in subjective beliefs independently of their truth or falsity; and an emphasis on discourse and language as opposed to the facts to which those discourses refer (or, worse, the rejection of the very idea that facts exist or that one may refer to them).[3]

The question is, how did such a highly esoteric theory become overtly leftist in its politics? There is, after all, no explicit political doctrine associated with postmodernism. Foucault and other French postmodernists were often politically radical, but many were critics of Marxism.[4] Most postmodernist thinkers were interested in art, literature, and theoretical questions, not politics. In fact, many saw themselves as wholly apolitical.

The answer is that the radicalism was built into their worldview. Postmodernists may have eschewed big ideas and grand theories such as Marxism, but their interest in how societies should be understood was inherently political. To wit, how a society is ordered culturally is as much a political question as deciding what kind of government is best for the people.

The deconstructionist method used by the postmodernists, albeit ostensibly theoretical in intent, is a powerful political weapon. It is a way to critique society without exposing oneself to easy counterattacks. By promising, for example, to tear away the veil of myth that supposedly props up capitalism and Western culture, it offers an all-purpose method of criticism that is political

without appearing to be political. Postmodernists present themselves as relativists, not dogmatists, and thus they can sling arrows
at the system from every possible angle. Since they are not held
responsible for defending anything that actually exists, they wear
their theoretical slipperiness as a badge of honor, as proof of a profound authenticity that is exceedingly difficult to disprove. They
are intellectual guerilla fighters in an asymmetrical war against
Western culture, only they often pretend not to be fighters at
all, but simply disinterested academics. They attack from the cultural flanks and then slip back into the cloistered protection of
the academy, professing an interest only in literary theory or the
nature of perception, language, and knowledge.

Practically every radical cause in America today shows the
influence of this postmodernist assault. From radical feminism to
racial and sexual politics, postmodern leftists blend their unique
brand of cultural criticism with the political objectives of these
movements. In their intellectual laboratories—the cultural studies
and humanities programs at American universities—they apply
theories of structuralism, poststructuralism, and deconstructionism to achieving the political objectives of the New Left.[5] The
results are a cornucopia of identity theories promising perfect diversity. They include radical multiculturalism, critical race theory,
African-American criticism, feminist theory, gender and transgender theories, gay and "queer" theories, Latino studies, media
"criticism," postcolonial studies, and indigenous cultural studies,
to mention only a few. The latest identity cause to add to the list
is the "neurodiversity" movement in which, as its supporters put
it, autism "ought to be treated not as a scourge to be eradicated
but rather as a difference to be understood and accepted."[6] All
adversity, even that which is biologically inherited, can be wiped
away by simply adjusting one's attitudes.

Every cause in identity politics owes its existence to this bevy
of critical theories. The whole notion of identity—the radically
subjectivist claim that "we are who we say we are; end of discus-

sion"—was invented by postmodernist identity theorists. So, too, were the notion of white privilege and the theory of "every-day racism."[7] Radical multiculturalism is an outgrowth as well. Such theories may have been designed in the rarefied air of the academic's study, but they have been wildly successful politically. They have entered the bloodstream of popular culture through movies, TV shows, satirical news programs, and pop songs, and most Americans have no clue where they came from.

Popular renditions of these ideas are everywhere. They are the stuff of conventional liberal wisdom: All cultures deserve equal respect, especially those that have been maligned by the evil influences of Western civilization. Not only Western culture but white people are congenitally racist. The notion of the "false narrative," so amply employed by activists and even some journalists, was perfected by the postmodernists. So, too, was the idea that the only "real" truth is "my" truth, which is the relativist proposition that all understanding of reality is nothing but a word game. In the postmodernist world of language, knowledge is objectively speaking a fiction, harboring some deeper reality that only the most astute philosopher (meaning a postmodernist) can dimly discern. No one knows for sure what anything means, but that does not stop postmodernists from loudly proclaiming the certainty of their views as if they were *fides ecclesiastica*.[8]

While philosophers such as Derrida and Lyotard cannot be held personally responsible for the vulgarization of their ideas, they are not entirely blameless either. The implications of what they say are not all that hard to discern. It was Lyotard who said there is no longer a coherent "master narrative,"[9] and Derrida preached that truth is only accessible in individual interpretations of "texts" and "narratives."[10] Their defenders may argue that Foucault and Derrida were misinterpreted, but the fact remains that the crude moral relativism of radical multiculturalists is not a far stretch from what these philosophers actually mean.[11] Even the campus fad of claiming a "microaggression"[12] is rooted in postmodernist theory.

It was Foucault who argued that language reflects the values of the existing power structures of society, which is seen by some as oppressive (for example, in defining what is "normal").[13]

These are not merely theoretical ideas worrying the curious minds of intellectuals. They are actually quite commonplace in today's politics and culture. When Bruce Jenner changes his identity from a man to a woman and is wildly celebrated as a hero, we are witnessing the complete triumph of the identity ideology. When FBI Director James B. Comey cites the lyrics of the song "Everyone's a Little Bit Racist" from the musical *Avenue Q*, he is echoing the "everyday race" theory.[14] When comedian Jon Stewart deflects criticism of his political statements by saying that he's (just) a comedian, he's channeling the postmodern habit of shifting perspectives to avoid accountability.[15] When a woman submits a factually incorrect and poorly researched article on an alleged fraternity rape at the University of Virginia to *Rolling Stone* magazine and its editors fail to check the story before printing it because they assume it must be true, they are mirroring a belief in the "larger truth" of their metanarrative.[16] When a Ferguson, Missouri, policeman shoots a black teenager in self-defense, and many people, including some in the Obama administration, jump to the conclusion that the white cop is racist, they are channeling the critical race theory notion that all white people must, regardless of their individual intentions or statements, be racist. When the character J.B. Richter in the TV series *Extant* proclaims, "certainty is the devil," he is reflecting the crude relativism of the postmodernist.

This is the cultural side of the postmodern left. It has an economic populist component as well. Represented best by the democratic socialist presidential candidate Senator Bernie Sanders of Vermont and the populist Senator Elizabeth Warren from Massachusetts, leftist populism is a powerful new force inside the Democratic Party. It is fiercely dedicated to attacking banks, redistributing income, and eliminating all income inequality in

America. In substance there is not much new here. The historical origins go all the way back to the prairie populists of the late 19th century who railed at banks and other fat cats. And there is a distinct neo-Marxist undertone of class warfare pulsating in the speeches of Warren and Sanders. As before, the power of the unions is supreme in this movement (although today they largely represent public service employees, not factory workers). So, too, is the alliance with Keynesian economists such as Paul Krugman and neo-Marxists such as Thomas Piketty.

But what is historically new is the alliance with the cultural left. Back in the 1960s, many economically minded New Deal liberals and even socialists wanted nothing to do with the cultural warriors of the New Left, thinking them shallow and feckless. No more. There is today not much distance between the postmodern cultural leftists and the democratic socialists like Sanders who want to focus mainly on economics. The two sides can run afoul of each other, as Sanders did at a Netroots Nation conference in July 2015 when black activists shouted him off the stage. But these disputes have more to do with different priorities than with ideological divisions. Philosophically there is not much daylight between Sanders and the hard-core cultural warriors of the postmodern left. The same is true for Hillary Clinton. She, in fact, tries to appeal to both sides at the same time. She sells herself not only as a postmodernist feminist candidate who will be the first female president of the United States, but as a classic fighter for the economically downtrodden. The fusion has been the strength of her candidacy, because it represents the broadest appeal to all the constituents of the Democratic Party.

The postmodern left is the new center of what is called progressive liberalism. It is the new "center left" in American politics. Debbie Wasserman Schultz, the current chairperson of the Democratic National Committee, may have a hard time explaining the difference between a Democrat and a socialist, but it is not because she fails to understand what a historical socialist is—

someone who wants to expropriate the means of production.[17] It is because she knows that many in her party actually support the self-avowed socialist candidate, Bernie Sanders. A decade ago that would have been unheard of. Today it is the new normal.

### ITS INTELLECTUAL ROOTS

The postmodern left has a distinct intellectual history. Understanding it can tell us a lot not only about where it came from but where it is going. The historical roots are twofold: 1) the tradition of radical egalitarianism that first surfaced over two centuries ago in the radical Enlightenment; and 2) various intellectual movements that arose as a negative reaction to the Enlightenment's rationalism, often lumped together in a movement called the Counter-Enlightenment. The first tradition is normally associated with the left, while the second is a phenomenon normally of the right, at least in Europe. The fusion of these two opposing intellectual traditions is a major reason why the postmodern left is so philosophically elusive. It is also a factor in why it has been so politically successful.

The postmodern left gets its particular brand of egalitarianism from the New Left of the 1960s.[18] It was then that neo-Marxism and other radical movements transformed the radical politics of America into something entirely new. The focus shifted from economics to culture. Old Marxist categories of class conflict were picked up and transformed into struggles over racial and gender identity and sexual politics.

The New Left had many variations. There was the Frankfurt School of neo-Marxism led by philosophers Herbert Marcuse, Theodor Adorno, and others who complained that capitalism was a source of cultural oppression. There were radical student movements like the Free Speech Movement at Berkeley and the Students for a Democratic Society that processed all sorts of radical historical influences, not only neo-Marxism but also American anarchism, the civil disobedience traditions of the radical abolition movement, radical populism, and the cultural critiques of radical progressives like Randolph Bourne. There were even radical libertarians like "anarcho-capitalist" Murray Rothbard, who sang the praises of capitalism but was intrigued by the grassroots democratic potential of the New Left; and his near opposite, the "libertarian socialist" Noam Chomsky, who hated capitalism but loved the absolute freedom of anarchism. The New Left was a veritable kaleidoscope of diverse movements. But they were united in one thing—the goal of overturning the traditional order in America.

The historical inspirations for the New Left were typically leftist. But the postmodern left was also fed by another set of ideas associated with the right-leaning Counter-Enlightenment. Partly a romantic rebellion against the rationalism of the Enlightenment, but also a continuation of some of its more radically egalitarian ideas, the Counter-Enlightenment was characterized by a distrust of rational discourse, a disdain for empiricism, contempt for Western liberalism, a hatred of modernity, and a tendency to glorify human passion as the mark of authentic individualism. The best-known modern philosophical proponents of these ideas were Arthur Schopenhauer, Friedrich Nietzsche, and Martin Heidegger. They and those who followed them were keenly interested in the radical possibilities of human freedom, which politically could go off in any ideological direction. They were also severe critics of modernity, believing it was destroying the authenticity that had been prevalent in earlier eras of human history (for Nietzsche, ancient Greece). On the right they spawned ideologies celebrating the heroic individual and the myths of the nation. On the left they gave rise to existentialism and its exploration of the radical freedom of the individual.

The most recent historical channel for these anti-modernist critiques of Western societies is the French postmodernists: Derrida, Foucault, Lyotard, and others. They were heavily influenced by Nietzsche, Heidegger, and other philosophers associated with the Counter-Enlightenment.[19] Their notions of the metanarrative and the inability to know reality objectively inspired the radically subjectivist views of the identity theorists and radical multiculturalism. Although first developed as abstruse theories of philosophy, their ideas were simplified, often crudely, by their academic followers into a political ideology.

Historically, the cultural side of the postmodern left is a hybrid movement of two very different modernist critiques of Western societies. On the one hand, there is the Nietzschean belief that the individual must be completely free of all ethical constraints—free to conduct one's own personal "transvaluation of values." This is the philosophical basis of the postmodern left's moral relativism. It is ethically nihilistic because it recognizes no standard or value other than its own freedom. It is radically individualistic because the individual alone, not society, gets to decide what is right and true. It is all about individual freedom, radically defined.

On the other hand, the individual's right to freedom is no longer just the individual's business. It is society's business too. This is where the principle of equality comes in. It is where the egalitarian imperative of Karl Marx meets the limitless possibilities of individual freedom imagined by Nietzsche.

Here is how it works: While in theory it may be up to the individual to decide the boundaries of personal morality, in certain cases such as sexual practices, recognizing marriage, or deciding racial or gender identities, personal decisions are not only an individual choice, but also socially constructed. In other words, if a gay or black person feels persecuted, they are being persecuted, full stop. Their personal feelings—their will to identity—are actually channeling the purported reality of their social construct into society. It is not the old Marxist notion of class consciousness, which was objectified in society and history. It is rather a new subjective kind of consciousness chosen by the completely free individual. Whatever that persecuted individual decides must not merely be tolerated but fully endorsed by others, often on pain of legal action. The demand for equality is now a mandate for cultural conformity. The personal views of identity claimants are not selfish whims but socially constructed civil rights—a plea for dignity, as Supreme Court Justice Anthony Kennedy describes it.[20] In this new matrix of rights what used to be civil-social rights based on people's objective place in society are now subjectively derived from people's own personal interpretations and feelings. It is an entirely new way of measuring human equality, because ultimately it is divorced from hard social reality.

At first glance the moral relativism of identity theorists may seem to be the same as the existentialists' ethics of absolute freedom—the view that the individual finds value only within himself. It is indeed similar, and both the existentialists and postmodernists were influenced by Nietzsche and Heidegger. But there are important differences between existentialism and postmodernism. Existentialists are concerned mainly with "being" (ontology) while postmodernists are interested in knowledge and perception (epistemology). Whereas the existentialist says "existence precedes essence" and therefore the individual is absolutely free to forge his or her destiny, the postmodernist says perception defines the operative equivalent of essence without actually being it. Thus the question of existence or anything objectively external to perception becomes essentially irrelevant. This is important because, in the postmodernist mind, it implies no limits whatsoever on what perception and interpretation can decide, ethically or epistemologically. The postmodernists argue that since what we say is true and real is a matter of perception and interpretation, we are absolutely free to chart our own ethics. Existentialists also believe individuals can make their own ethics, but only within the confines of objective reality. Essentially, postmodernists try to bypass the whole question of existence or any objective sense of the world because they contend it is unknowable beyond our relative interpretations of it.

But there is a problem. As existentialists such as Jean-Paul Sartre learned, radical individualism can be a dead end for social justice. It is not easy to establish a coherent ideology of social justice based solely on the radical freedom of the individual. Unlike Sartre, who eventually escaped into Marxism, postmodernist philosophers reject communism. But they do find refuge in the New Left, in which Marx's old economic class warfare has been replaced with identity-cultural warfare. This transformation gives them a way out of the individualist–relativist trap in which they found themselves. Instead of the proletariat, it is now cultural identity groups that are being oppressed. It is not workers but races, women, and ethnic and sexual minorities who are the new revolutionaries. Unlike classic Marxists, for whom class consciousness is a social phenomenon economically determined, identity theorists define it as a psychological phenomenon manifested in the culture. Identity solidarity is the equivalent of class consciousness, only it has no objective foundation, economic or otherwise, other than the perception of mutual grievance based on identity.

The philosophical leitmotifs of postmodernism are epistemic and ethical relativisms. But postmodernists are not the only ones to dabble in relativism. John Stuart Mill and other late classical liberals did the same. Modern liberalism (as opposed to 18th-century liberalism based on natural law) is quite ambivalent about whether absolute truth or justice exist. As Mill wrote in *On Liberty*, "There is no such thing as absolute certainty."[21] This is unmistakably epistemic relativism. But Mill was not a nihilist. In that same sentence where he disavowed absolute certainty he also said, "but there is assurance sufficient [of such certainty] for the purposes of human life." Whatever theoretical doubts he may have had about the existence of absolute moral standards, Mill still believed it was necessary for a moral person to act as if they did exist. Otherwise there would be the potential for a new and different kind of tyranny—the moral chaos of the nihilist, in which everything is permitted.

Postmodern leftists are vulnerable to the charge of nihilism, if for no other reason than that they loudly proclaim the death of all certainty. For this reason, they are also prone to the very kind of tyranny Mill feared. Whether they admit it or not, they assume that each local interpretation of truth is effectively an absolute in and of itself. In other words, it is objectively treated as a universal truth even though such a claim is supposed to be theoretically impossible. The difference with late classical liberalism is that, whereas Mill desired a pluralistic system to prevent the imposition of an infallible truth claim on everybody else, postmodern leftists believe they must control everything—the overall narrative of what is truth—in order to protect the validity of their own local truth claims. It is not pluralism, as Mill and others wanted, but a demand for conformity. Despite the theoretical position that "everyone is entitled to their own truths," the reality is that whatever local truth entitlement emerges as dominant must become the *final word for everyone.*

Postmodernists are essentially and perhaps even unwittingly treating the local truth as if it were an absolute truth. It is this bit of intellectual jujitsu (self-deception, really) that creates such nonsense as "intolerance in the name of tolerance" or trying to liberate free speech by controlling it. In the name of radical relativism, a new absolutism emerges in which a local truth is deemed infallible precisely because no one universal truth or moral position is allowed to challenge it.

Mill had something to say about what happens when someone thinks this way:

> There is a great difference between presuming an opinion to be true, because, with every opportunity for contesting it, it has not been refuted, and assuming its truth for the purpose of not permitting its refutation. Complete liberty of contradicting and disproving our opinion is the very condition which justifies us in assuming its truth for

purposes of action; and on no other terms can a being with human faculties have any rational assurance of being right.[22]

In other words, from the liberal point of view the moment you try to prevent a refutation of a truth claim, whether local or universal, you have forfeited your right to make any absolutist claim at all.

To be fair, relativism is a liberal as well as postmodern disease. From Hegel to the progressives in America, the belief that all truth was historically determined and thus relative killed off much of the Western world's faith in natural law. Indeed in the 20th century the relativist position in philosophy had become so commonplace that not only liberal philosophers like John Rawls but even conservative-minded liberals like Leo Strauss wrote about it.[23] With the exception of neo-Kantians, Marxists, and natural law conservatives, most modern schools of philosophy accept the relativist position. But this does not mean that all are equally comfortable with it. Both Rawls and Strauss were alarmed by the implications of a radical relativism. Rawls feared the loss of moral authority, while Strauss dreaded nihilism. Thus, like the postmodernists, they ended up accepting the position of acting as if it were true, even though theoretically they did not believe it was.

But, again, there is a difference. The liberal position may be logically problematic. It may even be morally hypocritical. But out of fear of tyranny, it is something liberals have lived with for centuries. They may be willing to tolerate the "gentle nihilism"[24] of a Nietzsche, which is a permissive kind of egalitarianism that may be hedonistic and even aimless in its values.[25] But at least it is not the hard, violent variety found in totalitarianism, where creating values is the sole right of the state.[26] Postmodern leftists unfortunately are more likely to lean to the compulsory rather than the gentle nihilism of the liberals, and this frankly makes them highly dangerous to both liberty and civil society. Their innovation is to pretend to be relativists when in fact they are closet absolutists. In the worst tradition of nihilism, they preach a new kind of harsh morality completely without limits, all in the name of having no morality at all.

### THE DIVISIVE LEGACY OF RADICAL MULTICULTURALISM

Cultural relativism permeates Western liberal thinking. No realm of human inquiry escapes it. Its origins can be found in the early 19th century, when Hegel developed historicist theories rejecting notions of universal, fundamental, and immutable interpretations of history and society. A few decades after Hegel's time, another new and powerful idea emerged. It was the philosophy of science known as positivism—the view that sensory experience is the exclusive source of all authoritative knowledge. Not only such pioneers of modern sociology as Auguste Comte, Emile Durkheim, and even Karl Marx but also anthropologists like Franz Boas in the later 19th century partook of the positivistic spirit, believing that societies and cultures could be scientifically dissected and understood.

These two intellectual traditions come together in what we today call multiculturalism. On the one hand multiculturalists believe that cultures and societies can be studied with the scientific method; that is, after all, what sociology and anthropology are all about. On the other hand, they also believe that cultures exist in a vast continuum of historical change that prevents any one immutable "scientific" interpretation from emerging. In other words, even though multicultural-minded sociologists use scientific methods of research, they believe that no absolute laws for all societies and cultures exist for all time. Thus, in multiculturalism, the scientific "objectivity" of sociology meets the idealists' phenomenology and ethics of relativism—the view that truth and ethics change over time.

Karl Marx was the first to try to fuse these two traditions. He rejected Hegel's idealism but kept his dialectical method and then posited it as objectively scientific. But he was not the last. Today the radical multiculturalists do the same. They argue that in theory all cultures are equal, but some cultures are "more equal" than others. Radical multicultural theorists can be found all across the academic world, for example in English, sociology, and law departments. Like all deconstructionists, they use the social sciences, literary theories, and new legal concepts to dismantle Western culture and its value systems. In terms of intellectual history, they try to bridge the theoretical gap between the hard claims of science and the philosophical assertions of historical and epistemological relativism.

While much of the theoretical work has been done in academic cultural studies departments, multiculturalism's most successful area of research is the law. It is an ideal target for a number of reasons. One, law is where theory meets the possibility of real change, making it the ideal discipline with which to force a revolutionary makeover of society. Two, study of the law allows people to sidestep thorny theoretical questions of epistemology and to focus instead on outcomes. It also enables them to be critics instead of system builders, a mistake many postmodernists believe Marxists have made. By going the legal route, the system can be deconstructed gradually while avoiding the dangers and blowback from being an outright revolutionary.

Radical multicultural law has two specific historical origins. The first is not radical or even postmodern. It was the legal realist movement that arose in the 1920s with such figures as Karl Llewellyn at Columbia University and Jerome Frank and Morris Cohen at Yale.[27] They argued that there were no such things as neutral legal opinions based on general principles derived from cases over time. The law and discretion are arbitrary. The second origin was the (by now) familiar assortment of radical identity theorists, especially feminists, who took the postmodernist idea that reality is a social construction and built whole theories of law around it.[28] Radical multiculturalists left the "naïve" empirical methods of the realists behind, but they kept the nihilistic implications that the law ultimately is relativistic. It was an auspicious revision, because it gave the radicals a "leg up" in legal debates. It gave them the perfect weapon—deconstructive (i.e., destructive) criticism—to tear down old laws while avoiding the appearance of being wild-eyed revolutionaries. The law was seen as a tool to be co-opted and used as a weapon to force social change (sometimes called "lawfare").

Who are the radical multiculturalists? They are legal theorists such as Derrick Bell (now deceased), Catharine MacKinnon, Patricia Williams, and Richard Delgado, who are or were very influential in American legal circles. It is difficult to exaggerate their impact. Without them and others like them, there would be no talk of "hate speech" or "hate crimes." There would be no expansive judicial interpretations of Title IX to force universities to act like courts in rape cases, a development that is the direct result of treating sexual violence as a form of sexual discrimination.[29] Nor would the rights of free speech be so easily attacked on America's campuses and elsewhere. In fact, MacKinnon and legal scholar Stanley Fish believe that free speech is a myth, which is why they do not worry very much about banning it.[30]

The greatest impact of the multiculturalists has been in changing the notions and standards of civil rights and discrimination law. This influence goes beyond defining legal rights as group rights. It extends into providing elaborate defenses of affirmative action, especially racial and other quotas, against the charge of profiling. For example, believing a school district's school board underrepresented blacks, ACLU lawyers argued in a case in Missouri in 2014 that the electoral system dilutes "African-American voting strength," as if they knew exactly how every black person would vote.[31] This viewpoint is, by any reasonable definition, stereotyping black people, even profiling them, if you will. Similar arguments have been heard in defense of federal contracting rules based on racial quotas that continue to persist despite court rulings against them.[32] A similar logic was used by the Obama administration in its proposal to induce local communities to include low-income housing in wealthy neighborhoods.[33]

The real-world impact of multiculturalism is significant. There are precious few American public school systems today that lack a mission statement dedicated to cultural diversity. The federal government and most state governments have adopted diversity as an official employment policy. Corporations and businesses all over America preach diversity in their mission statements, employment policies, and even advertising campaigns. Cultural diversity is practically a sacred principle in the universities and in the entertainment industry, except in the Hispanic and African-American networks, where exclusivity is the rule.

## THEORETICAL CONTRADICTIONS

Radical multiculturalists have always been beset by a theoretical contradiction. It is derived, in part, from a deceptive claim. While they act as though all cultural values are equal, what they really believe is that Western values are inferior. Hence the problem: they pose as if no permanent cultural truth is possible and yet argue from a standpoint that implies a superior and therefore universal moral judgment. Essentially, they want to have their cake and eat it too. Channeling a faux scientific positivism, they claim to know the objective truth about all cultures, including our own, but they also argue that no such universal truth or moral standard can possibly exist.

This presents a serious dilemma. Multiculturalists cannot give up the relativist position because that would deprive them of their main critical weapon to deconstruct Western values. But at the same time they will not admit to being old-fashioned moralists or even positivists, because that contradicts their theoretical positions of ethical and epistemic relativism.

To resolve the dilemma they escape into the brazen double

standard. They pretend as if their own narrow point of view cannot be anything but true. Thus we get the patently absurd "black lives matter" campaign, which takes offense when someone like former Baltimore Mayor Martin O'Malley claims "all lives matter." Worse, O'Malley is shouted down when he claims that "white lives matter."[34] The only answer to alleged racism is racism in return. In their zeal to maintain an incoherent narrative, these demonstrators cannot tolerate even the most elemental and obvious statements of truth and decency to the contrary. They must shut down all dialogue (ridiculously called a "conversation") and storm stages to force their own point of view on everyone else.

There is no other way to put it: radical multiculturalism is a fraud. It claims to be something it is not—a compassionate worldview in which everyone gets a fair shake. It is actually a rigged system in which some people enjoy favor over others. It is the mirror image of the old hierarchy it wants to overturn: it now wants to put previous minorities on top, making them the new majority—if not in number then at least in enjoying government favor. As far as the law is concerned, no system of law can survive a radically relativist view of the world.

The same shaky foundation that barely holds up postmodern philosophy is much more vulnerable when it comes to legal theory. If all truth and the law are *socially* constructed, then knowledge and the law as we normally understand them cease to exist. Completely divorced from any ethical standards, the law becomes purely political and merely administrative, a system of arbitrary rules by which rulers impose their will. It is not only theoretically unsustainable but profoundly anti-democratic and illiberal.

Given its postmodern origins, we should not be surprised that some radical multiculturalists take highly disturbing views of race and ethnicity. Derrick Bell, for instance, believed that high academic standards discriminate in favor of Jews. Other radical lawyers complain that higher-scoring Asian students get a racial preference over lower-scoring blacks.[35] By taking up the defense of one racial group against another, Bell and the others like him have been feeding into the tendency of postmodernists to engage in negative racial stereotyping. As Daniel A. Farber and Suzanna Sherry observe in *Beyond All Reason: The Radical Assault on Truth in American Law* (1997), the racist implications are troubling:

> [I]n our view, the radical attack on merit has implications that should appall the radicals themselves. If merit is nothing but a mask for white male privilege, then it becomes difficult to defend the fact that Jews and Asians are quite disproportionately successful. If their success cannot be justified as fairly earned, it can only be attributed to a heightened degree of entanglement with white male privilege. In short, we believe that radical multiculturalism implies that Jews and Asian Americans are unjustly favored in the distribution of social goods. These anti-Semitic and racist implications of radical multiculturalism are unavoidable, and lead us to condemn radical multiculturalism itself as unacceptable.[36]

The implications are unavoidable because, in the mindset of the radical multiculturalist, some folks are quite simply more deserving than others.

# THREE

# Why the Postmodern Left Is Not Liberalism

The postmodern left is the latest in a long line of radical movements. It draws on a wide array of eclectic historical sources, including not only the egalitarianism of the radical Enlightenment movement but also the irrationalism, radical individualism, and rejection of modern life found in some parts of the Counter-Enlightenment. Despite their different ideological pedigrees, both of these movements were opposed to the liberal direction of Western civilization. Both rejected classical liberalism. The far right and far left despised all the major tenets of liberalism, especially natural law, natural rights, and the idea that liberty must be protected from government tyranny. Despite their differences, each movement was fundamentally illiberal in their mutual scorn for liberalism.

As heir to these two very different traditions, the postmodern left is also illiberal. Illiberalism, in fact, captures best the overall posture of the postmodern left. It incorporates the bipolar ideological nature of its radicalism and reveals that, at bottom, it is a hybrid movement united by hatred not only of hierarchical conservatism but of classical liberalism. Often mistakenly equating the two, the postmodern left wishes to undo the liberal (and capitalist) democratic order.

What does "illiberalism" mean? Webster's Dictionary defines

it as "opposed to liberalism." In popular usage it has come to mean closed-minded, intolerant, and bigoted, or "not allowing people to think and act as they choose." But there is a broader meaning. In a 1997 article in *Foreign Affairs*, Fareed Zakaria describes the "illiberal democracies" of Russia and Venezuela as regimes that suppress dissent, bend the law, and hold sham democratic elections.[1] In a 1964 *Harper's Magazine* article, Columbia University professor Richard Hofstadter described the "paranoid style" of American politics that closely resembles the worldviews and conspiratorial fantasies of the illiberal mindset.[2] Though Hofstadter (and others) associated the paranoid style with the American right, even he, a liberal, admitted that it "is not necessarily right wing." Indeed, as historian Richard J. Ellis describes in *The Dark Side of the Left: Illiberal Egalitarianism in America* (1998), illiberalism has a long track record in the history of the American left.[3]

### THE HISTORICAL ORIGINS OF THE
### POSTMODERN LEFT'S ILLIBERALISM

In Europe, illiberalism has been mostly associated with right-wing authoritarianism. Historian Fritz Stern saw it in the political culture and structures of imperial Germany prior to World War I. "The ruling classes," he asserts, "disdained the liberal habits of tolerance, dissent, debate, openness as well as the politics of liberalism."[4] Politically, these attitudes found expression in the German Right's distrust of democracy and support for authoritarianism, nationalism, and militarism. This mindset earned the name "illiberalism,"[5] according to Stern, because it was the near polar opposite of the Western liberal political order that affirmed democracy and the liberal-minded openness prevalent in America and Great Britain. In the absence of pluralism and free and open debate, a German authoritarian political culture created what Stern calls a "negative utopia" that was prone to illusions. Although on the surface it looked strong and forceful, it actually masked the deep-seated fear of the ruling class that was, at root, the main motivation behind the urge to coerce and condemn. This political culture, according to Stern, set the table for the rise of Nazism in the 20th century.

In American history, illiberalism is also often associated with the far right. First and foremost, the institution of slavery in the antebellum South was quintessentially illiberal, dedicated to maintaining a fiercely hierarchical society by force. After the Civil War, the Ku Klux Klan carried on the cause of white supremacy. The 19th-century Nativist movement against Catholic and non-English-speaking immigrants was equally illiberal.[6] It spawned the Know Nothing or American Party in the 1850s and the Immigration Restriction League in the 1890s. Steeped in religious and racial bigotry, these groups are also examples of what some historians call hierarchical illiberalism. They cling to inequality as the natural order of things, and they are often quite willing to use violence to prevent hated groups from rising in society. They are the closest thing America has to the illiberalism of the German Right as described by Stern.

While there is a long history of illiberalism on the right in America, a leftist illiberalism exists as well. All too often historians underestimate or even ignore it. They assume rather simplistically that left-wing illiberalism is an ideological impossibility—that authoritarian illiberalism can only exist on the right. They are mistaken. There are degrees of illiberalism to be sure, but an anarchist or communist can be every bit as authoritarian and illiberal as a nativist or slave holder. They can be as violent as well. Both are willing to use coercive measures against innocent people in ways that deprive them of their most basic human rights. We should not be blinded by the ideological prejudice that excuses authoritarian values in one while condemning them in another. Authoritarian—even totalitarian—thinking is an equal-opportunity scourge that can infect the far left as well as the far right.

There were two basic kinds of radical illiberalism in 19th-century America. As Ellis points out, one was radical abolitionism. Because of the righteousness of their cause, abolitionists are normally portrayed in American history as near saints. While it is certainly true that many abolitionists were motivated by sincere religious and/or liberal principles and thus deserve the heartfelt thanks of generations of freedom-loving Americans, the most radical among them were not just critics of slavery but also utopian revolutionaries. They believed that slavery was the tip of the iceberg in a society that was steeped in corruption and iniquity. They rejected not just slavery but the very authority of the U.S. government. They often railed against capitalism as much as any communist would. Some, like radical abolitionist Stephen Foster, whom every American schoolchild knows solely as the composer of sentimental American folk tunes, were as radical as any New Left critic of the family. Foster not only viewed marriage as an oppressive institution but said "every family" is little more than an embryo plantation.[7] John Brown may be celebrated as a great abolitionist, but he was also a cold-blooded murderer responsible for some of the "bloody Kansas" massacres in the run-up to the Civil War. While most radical abolitionists were pacifists, others were anarchists who gloried in the brutality of the Civil War. Seward Mitchell, a supporter of William Lloyd Garrison who had once counseled nonresistance, changed his mind once the war broke out. Slavery, he said, might be the cause of the war, but that was "not going to the bottom of our troubles. Something must come to destroy these governments, and make money worthless; and I am happy to see them dashing out each other's brains. In their self-destruction is the hope of the world."[8]

Another type of radical illiberalism in America was associated with anarchism. Nineteenth-century America was awash in all kinds of Utopian social experiments that Ellis describes as illiberal. In the 1880s and 1890s, socialist Utopian colonies cropped up all over the country. Among them were Julius Wayland's Ruskin Colony in Tennessee, the Christian Commonwealth Colony in Georgia, the Kaweah Cooperative Commonwealth in California, and the Washington colonies of Equality, Burley, and Freeland.[9] Many of these communes were religiously inspired. Some of the more radical utopians in these years were anarchists like Lysander Spooner and Benjamin R. Tucker.[10] Most were not violent, but they believed that only a complete destruction of the existing system would make them free. Although Randolph Bourne is best known in American history as a critic of U.S. involvement in World War I, he also was a radical cultural critic of American society. His solution to overcoming the "atomistic" society of individuals that he believed plagued America was as simple as it was dictatorial: "Abolish this hostile attitude of classes towards each other," he said, "by abolishing class struggle. Abolish class struggle by abolishing classes."[11]

In Europe, the illiberal egalitarianism of the far left went in a different direction. First surfacing in the Terror of the French Revolution, it was much more prone to violence and a radical leveling of society than its American counterpart. In the most extreme cases of Stalinism and other communist regimes, few if any limits were placed on the use of force, violence, or coercion. In the 20th century, European socialism and communism made their way to America's shores, reflected not only in the rise of the Communist Party of the U.S.A. but also in various neo-Marxist movements that gave birth to the New Left and antiwar movements in the 1960s. Although far-left radicalism always existed on the fringe of American progressivism, it was not until recently the dominant faction.

### THE ILLIBERAL CHARACTERISTICS
### OF THE POSTMODERN LEFT

The historical movements that give us the postmodern left were illiberal, but what does it mean today to be illiberal? Not all left-leaning political movements are illiberal. A political ideology such as social democracy can be called "not liberal" without being "illiberal." On the other side of the ledger, traditional conservatives do not like the current form of liberalism in America either, but it would be wrong to describe all conservatives as illiberal. It is not really a question of degree—of how extreme someone is in his views—but rather whether the ideology endorses the suppression of human rights and freedom.

Before we answer the question of what it means to be illiberal, we need a working definition of illiberalism. First, there are hard and soft forms of illiberalism. The former represents the mindset and political styles of dictators ranging from Stalin to Putin. The latter is not prone to violence or even collective oppression, but its adherents are content to cut corners in order to undermine democracy and deprive people of their natural rights. The postmodern left in America today is of the soft variety. It embraces principles, attitudes, and practices that sanction the use of coercive methods, either through legal means or public shaming rituals, to deny certain people their rights and civil liberties, particularly freedom of speech and conscience, in ways that undermine American democracy and the rule of law.

With this definition in mind, let's review in what ways the postmodern left is illiberal.

*Racial Stereotyping.* For Martin Luther King, Jr., and other civil rights leaders, the sin of white racism was stereotyping all black people as inferior. It was a prejudice to be sure, but it was predicated on the assumption that all blacks were the same. King objected to stereotyping because he wanted blacks to be treated as individuals and not reduced exclusively to their racial identity (hence the meaning of his famous statement about the content of one's character taking precedence over the color of one's skin).

The postmodern left turns the civil rights model on its head. It embraces racial stereotyping—racial identity by any other name—and reverses it, transforming it into something positive, provided the pecking order of power is kept in place. In the new moral scheme of racial identities, black inferiority is replaced by white culpability, rendering the entire white race, with few exceptions, collectively guilty of racial oppression. The switch is justified through the logic of racial justice, but that does not change the fact that people are being defined by their racial characteristics. Racism is viewed as structural, so it is permissible to use overtly positive discrimination (i.e., affirmative action) to reorder society.

This end-justifies-the-means mentality of course predates the rise of the postmodern left. It can be found in the doctrine of affirmative action. But the racial theorists of identity politics have taken "positive" discrimination to a whole new level. Whereas affirmative action was justified mainly in terms of trying to give disadvantaged blacks a temporary leg up, the racial theorists of the postmodern left see corrective action as permanent. The unending struggle that ensues necessitates acceptance of a new type of racial stereotyping as a way of life and increasingly as something that needs to be enshrined in administrative regulations and the law.

The idea of positive stereotyping contains all sorts of potential for illiberal troublemaking. Once one race is set up as victim and another as guilty of racism, any means necessary are permitted to correct the alleged unjust distribution of power. Justice becomes retaliatory rather than color blind—a matter of vengeance rather than justice. The notion of collective racial guilt, once a horror to liberal opinion, is routinely accepted today as the true mark of a progressive. Casualties are not only King's dream of racial harmony but also the hope that someday we can all—blacks and whites—rise above racial stereotypes.

*Double-Standard Bigotry.* It is not uncommon within progressive circles to find the assumption that certain kinds of people are less equal than others. White people are assumed to be racist, for example, and they must be watched closely lest they abuse their position of power at the expense of people of color. This viewpoint is so common today that even mainstream liberals like Hillary Clinton buy into it.[12] It is most often true for black–white relations, but the double standard extends into other areas as well. Jews, for example, are often accused of bias on matters in the

Middle East, while Arabs and Muslims, occupying the morally advantageous position of victimhood, are not. It is so natural to slice the world into privileged and underprivileged groups that one no longer gives a second thought to the fact that a man would never be invited to lead a woman's organization. By the same token, a black caucus in Congress is welcome but a white caucus would be dismissed out of hand as racist. The double standard is tolerated because it is seen *in and of itself* as a form of corrective justice. But the fact remains that it is validating a double standard of bigotry, no matter how benign the intentions may be.

For the true liberal, double standards are poisonous regardless of their professed good intentions. They inevitably lead to an arms race of competing bigotries vying to outdo one another in escalating claims of victimhood. For classical liberals, power relationships between social groups should be fluid. They should never be made permanent based on characteristics of race, gender, sexual orientation, or even wealth. Society must be open and dynamic. Once it is assumed that the government's place is to establish and maintain a static power structure based solely on fixed social categories, the way to the abyss has been opened. Everything becomes a fight over group rights, which pits one side against another as if they were warring tribes. It is inevitable that such a system should be illiberal. It assumes winners and losers, decided not by open competition but by government fiat. Whereas in a liberal society classes and groups are not supposed to be permanent, in a postmodernist egalitarian society they are not only locked in perpetual conflict; they are openly accepting of the fact that coercion is needed to make sure only the right sort of group wins.

Ultimately, the double standard is embraced because of a misunderstanding about equality. It involves a mistake in logic—a categorical error, according to philosophers—in which things belonging to one category are mistakenly said to belong to another. It is the belief that things that are fundamentally different are, or should be, treated the same. For example, consider this question: Is the transgender person's demand that government pay for a sex change operation really a "right" on par with a woman's right to be free from job discrimination? The cases are completely different. The woman's right arises from civil rights she shares with all Americans. The transgender person, on the other hand, is demanding special treatment—something (having taxpayers foot the bill for a sex change operation) that all other Americans cannot possibly be given. There is a superficial appearance of equality ("you get to be who you are so I have the same right"), but the reality is a demand to treat different things the same. In essence, it is not a plea for equality, but a demand for privilege.

In practice, identity and equality work against each other. The more the former is pushed, the more the doctrine of equality is Balkanized. It becomes a contest between competing demands for recognition and privilege. For example, when feminist-lesbian activists take umbrage at a transgender man trying to transform himself into a woman (as a feminist did in a *New York Times* op-ed),[13] they reveal they are more concerned about who gets to decide what those identities are than about the principle of equality. Even Germaine Greer, the Australian-born icon and inspiration for many of America's most ardent feminists, is being called "transphobic" for questioning transgenderism.[14] The lesbian feminist wants full equality with men, but only for those who are actually born female. For all the talk of equality defined by identity, in the face of transgenderism some feminists are forced to take a separatist position—defending what makes them distinct. Separatism is the only line of defense left against transgender men who are encroaching on their territory.

The same thing is happening with some black activists, such as those at the University of Missouri who asked white student protesters to leave their "black-only healing space."[15] Oddly, in the name of equality, these activists have upended the original purpose of the civil rights movement, effectively embracing the position of segregation that had been the nemesis of Dr. King and other early fighters for civil rights. Whether the issue is race or gender, the war for equality is now all about who gets to define and control the claim of identity, which from the postmodern-ist perspective is the only acceptable way to look at the issue of equality. It is a fight, not for actual equality but for special rec-ognition of privilege. It is a campaign that inevitably exacerbates differences, sometimes even leading to calls for racial and gender separatism.

*Disregard for Democracy.* America's constitutional order has al-ways been a delicate balance between protecting rights and re-flecting the will of the majority. In this respect, democracy as we generally understand it is not the only or even the highest principle in American government. More important is the prin-ciple of self-government, which assumes constitutional limits on what government can do. To maintain a proper balance between individual rights and the will of the people, it is necessary that the federal government always respect the will of the people, pro-vided it does not violate some cherished right laid out in the Bill of Rights. Rights are sacrosanct, but so too is the presumption that laws should be made by legislatures and implemented by the elected executive. They should not be made up by the courts. It would be impossible to be a self-governing people otherwise.

The postmodern left did not invent judicial activism, but it embraces it with a vengeance. It is the weapon of choice in the same-sex marriage fight. All too often laws are overturned on legal technicalities. In the American system, the Constitution is the protector of our most fundamental rights, and the law is sup-posed to reflect the will of the people, not the whims of unelected judges. Laws should be made by the people's democratically elected representatives in the legislatures, not by the courts. When judges deign to speak for the people in the capacity of legislators, they not only usurp the constitutional rights of the legislature but subvert the democratic will of the people.

## WHY THE POSTMODERN LEFT
## IS NOT TRADITIONAL PROGRESSIVISM

Progressive liberals believe their views are well grounded in American history. They point to the Progressive Era as their source of inspiration. But there is a serious problem with this argument. The views of progressives a century ago were quite different from the views of those who call themselves progressives today. There are indeed similarities: the spirit of Herbert Croly, Charles Beard, John Dewey, Woodrow Wilson, and Walter Lippmann lives on in the progressive liberal's love of centralized governments and disdain for individualism and original constitutionalism. But there are important differences as well, and this historical discontinuity is significant; it shows how radical today's progressives have become.

*Progressives vs. Postmodern Leftists.* What are the main differences? For one thing, the philosophical assumptions are completely different. The postmodern left's ethical relativism, which assumes individuals literally create their own "truths," is at odds with Croly's and other progressives' distrust of individualism. The notion that individuals can choose their own identities and then foist them on the rest of society would seem bizarre to Croly or Wilson. From the original progressive point of view, the radical individualism of the ethical relativist would be antisocial. It does not matter that it is shrouded in the rhetoric of equality. Its focus on the individual's subjective choices is contrary to the progressive spirit of worrying about the impact of individual decisions on the society at large. Gay activists may argue that their rights are good for the rest of the society because they advance the principle of marriage equality, but what of the impact on children and society as a whole? Is there not a collective good in maintaining the structure of the traditional family? The radically free ethics of multiculturalists would have them say no, mainly because they believe their personal liberty trumps all considerations of the common good.

Progressives were interested above all in building a new community. They could not have imagined an unending conflict between identity tribes trying to capture the state for their own narrow group interests. Yes, they championed the poor and the union movement, which in some cases gave rise to the class-conflict mentality we know to this day. But progressives were still liberal enough to believe in universal justice. Multiculturalism, for example, stands completely opposed to the progressive vision of community. It promises not to build a common vision for everyone but to tear the community apart in an ethnic and racial conflict of all against all.

There is another important difference. The postmodern left's hostility toward values long championed in Western civilization would be totally out of bounds to most traditional progressives. They were indeed critics of capitalism, individualism, and traditional constitutionalism, and it would even be correct to describe some of them as trying to develop a uniquely styled American social democracy. That was the essence of Herbert Croly's New Nationalism.[16] But progressives accepted the basic cultural and moral frameworks of Western civilization. Postmodern cultural critics do not. It would not have occurred to progressives to question the value of the family, for instance. Nor could they relate to the postmodernist's nihilistic relativism. To understand the progressives' view of the civilizing influence of community, for example, consider how John Dewey explains the importance of historical continuity to community in *Democracy and Education* (1916):

> Men live in a community in virtue of the things which they have in common; and communication is the way in which they come to possess things in common. What they must have in common in order to form a community or society are aims, beliefs, aspirations, knowledge—a

common understanding—like-mindedness as the sociologists say. Such things cannot be passed physically from one
to another, like bricks; they cannot be shared as persons
would share a pie by dividing it into physical pieces. The
communication which ensures participation in a common
understanding is one which secures similar emotional and
intellectual dispositions—like ways of responding to expectations and requirements.[17]

This passage would be anathema to cultural critics of the postmodern left. Its talk of a "common understanding" would be dismissed out of hand. The respect for a common heritage would
be ridiculed as too accepting of historical "myths" or too tolerant
of an unjust gender or sexual orientation hierarchy. The bow
toward community as a civil society of shared values would be
abhorrent to the radical multiculturalist who believes that no such
shared values exist.[18]

For all their admiration of European social democracy, progressives were still grounded in the American liberal tradition.
They were severe critics of the Founders' liberalism—America's
classical liberalism. It is true that some on the far left, like Randolph Bourne, engaged in a kind of cultural criticism that fore-
shadowed the New Left of the Sixties and the postmodern left of
today.[19] But most progressives kept one eye on America's liberal
tradition as they constructed their new social democracy. After
all, Croly's hero was Alexander Hamilton, not Karl Marx.[20] Even
the more liberal of them, who ended up challenging old guard
progressives like Woodrow Wilson—writers such as Theodore
Dreiser, Upton Sinclair, and John Dos Passos—staked much of
their claim as liberals on their passionate embrace of the First
Amendment's freedom of speech and assembly, which of course
was grounded in America's founding liberalism.

*European Liberals vs. Postmodern Leftists.* A comparison between the postmodern left and the European liberal tradition reveals similar contrasts. Let's review the liberal masters as described by Edmund Fawcett in his book, *Liberalism: The Life of an Idea* (2014):

> Against that historical and conceptual background, we have met in the course of this first part a nineteenth-century liberal who prized the open-endedness of human capacities (Humboldt), one who stressed the absoluteness of people's privacy (Constant), as well as liberals who urged people to show initiative and take responsibility for their lives, either materially by inventiveness and hard work (Smiles) or morally by civic engagement and commitment to great causes (Channing). We have met a liberal who called for ethical experimentation and the promotion of individuality (Mill). We have met a liberal preoccupied by how unchecked power may grow to dominate unless talked back to by critics with awkward opinions and unorthodox beliefs (Guizot). We have met liberals preoccupied by how obstructive or superannuated rules may interfere with people's innovations and commercial aims (Cobden), how the pressures of majorities may jeopardize the pursuit of excellence (Tocqueville), and how the twin growth of big business and centralizing government may crush small-scale enterprises and local control (Schulze-Delitzsch). All were in some way speaking up for the worth of human projects and capacities, and for the need to protect them from cramping or controlling power. It is natural by contrast to ask in which of those many tasks, and in what way, those liberals were all standing up for individuals. How and in what sense was it that the liberal's enlightenment inheritance—religious toleration and free speech—came to be thought of as "individualist"?[21]

Postmodern leftists have no such reservations about controlling power. In fact, they wish to gain and expand that power in order to force their agenda on the rest of society. There may be some of Benjamin Constant's belief in absolute privacy when it comes to abortion and national security, but not when it involves criticism of gay marriage. There may be admiration for John Stuart Mill's individuality when it involves the freedom to choose one's sexual identity, but not when it comes to defending the right of other people to speak out against that identity. The fear of central government seen in Alexis de Tocqueville, Richard Cobden, and Franz Hermann Schulze-Delitzsch is practically nonexistent in the postmodern mind, mainly because postmodernists envision themselves as always in charge of that same government. And, finally, the championing of unorthodox views, although seemingly alive in the promotion of ever-changing value systems, becomes problematic on campuses and elsewhere when their own progressive views are challenged.

There is a lesson to be learned here. The loss of historical memory as to what liberalism *was* is actually a key to understanding what it *is* today. The amnesia is quite intentional. It is the very purpose of historical revisionism. For example, when a prominent professor of politics and sociology, Steven Lukes, casually dismisses the old categories of economic or religious individualism as irrelevant to defining today's liberalism and states that what matters instead are concepts like human dignity and personal growth, he is letting us know that he thinks the old liberalism is dead.[22] He is also signaling that the social democratic version of liberalism is the only game in town—it *is* the new liberalism. He suggests he is merely "updating" liberalism when in fact he is altering it. For Lukes and others who have written on the history of liberalism, including Fawcett and British historian Alan Ryan, no matter what happens, liberalism (like "progress") is always marching in a social democratic and postmodern direction.[23]

In case there is any doubt that liberals today are jettisoning their progressive past, consider the renaming movement. Liberal democrats are not only talking about renaming the annual fund-raising Jefferson–Jackson Day dinners. Some are lobbying to expunge the name of iconic progressive Woodrow Wilson as well.[24] Like any cause prior to the postmodern left's takeover of American liberalism, old-fashioned progressivism is treated as a reactionary embarrassment. To some, it is no better than the Confederate ex-generals who started the KKK. To others it is simply passé, a moment in time superseded by the latest phase in that inevitable dialectical movement called progress.

### OBAMA'S REJECTION OF BILL CLINTON'S LIBERALISM

To get an idea of how far down a leftward path the postmodern left has taken modern progressive liberalism, a review of the history of the Democratic Party after Bill Clinton left office is helpful. For most of the 1980s and 1990s leftists worked, if not underground, then certainly below the political radar. They were still operating in a Reagan or post-Reagan era. They inhabited universities and activist organizations that had existed on the fringes of American liberalism since the 1960s. This marginal existence ended in the 2000s under the presidency of George W. Bush. Progressive activists launched a movement against the war in Iraq, and eventually the Democratic Party broke with the moderation of the Clinton years. Energized and radicalized, Democrats moved far left and began to take on the old liberal establishment, much as the New Left had done in the Kennedy and Johnson years. The result is a far more aggressively liberal party. This cause triumphed with the election of Barack Obama, a quintessential postmodern leftist, to the presidency in 2008.

Once in office President Obama repudiated the moderate liberalism of the Clinton era. Unlike Clinton, who worked with Republicans on welfare reform and the North American Free Trade Agreement (NAFTA), Obama stonewalled Republicans at every opportunity. He dropped the work requirements for welfare and aggressively began expanding the welfare state, repudiating Clinton's declaration that "the era of big government is over."

After equivocating on same-sex marriage in his first term, he fully embraced it in his second. He overturned the religious liberty provisions Clinton had established in the 1993 Religious Freedom Restoration Act. He pushed a culturally progressive agenda not only in the courts but through his education regulatory policies.

Whereas Clinton had his "Sister Souljah moment" and publicly rejected the hip-hop artist's condoning of retaliatory black violence against white people, Obama refused to denounce similar statements made by protesters in Ferguson, Missouri. In fact he invited one of the more incendiary Ferguson protest leaders, Al Sharpton, to the White House for consultations.[25] The rout extended to economic policy. Clinton balanced budgets, while Obama added trillions of dollars in new debt, breaking all records. It is true that both presidents wanted health care reform, but Clinton pulled back his bill when it failed to generate bipartisan support. Obama rammed his bill through Congress without a single Republican vote.

All in all, Obama is the anti–President Bill Clinton of Democratic politics. He has changed not only the Democratic Party but progressivism profoundly. Gone is the "New Democrat" moderation of the Clinton era. The Democratic Leadership Council, the intellectual force behind Clinton's rise, closed shop in 2011. Even Bill Clinton's wife, Hillary, ever watching the socialist Bernie Sanders over her left shoulder, has disavowed her husband's legacy. It may be, as liberal columnist Dana Milbank crowed in an article titled " 'Liberal': So Hot Right Now,"[26] that liberal is no longer a dirty word; yet the movement that he describes is liberal in name only. The postmodern left, the driving force of progressivism and the dominant voice of the Democratic Party today, has triumphed over liberalism.

## THE PHILOSOPHICAL WAR ON LIBERALISM

There is a philosophical corollary to the Democratic Party's abandonment of Bill Clinton's legacy. As mentioned earlier, one of Clinton's favorite intellectuals was John Rawls. It is fair to say that his work mirrors the moderate turn of liberalism represented by Bill Clinton in the 1990s. But by 2008, like Clinton's neo-liberalism, Rawls's moderate liberalism had already gone out of style. The culprits in his demise are the same people who eroded Clinton's moderate liberalism—the postmodern leftists.

The philosophical issues are subtle and complex, but the most common theme running throughout postmodernist critiques of Rawls's thought is this: Rawls mistakenly believed in the existence of universal justice objectively arrived at by human reason. Though this was a landmark principle of liberalism for centuries, it is too much for postmodernists, who recoil from anything that smacks of natural law. For example, philosopher David Gauthier, who tries to invent a neo-Hobbesian view of the social contract, complains that Rawls assumed there is only one possible rational agent in deciding the nature of justice. Gauthier believes no such single agent exists, and therefore there is no agreement on what the "original" position of justice is. There is rather only the "initial bargaining position."[27] Another philosopher, Ronald Dworkin, also maintained that there is no such thing as an original agreement on justice; there are simply too many local variations of what the truth is, he says, to settle on any single viewpoint.[28]

Dworkin and Gauthier are evoking postmodernism's quintessential idea—epistemic relativism—in their criticisms of Rawls. Their philosophical bête noire is the moral certainty inherent in natural law, which they seem to sense lurking in the background of Rawls's philosophy. Rawls never advanced a theory of natural law, but he did want to find its equivalent (insofar as he assumed the existence of rational agents agreeing on what universal justice actually is). He had the moralist's intuition that any kind of morality necessitates a universal position. But nothing could be more offensive to a postmodernist. The philosopher Michael Walzer, for example, faults Rawls for adopting a "transcultural, ahistorical, universalistic perspective," as if the mere recantation of these words should strike horror in the heart of all intellectuals.[29]

Epistemic relativism is not the only postmodern idea used against Rawls. Also common is the argument that he fails to understand the nature of power in identity politics. For example, critical feminist theorists Susan Okin and Martha Nussbaum complain that Rawls allows for the perpetuation of an unjust gender hierarchy.[30] Others blame him for insufficiently appreciating the role of economic equality in establishing social justice.[31] Canadian philosopher Will Kymlicka contends that liberals like Rawls should abandon their notion of neutral liberal state action acting on behalf of the entire population, and instead adopt the view that the state should take action to immunize the lifestyles of cultural minorities from the majority.[32]

The assault against Rawls was unrelenting, but he was not the only liberal philosopher in this period trying to save liberal principles. Another was Richard Rorty,[33] a professor of philosophy who taught at Princeton and other prominent universities. Rorty is known for trying to update the philosophy of pragmatism with insights from postmodern philosophy. On the one hand, like the postmodernists, Rorty embraced epistemic relativism, believing that there is no worthwhile theory of truth other than what can be established semantically. He also was fascinated by the postmodern sense of irony; he believed that the attempts to see the world empirically and representationally were responsible for most of the ills of the world. On the other hand, he was openly critical of postmodernists' theoretical flights of fancy, accusing them of failing to answer the world's problems. He was particularly upset that they failed to appreciate human rights. His equivocation even went to the point of defending John Rawls from his critics. Even though he did not agree with Rawls's philosophy, he admired his attempt to find a common ground upon which to build a political philosophy.

Rorty is, like Rawls, a transitional figure. Whereas Rawls stood between liberalism and the welfare state, Rorty is positioned midway between Rawls and the postmodern philosophers. On the one hand Rorty wanted to cling to the optimistic progressivism of Rawls and earlier liberals such as John Dewey; it is as if he did not want to give up on some sense of universalism, despite the fact that his epistemology told him adhering to it was a fool's errand. On the other hand he was a man of the postmodern age, unable to pull himself out of the epistemological quagmire into which Jacques Derrida and the others had sunk Western philosophy.

Unlike Rawls, Rorty is a man who could not make up his mind. There is no middle ground between liberalism and postmodernism. By the time both men died (Rawls passed away in 2002 and Rorty in 2007), their time was pretty much up. The postmodern leftists had triumphed. They had largely taken over the humanities and cultural studies departments of the American academy and their epistemological assumptions were, despite the widespread existence of analytical and other non-postmodernist schools of philosophy in America's universities, the predominant worldview of progressive liberals.

## THEORETICAL DIFFERENCES BETWEEN
## LIBERALISM AND POSTMODERN LEFTISM

Many, but not all, of the postmodern left's arguments against liberalism can be traced back to epistemic relativism. They also are derived from the different interpretations of man, law, and society debated for centuries inside the Western Enlightenment tradition. A review and comparison of the main philosophical differences between liberalism and the postmodern left is useful.

*The Problem of Power.* For liberals like Alexis de Tocqueville and François Guizot, unchecked power was a problem—it was, in fact, *the* problem. Guizot believed the only way power could be kept in check was to tolerate unorthodox and uncomfortable opinions. Looking back fearfully on the French Revolution, Tocqueville thought much the same, fearing that a concentration of power, even in the name of the people, would lead to tyranny. Liberal economists from Adam Smith to Schulze-Delitzsch worried that over-centralizing government power would hamper economic innovation and threaten local control of the economy. There are few liberal principles more enduring historically than the distrust of centralized power.

Clearly the postmodern left has no such qualms. They may have unique cultural concerns, but postmodern leftists, like socialists, are all too happy to use state power to force people into line. Unlike socialists, postmodernists are not interested in nationalizing the means of production or even creating large centralized bureaucracies. In fact, in their embrace of technology and constant social change they are more like anarchists and libertarians than 19th-century socialists.

Revolutionaries of all stripes promise that things will be different once they are in charge. This is an argument heard from radicals throughout the ages, and it is heard from the democratic socialists and identity radicals of the postmodern left today. But as we know from history, it hardly ever turns out that way. Once in power the victims act worse than their oppressors. It is the age-old story of the revolutionaries storming the ramparts but then pulling up the drawbridge behind them after the castle has fallen. As George Orwell once wrote, "[m]ost revolutionaries are potential Tories, because they imagine that everything can be put right by altering the shape of society." However, he added, "[o]nce that change is effected, they see no need for any other."[34]

*Inclusiveness.* As we have seen, according to Fawcett, one of the central ideas of late liberalism (from John Stuart Mill onwards) is the notion of inclusiveness—that is, devising ways to include as many people as possible in social intercourse and government. This is an important liberal principle, but it has to be put in context. People should be included in society's decision making, but there must also be a private sphere for ethical choices and also for civil liberties like freedom of speech.[35]

There has always been tension between these two principles— between "social" liberalism that emphasizes democracy and equality and "political" liberalism that values individual liberty. But for most liberals, if trying to "include" people in the name of equality ran afoul of the liberty principle, then the liberty principle usually prevailed. Indeed, what we call inclusiveness today was for most of modern liberalism's history understood negatively as nonexclusiveness, i.e., the notion that people should not be excluded from society or the polity because of their views or social circumstances. It did not mean absolute social equality. This difference defined liberalism's central historical distinction not only from socialism but also from its more modern offshoot, social democracy.

The postmodern left's notion of inclusiveness could not be more different. It means absolute social equality, both in terms of social status and income level. There is no respect for the liberty principle as traditionally understood by classical liberals, because the postmodern impulse is not liberal at all, but radically egalitarian. Whereas the liberal would worry about someone being intentionally excluded from society by the willful actions of individuals and the government, the postmodern leftist, like a social democrat or even a socialist, would demand the government take direct action to force society to accept them as an equal. There is no interest in a trade-off or balancing of liberty and "social" justice, because to the postmodern leftist individual liberty is considered a social fiction.

*Nonobstructionism.* Another difference involves the liberal principle of nonobstructionism.[36] It establishes that neither the state nor society should obstruct the private lives of individuals unless there is an overriding and compelling reason to do so. Once again, in the interest of balance, the modern liberal accepted some limitations on individual liberty in order to serve the greater public good. The two most notable areas where this has occurred are national security and the welfare state. But whereas liberals such as John Rawls and Ronald Dworkin seek some balance between liberty and social democracy in their approach to the welfare state, the postmodern left completely dismisses the principle of nonobstructionism. It not only adopts a radically egalitarian view of social welfare policy, it also disregards the right of free speech, which in some quarters of the left is seen as a potentially antisocial principle.

*Sovereignty of the Individual and the Noninstrumentality of Man.* Most people recognize that liberals care about individual freedom. It is one of liberalism's signature principles. But as a philosophical idea, individualism has had a rough time. It can mean either the classic liberal individualism of natural law or the radical individualism of Nietzsche or an existentialist. Nevertheless, despite its philosophical slipperiness, most liberals at least try to maintain a respect for the right of the individual to make up his or her own mind about how to live and what to believe. Call it civic respect as Edmund Fawcett does or human dignity as Steven Lukes does, but liberals of all stripes have more or less believed that individuals have some degree of moral freedom and are not to be treated as mere instruments in a social game.[37]

As Fawcett points out, Immanuel Kant summed up the sovereignty of the individual in *Groundwork of the Metaphysics of Morals* (1785):

> Man, and in general every rational being, exists as an end in himself. This notion that man should never be treated as a mere instrument is nearly universally accepted as a liberal principle. He does not exist to represent some class or race. Nor does he find meaning or redemption in some political cause. His rights are endowed either by nature, God, or the very least as a consensus arrived at by some form of social contract, and it is up to the government to protect those rights.[38]

Postmodern leftists, like leftists in general, have no such qualms. Individuals are supposedly fictitious social categories created by the ruling class to protect their selfish interests. People's identities are socially constructed things that solely reflect the interests of race, class, or gender. Since individuals are simply social constructs, it is perfectly acceptable to treat them as mere instruments of power and society. They have no rights except those granted by society and the state. For postmodernists, there is no question of a morally conscious individual *choosing* right or wrong; he or she is merely acting out some predetermined class, racial, sexual, or gender outlook. Since the person is a social object and not a sovereign subject in charge of his or her own destiny, freedom is defined by how closely the individual's will conforms to the general will of the collective.

This creates multiple problems for the liberal. There is not only a lack of civic respect for a person's ethical freedom. There is also the loss of universal justice as a basis for civil rights in general. Progressives today are fond of saying that gay, gender, and transgender rights are the new frontier of civil rights. But their version of civil rights is not the same as those of Martin Luther King, Jr., and other pioneers in eliminating racial discrimination. As King saw it, blacks deserved equality before the law because of their humanity—the human dignity they share with all human beings as individuals. The same is true for women. They deserve protection against discrimination not because they are women per se but because they are human beings. Being black or female is nothing more than an attribute of being human; and a liberal society has an interest in ensuring that no one deprives them of the human rights they share with everyone else. In this respect, to the liberal, all human rights are individual rights.

*Relativism vs. Pluralism.* The liberal's embrace of individualism may appear on the surface to be relativistic, but it is not. It is pluralistic. Liberal philosophers Isaiah Berlin and Karl Popper are the most famous proponents of pluralism as a philosophical idea.[39] Berlin mentioned it by name, while Popper spoke of the need for an open society. Berlin believed that any attempt on the part of society or the state to define personal ethics for people would inevitably lead to tyranny. Popper agreed; otherwise societies could sink into totalitarianism. Both believed that some universal ethics existed, but it was up to a free people to discover what they were.

The postmodern relativist could not be more different. While the "let a thousand flowers bloom" relativism may appear at first to be pluralistic, it is actually the opposite. Since there is no central moral reference point, and any one view is theoretically as good as any other, there are no ethical limits to what any group can do inside its own ethical domain. All that is necessary is to assert an overriding need to rectify a social injustice. Relativism appears to be about letting everyone be or do anything they want, but as we see with speech codes and reverse social stereotyping, that is not what happens in practice. Lacking a civic respect for everyone's point of view, which is the liberal position, cultural relativism falls back on the default of illiberalism—that of imposing its views on everyone.

*In Sum.* The differences between the postmodern left and liberalism cut across the entire spectrum of intellectual thought. Liberalism is rational; the postmodern left is irrational. Liberalism is empirical, believing in objective facts; the postmodern left is radically subjective, arguing that all truth is merely a matter of interpretation. Liberalism is totally committed to science and the scientific method of rigorous empirical research; the postmodern left in some cases treats the scientific method as mere fiction, while in others uses it deceptively and opportunistically to advance a political agenda. Liberalism is legally positivistic, while the postmodern left is happy to sacrifice legal facts for some preferred ideological narrative. Liberalism treats people as individual moral beings capable of making rational moral decisions, whereas the individualism of the postmodern left defines morality as purely subjective and relative to the situation of the group. Liberalism thrives on open-ended debate; the postmodern left is suspicious of open inquiry, fearing it will legitimize some idea whose very existence is considered a sign of oppression.

## A QUESTION OF BALANCE

So long as America's social liberalism was working in tandem with political liberalism, the American left and America's classic liberal traditions existed in a rough and contested balance. They were seldom in agreement, but at least they were not waging total war against each other. That is no longer the case. Today the postmodern left is engaged in open warfare against what remains of the American liberal tradition.

We should remember that it was Andrew Jackson, the democrat, who first expanded democracy in American life. Jackson saw himself as the political heir to Thomas Jefferson, the classic American liberal. He established the standard by which social inclusion in the name of democracy also meant extending Americans' liberal political rights. It was a principle of American democracy grounded firmly in the American classical liberal tradition, one whereby equality was defined as equal political rights for all people. It would take the Civil War and the civil rights movement to fully achieve this principle for all Americans, but it was a principle—a question of balance, really—that endured for most of American history.

Endured, that is, until recently. Now the balance between liberty and equality has broken down completely. For the postmodern left, equality no longer means equality of opportunity, but equality of results. Opportunity for all means a government that favors some over others. Liberty means the right to force one's views on other people. And tolerance actually means intolerance.

It is Orwellian doublethink. What we call progressive liberalism in America today is actually a bitter ideological enemy of liberalism. It not only is illiberal; it is only partly American. It is ideological bread first mixed and rolled by French and German philosophers; kneaded with the American traditions of anarchism, progressivism, and the New Left; and then over-baked by academics and activists into a black-crusted loaf of anti-Americanism. Some libertarians argue that American liberalism started dying the moment the U.S. government was formed.[40] That is only partially true. American liberalism lived on well into the 20th century. But in the past decade it has been rapidly disappearing. Gone is any concern for balancing the social democratizing tendencies of progressivism with the American instinct to preserve individual liberty.

# FOUR

# The Illiberal Style of Liberal Politics Today

Intolerance is a hot topic in America. Liberals accuse conservatives of intolerance and conservatives return the favor. Most academics blame conservatives, especially religious ones. Amos N. Guiora, a professor of law at the University of Utah, attributes the "new" intolerance spreading across America to religious "extremism," by which he means not only radical Islamism but devout Christianity.[1] Martha C. Nussbaum, professor of law and ethics at the University of Chicago, argues that American fear of Muslims is contributing to the new intolerance.[2] But not everyone thinks the new wave of intolerance in America is religiously inspired or coming from the right. D. A. Carson, a Canadian theologian, argues the opposite. In *The Intolerance of Tolerance* (2013), he concedes that intolerance is indeed on the rise, but it is not Christians who are at fault; it is secular liberals who are intolerant of Christians. A "disproportionate part of the intolerance that masks itself as (the new) tolerance," he says, "is directed against Christians and Christianity."[3]

Carson is on to something. Much of the chauvinism you see in America today has nothing to do with religious extremism or the American right. It is in fact increasingly coming from the left. There are numerous examples. A prominent liberal blog, *The Daily Kos*, posted a call for the arrest of Senator Ted Cruz for treason.[4] During the government shutdown debates of 2013, then Senate Majority Leader Harry Reid, a Democrat, labeled Tea Party activists "anarchists," "radicals," "fanatics," and "extremists" who, like a bad disease, had "infected" the Republican Party.[5] The President of the United States, Barack Obama, referred to his opponents as "enemies"[6] and "hostage-takers."[7] Democrat gadfly Representative Alan Grayson of Florida, who is known for his incendiary rhetoric, exclaimed that he cannot listen to former Vice President Dick Cheney speak "because of the blood that drips from his teeth."[8] Grayson attracted widespread condemnation during the debate over Obamacare when he remarked that "the Republicans want you to die quickly if you get sick."[9] Progressives routinely label religious conservatives who question same-sex marriage as hateful bigots. In the days after the Supreme Court ruled in favor of same-sex marriage, a priest was spat upon on the streets of New York City[10] and former *Star Trek* actor George Takei called Supreme Court Justice Clarence Thomas a "clown in blackface."[11] Even the comedian Jerry Seinfeld has lamented how difficult it is to do comedy because of the political correctness on the left.[12]

A conclusion is inescapable: intolerance is on the upswing, and the cause is not a sudden new outburst of right-wing radicalism, but an aggressive new boldness growing inside the modern progressive movement.

The purveyors of liberal intolerance are not bit players. They are political leaders, public officials, teachers, intellectuals, corporate tycoons, famous celebrities, and the leading voices of the U.S. media. They are mainstream figures in public life, not fringe elements crying in the wilderness or baying from the fringes of American politics. Pollster Frank Luntz spends a great deal of time taking the pulse of the country, and he is alarmed by how divided it has become. The Americans he polls "want to impose their opinions rather than express them," he observed. "And they're picking up their leads from here in Washington." When asked if it hadn't always been this way, he answered, "Not like this. Not like this."[13] Even TV host Bill Maher senses something has gone wrong; during the 2013 Paula Deen controversy over remarks she made about her views of blacks as a child, he asked: "Do we always have to make people go away?"[14]

American politics has always been a rough sport. But the chauvinism inside progressive circles today is markedly worse than it was even a decade ago. Liberals blame conservatives for the bitter new environment; they often cite Bill Clinton's impeachment as the starting point for the angry turn in politics. But conservatives fire back that before that there was Senator Ted Kennedy's character assassination of Robert Bork, and after that the horrible way Clarence Thomas was treated in his confirmation hearings. So there is plenty of blame to share on both sides, but frankly these events were a long time ago and cannot really account for the negative turn of events over the past eight years.

The shift has been not only more recent but more fundamental, having mostly to do with the changing face of America's political culture. Progressive liberals always have had a low opinion of conservatives, but their disdain is now a bitter, dark kind of revulsion. The more their views have gained public acceptance, especially on sexual rights issues, the more brazen they have become in expressing their vitriolic hatred of conservatives. The result is a profound change in the balance of power in the culture wars. The battlefront in the war on intolerance that once was fought by battered liberals against an established, dominant conservative culture has shifted. Today it is the warriors of an established, dominant liberal culture fighting against embattled conservatives.

This is not to say that intolerance and bigotry have disappeared on the right. The 2015 attack by a white supremacist on a black church in Charleston, South Carolina, shows that a violent strain of racial hatred still exists on the far right in America. The attempt to accuse all Southern conservatives of racial hatred is unjust, but it is nonetheless true that some conservatives have been too quick to dismiss the complaints of black people who are offended by symbols of the Confederacy. When in the summer of 2015 Donald Trump spoke of Mexican immigrants as rapists, his popularity spiked. Trump may be more of a populist than a conservative,[15] but his rhetoric undoubtedly awakened and even empowered intolerant voices on the right. It is equally true that some right-wing commentators go over the top in accusing President Obama of treason or some other abominable crime. And trolls on Twitter and other social media can be every bit as nasty as any left-wing radical. Most conservative Americans are decent, law-abiding citizens, but some activists and media types push the envelope of intolerance.

Populism of the kind represented by Donald Trump knows no ideological boundaries. Trump's positions on Planned Parenthood or foreign trade are roughly the same as any Democrat's. Bernie Sanders's socialism is as populist as Trump's pseudo-conservatism. Regardless of ideological differences, there is a common source of these phenomena. People across the political spectrum are fed up with the American political system. They may very well have reason to feel this way, but the very nature of the emotions involved tend to stoke a zero-sum mentality in the way they view politics. Like all populists down through history they are prone to respond to fiery speeches more than to data-laden white papers and in the heat of the moment to surrender to the belief that all the problems in America are caused not by misguided policies, but the dark motives and conspiracies of political enemies.

Despite the existence of populist intolerance on the left and right, it is the intolerance of the left that poses the greatest danger to the American republic. For one thing, progressives have shown little interest in policing the illiberalism on their far left flank. Unlike Republican presidential candidates Ted Cruz, John Kasich, Rand Paul, and Marco Rubio, who have rebuked intolerant statements made by Donald Trump, Democratic candidates Hillary Clinton and Martin O'Malley have treated socialist candidate

Bernie Sanders with kid gloves and refused to repudiate the blatant illiberalism of, for example, the "black lives matter" movement.[16] The "no enemies to the left" mentality of progressive liberalism is widespread and growing. It is increasingly becoming entrenched in the American system itself—in its laws, its policies, and the culture and institutions of mainstream America. In the Democratic Party, the government, the courts, the media, the entertainment industry, the universities, and the corporate world, there is a new aggressive edge to progressive politics. Political opponents must not be merely challenged, but silenced. People with different views must not be debated but ostracized. Speech must be controlled. Rules, constitutional law, and democratically enacted laws must be bypassed. Entire classes of people are accused of guilt by association. Such tactics are all too familiar in the history of American radicalism, but today they are mainstream. They are the ugly face of a progressive movement that once prided itself on compassion, openness, and generosity.

### THE POLITICS OF INTOLERANCE

Regardless of who is to blame, the country is deeply divided. Alan Abramowitz and Steve Webster of Emory University argue that the two political parties' dislike for each other has grown. They note that there has been "a very large increase in ideological distance between supporters of the two parties," doubling over the past forty years.[17] Not only has the distance grown but so too has the depth of dislike people have for the opposing party. Abramowitz and Webster call this new condition "negative partisanship." One of the biggest political motivators to win elections is not in order to get something done, but to stop the other side from gaining power. Underpinning this political negativity are growing divisions in racial, cultural, and economic attitudes. Not only is racial tolerance weakening—for whites as well as for blacks—but the cultural wars over abortion and same-sex marriage are more heated and personal.

Political polarization is not just political, but social. More and more, people are segmenting themselves culturally into homogeneous value tribes. They are choosing neighborhoods, jobs, and schools for their children that reflect their own values and prejudices. They associate mainly with their own kind, and tend to look down on people outside their own cohort. The impact on the political culture is palpable. Empathy is in short supply. With rising intolerance comes declining community values. People are increasingly impatient with the "otherness" implied by different opinions and lifestyles. Each side battles to control the definition of normalcy and the political middle as a tactic to accuse their opponents of being crazed radicals. Put simply, intolerance is not just ideological but increasingly a cultural norm that cuts across all ideologies. It is becoming more culturally acceptable to demonize someone who thinks and acts outside of one's own clique, group, or cohort.

A contributing factor is the coarseness of America's popular culture. People have complained for decades about violence in movies and TV shows, hard-core rap, and antisocial hip-hop music. Sexually explicit themes have been around a very long time, even though they are far more pervasive and vulgar today than twenty or thirty years ago. It all has taken a terrible toll on the culture. Violent images and narcissistic values have lowered the threshold for indulging in outrageously selfish behavior. It is now quite normal to view human beings as nothing more than a collection of appetites and needs that, if denied, justify all sorts of protests, petitions, and, in extreme circumstances, even the threat of violence.

Take, for example, the prominence of vengeance as the central theme in successful movies such as *Dead Man Down*, *Iron Man 3*, *Star Trek Into Darkness*, *The Lone Ranger*, *The Wolverine*, *Gangster Squad*, and even *Hansel and Gretel: Witch Hunters*. Revenge in various states of violence is the leitmotif of the HBO hit series *Game of Thrones*, whose characters are defined by how well they execute their exquisite plans of revenge. The overall impression is one of doing anything for justice. Entertainment is entertainment, and it occupies a different world from that of politics. But it is still true that much of what happens today in the movies and on TV mirrors and impacts the hopes and fears of our culture, as well as our illusions and prejudices. One of those illusions is that justice is simply another kind of vengeance. Severe payback is now okay, provided the victim can be made into a social villain. It is not much of a stretch to turn "vengeance is mine," a rather selfish and stupid kind of morality, into something a bit more sophisticated—into, say, "no justice, no peace."

The popular culture has also lowered the threshold on public shaming rituals. It is not only suppressing certain speech on college campuses, but making public denunciation of certain classes of people into a form of popular entertainment. The masters of the funny cheap shot are comedians Jon Stewart and Stephen Colbert, who routinely and cleverly skewer conservatives as stupid bigots. After the Supreme Court ruling on same-sex marriage, for example, Stewart asked what was wrong with opponents of same-sex marriage, as if a view held for thousands of years, even not very long ago by both Barack Obama and Hillary Clinton, were incomprehensible. The use of humor is a cultural trick. It provides a cultural permission slip to be nasty because, or so the assumption goes, the enemies of "the people" are so unattractive that they deserve whatever Stewart or Colbert throws at them. When Stewart compares Senator Ted Cruz to the *Harry Potter* character Voldemort,[18] he knows we will then think of Cruz as the book's author describes Voldemort, "a raging psychopath, devoid of the normal human responses to other people's suffering."[19]

It may seem futile to complain about the crudeness of American mass culture. It has been around for decades, and it is not about to change anytime soon. The thin line that exists these days between politics and entertainment (witness the rise of Donald Trump) is undoubtedly coarsening our politics. It is becoming more culturally acceptable to split the world into us–versus–them schemata and to indulge in all sorts of antisocial and illiberal fantasies about crushing one's enemies.

Only a few decades ago most liberals had a different idea of tolerance. Most would explain it with some variation of Evelyn Beatrice Hall's line about Voltaire's philosophy of free speech: "I disapprove of what you say, but I will defend to the death your right to say it."[20] That is no longer the case. It is now deemed necessary, indeed even noble, to be intolerant in the cause of tolerance. Any remark or viewpoint that liberals believe is critical of minorities is by definition intolerant. A liberal critique of conservatives or religious people, on the other hand, is, again by definition, incapable of being intolerant. It is a willful double standard. For liberals, intolerance is a one-way street leading straight to conservatism.

The liberal view of tolerance can be broken down into three categories. The first is *mandated tolerance*: You are not entitled to your opinion at all; some ideas, especially those involving sexual politics, religion, and anything that can be labeled as "hate speech," can justly be suppressed, even by force of administrative rule or the law. It is the most radical of all the categories and is seen in campus speech codes, microaggression charges, "trigger warnings," and various attempts to control "hate speech" (which are discussed more thoroughly in another chapter). It is patently authoritarian, a familiar refrain sung countless times throughout history by revolutionaries and totalitarians.

The second category is slightly less in-your-face, but it is still implicitly authoritarian. It is *self-censorship tolerance*: You may be entitled to your opinion, but you must keep it to yourself. You may think whatever you like in the privacy of your home, but once you step into a public space—or even a private meeting outside of business hours—your opinions can be regulated and controlled. Examples include university diversity rules restricting what employees can say outside the workplace about minorities and same-sex marriage; similar rules governing what employees can say privately on Facebook or Twitter; and most recently, new anti-discrimination laws and regulations aimed at protecting LGBT (Lesbian, Gay, Bisexual, Transgender) people that force others to divorce their religious convictions from their public actions, even inside their privately owned shops. On the surface this view appears to respect freedom of opinion, but it does nothing of the sort. Its real purpose is to shame people into exercising self-censorship. Freedom of opinion is a meaningless gesture if you cannot express yourself openly in public. As Supreme Court Justice Samuel Alito observed after *Obergefell v. Hodges* (2015), the Supreme Court ruling that established same-sex marriage as a "constitutional" right, dissenters now will only be able to "whisper their thoughts in the recesses of their homes."[21]

The third category is far more subtle. It is *peer pressure tolerance*: You are entitled to your opinion, but I am not obligated to take it seriously. The tactic is to shrink the space in which contrary views are deemed socially acceptable. There are numerous examples. An academic department subtly excludes professors with contrary views but justifies it on grounds other than ideology (for example, hiring only the "best" people from liberal Ivy League schools). A study written by a conservative professor from a small Midwestern college is rejected for consideration at a Davos or Aspen Institute conference, not on its merits, but because the professor's credentials do not compare with those of the multimillion-dollar-endowed professor from Harvard or Yale. A climate change scientist not only tries to crush dissent inside his profession but uses his credentials to advance political agendas with implications far beyond science. The academic and scientific peer-review processes are stacked with political and professional allies. Journalists serve as strict gatekeepers for the news, only letting through what serves their prejudices.

The new intolerance would not exist were it not for a profound confusion. Every decent person wants to be compassionate. It is one of the traits that distinguish good people from bad. But what if that sense of compassion is driven not by ethics—or conscience—but by politics and power? It then becomes something altogether different. What if what is otherwise a virtue gets transformed into the vices of irresponsibility and malice? Instead of focusing on actually helping people, you shift the responsibility away from yourself and onto others. Instead of being charitable with your own money, you demand that others or the government step in and help. You become far more concerned with punishing alleged transgressors than with helping people. Either way, you have slipped over into selfish and venal kinds of behavior, all the while morally preening yourself as a good person.

There is another misunderstanding. The psychology of guilt is normally associated with personal failings. The conscience can be quite tough and even cruel when it thinks we have fallen short of our ideals. But what happens when the psychological mechanisms of guilt are projected not inwardly but outwardly, toward other people? Guilt then becomes not an agent of morality and self-improvement but of social control and civil vengeance. As Joseph Epstein observes:

> Victims of an earlier time viewed themselves as supplicants, throwing themselves on the conscience if not mercy of those in power to raise them from their downtrodden condition. The contemporary victim tends to be angry, suspicious, and above all progress-denying. He or she is ever on the lookout for that touch of racism, sexism, homophobia, or insensitivity that might show up in a stray opinion, an odd locution, an uninformed misnomer. People who count themselves victims require enemies. Forces high and low block their progress: The economy disfavors them; society is organized against them; the malevolent, who are always in ample supply, conspire to keep them down; the system precludes them.[22]

As a result, Epstein continues, "the roles of victim and supposed antagonist are reversed. Today it is the victim who is doing the bullying—threatening boycott, riot, career-destroying social media condemnation—and frequently making good on their threats." It is quite simply a moral inversion: one can blame others for one's own failings, moral or otherwise. We have arrived at the dark heart of this notion of illiberal liberalism. It is what gives liberals the permission to be so bloody intolerant of others. Fire can now be used to fight fire, and truly the end justifies the means.

◆ ◆ ◆

In the early 1960s, political scientist Richard Hofstadter developed a theory about what he called the "paranoid style" of American politics.[23] It is an apt description of politics in America today. He had mostly right-wingers like the John Birch Society in mind, but he also believed the paranoid style could exist on the far left. It is the paranoid style of left-wing politics that is most influential today. Many of the paranoid habits of the 1950s that Hofstadter described are prevalent in the far-left reaches of today's progressive movement.

Liberal populists, like the populist right-wingers of the Fifties, are big believers in conspiracy theories. Hillary Clinton once spoke of a "vast right-wing conspiracy" against her and her husband, and she is not alone in her paranoia. Senator Elizabeth Warren of Massachusetts (whose financial disclosure reports showed her to be worth about $8 million in early 2015[24]) believes businessmen, bankers, and the rich are irredeemably selfish and make decisions solely for their own benefit, which hurts the poor.[25] To many progressive liberals, opponents of same-sex marriage are not honest people guided by conscience, but malicious bigots out to do harm. American history is not a complex unfolding of events but a cynical conspiracy driven by rich white people whose only interest is to keep their racial and economic privileges. Since the "enemy" is in control of everything—the radio waves, the churches, and the banks—they are thought to be all-powerful. It is therefore perfectly acceptable to apply any means whatsoever to dislodge them from power. It is justice of the revolutionary sort, because according to the paranoid's viewpoint, one's political opponents are simply too evil to be given a fair shake in the debate. They must not be merely opposed. They must be silenced and removed.

The paranoid mindset is not always plain to see. The chair of a "queer studies" academic program may be calling for a sexual revolution, but you would not know it by the pseudo-scientific jargon used in the classroom. Nor would you know it from appearances. The days are long gone in the American academy when radical professors wore sandals, sported long hair, and acted like angry outsiders. They are today insiders and they act the part. Their outward style is thoroughly anodyne, which makes their whole campaign for radical change look staid and even middle-class. Many radicals, not only those on campus, have become gentrified. Following the advice of Saul Alinsky, who wrote *Rules for Radicals* (1971),[26] they long ago gave up the call for total revolution and decided to march slowly through the institutions, trimming and compromising whenever they must but never giving up on their old radical dreams.

These people are today the new ruling class in America, with even one of their own, Barack Obama, as president of the United States. It is a long way from the front steps of Berkeley in 1964, where the radical student movement of the 1960s was born. But all in all the New Left of that era, after having failed miserably in the 1970s, has today finally prevailed in making its cultural revolution in America.

The key to making this revolution work is to transform the meaning of normality. If you were to ask gay activists what they want, their most likely answer is to be treated as normal persons. That is what they mean by equality. But there is a catch: For them to feel normal their critics must be abnormal. For them to be equal their opponents must be treated unequally. Religious opponents of same-sex marriage must be thoroughly delegitimized. They cannot be accepted as merely holding a different opinion, but tarred as hateful bigots and denounced as social deviants, just as gays say they were themselves ostracized by religious conservatives in the past. Similarly, the entire white race must be said to be racist, and not just a few misguided individuals. The whole basis of social morality must be turned upside down, to the point that churchgoing people are painted as social villains if they question gay rights. Meanwhile people who used to be seen as deviants are now the new normal.

The moral energy required to sustain the inversion gets transformed into paranoia. In its fragility, this moral inversion can only be maintained through eternal vigilance against even the slightest deviation. In order to "trans-evaluate" all values—that is, overturn old ones and create a whole new set of values—the definitions of right and wrong must be turned upside down. Tolerance is not enough. Total submission is required. People must be divided into friendlies and enemies. As Hofstadter observes:

> The paranoid's interpretation of history is distinctly personal: decisive events are not taken as part of the stream of history, but as the consequences of someone's will. Very often, the enemy is held to possess some especially effective source of power: he controls the press; he has unlimited funds; he has a new secret for influencing the mind (brainwashing); he has a special technique for seduction (the Catholic confessional).[27]

To a progressive liberal inclined to think this way, America is always on the verge of a theocratic takeover by the evangelical right. Former Arkansas Governor Mike Huckabee and other evangelicals are ten feet tall and about to storm the White House. Evangelicals want to criminalize homosexuality, and conservatives want, as Vice President Joe Biden once said, to put black people "back in chains."[28] It matters not that evangelicals are a shrinking force in American politics and do not even enjoy a majority among the Republican electorate. Nor does it matter that progressive views on marriage are clearly gaining ground. To progressive liberals, it is still 1923, when KKK rallies were held across America. Every new day is just as it was in Selma in 1965, a showdown between the forces of good and evil.

There is only one way to defeat such a horrible enemy: to become like him. Hofstadter called this way of thinking "emulating" the enemy. As examples, he noted that in the 1950s the John Birch Society established front groups that mimicked Communist Party cells, and the KKK imitated Catholicism by donning priestly garments.[29] Today progressives habitually project their own hatreds onto others. If gay activists assume a Christian opponent of same-sex marriage is a bigot, then they feel perfectly within their rights to treat Christians in a bigoted way in return. If a radical feminist assumes all men hate women, then she is entitled to hate men back. If a racial activist believes all white people are racist, then he or she can engage in blatant racial discrimination against white people without the slightest twinge of guilt.

At the most basic level it is the logic of the military conflict. If you do not get your enemies first, they will get you. As Hofstadter explains:

> Since the enemy is thought of as being totally evil and totally unappeasable, he must be totally eliminated—if not from the world, at least from the theatre of operations to which the paranoid directs his attention. This demand for total triumph leads to the formulation of hopelessly unrealistic goals, and since these goals are not even remotely attainable, failure constantly heightens the paranoid's sense of frustration. Even partial success leaves him with the

same feeling of powerlessness with which he began, and this in turn only strengthens his awareness of the vast and terrifying quality of the enemy he opposes.[30]

The paranoid style still exists on the far right in America. What is new is not only how pervasive it is on the far left, but also how acceptable it has become in the mainstream mentality and practices of progressive liberalism.

◆ ◆ ◆

The left's intolerance raises a question: Is progressive liberalism becoming totalitarian? Is the illiberalism described here turning that movement into something downright dangerous? A lot of conservatives think so.[31] They sense a new mean-spirited urge to control all aspects of people's lives that goes far beyond the authoritarian streak one normally finds in progressive liberalism.

Some distinctions are in order. The actual historical instances of fascism in Italy, Nazism in Germany, and communism in the Soviet Union and China were distinctly brutal and truly totalitarian in their bids for absolute control of society. They each had their own unique set of characteristics and were set in a different time of history. Illiberal liberalism in America is indeed becoming more intolerant and authoritarian, but it is not nearly as bad as these totalitarian movements. The elements of genocide, violence, and mass detention are not present; and the specific ideologies of fascism, Nazism, and communism are not relevant to progressive liberalism (although neo-Marxism is pertinent). As we discuss elsewhere, progressive liberalism today is ideologically postmodern, which separates it from the old ideologies of totalitarianism. It may share contempt for capitalism with socialism, but it is not calling for the nationalization of the means of production or the abolition of all private property. It may be paranoid and conspiratorial, and may even appropriate some of the philosophical ideas of the European far right, but progressive liberalism has not descended into the moral abyss of the Nazis' Nuremberg laws or the Soviet Union's imprisonment of political prisoners in Gulags.

But here is the rub: progressive liberals may not be identical to the old totalitarians, but they *are* willing to dip into the totalitarians' illiberal tool box. This has to do with the logic of making a big revolution. If you want to transform society, as gay activists and even President Obama want to do, then clearly some eggs will have to be broken to make the omelet. After all, it is a tall order to change the way society thinks about values (on sex and marriage, for example) that have been around for millennia. It requires a fairly heavy dose of reeducation if your goal is nothing less than a cultural revolution. Increasingly universities, workplaces, and even the U.S. armed forces are forcing employees to attend sensitivity training seminars on controversial moral issues that used to be entirely private affairs. These training sessions are not the equivalent of Maoist reeducation camps that threaten you with execution if you do not attend, but they are necessary if one wants to keep his job or get promoted. It is all done with a friendly, smiling face, but the underlying threat of illiberal coercion is unmistakable.

Transforming society also involves historical amnesia. Since progressives have convinced themselves that they are forever marching the country toward progress, nothing that has ever happened in the past has anything whatsoever to do with them. Being the good postmodernists that they are, every day is new, and if a training seminar reminds you of a reeducation camp, it is not their concern. All history's lessons about threats to free speech or concentrating power in the hands of the few are ignored. Like the future, history is a blank slate on which progressives can write their dreams and desires. Its only use is as a weapon in a political struggle, not as a source of wisdom or counsel on the harm the politicization of knowledge can do to societies and civilizations.

Treating knowledge and politics in such cavalier ways is dangerous. It may not be totalitarian in a historical sense, but it is frankly getting too close for comfort. Indulging the illiberal impulse is like touching a hot wire; it can shock and even kill, depending on how long you hold on to it. Until recently, progressives refrained from grabbing the wire with both hands and holding on. Unfortunately, that is no longer true.

### WHEN BIGOTRY IS OKAY

Of all the excuses used to restrict speech and freedom of expression, none looms larger than the charge of bigotry. It is the sine qua non of attempts not only to ban "hate speech" but to control and regulate political opinions on campus and force religious people to participate in activities that violate their consciences.[32]

But what exactly is bigotry? The *Merriam-Webster Online Dictionary* in 2015 defined a bigot as a person "who hates or refuses to accept the members of a particular group (such as a racial or religious group)" or "who is obstinately or intolerantly devoted to his or her own opinions and prejudices; *especially*: one who regards or treats the members of a group (as a racial or ethnic group) with hatred and intolerance." Bigotry can be found in any ideological movement, including those on the left. It is an equal-opportunity vice that knows no political boundaries.

The essential part of the definition is not the examples but the principle of aiming hateful or intolerant attitudes toward *members of a group*. That could include any collection of people. It is the negative stereotyping with harmful intent that defines the act of bigotry, not the political or social character of the targeted group. Progressives try to narrow the definition to politically preferred victims, such as sexual and racial minorities, but it is possible for a minority or oppressed person to exhibit bigoted behavior on his or her own. A black person who thinks all white people are racist is no less bigoted than a white who thinks all black people are inferior. Quite simply, bigotry is a negative bias against persons based on their association with a group that is negatively stereotyped and is seen as being collectively guilty of doing something bad.

By this definition, progressive liberals have got a problem. They have developed a bigoted attitude that dare not speak its name—that is, anti-Christianity, or to use a progressive turn of phrase, "Christophobia." Once you refuse to accept the progressive notion that only certain designated groups—women and racial, sexual, and ethnic minorities—are by definition exempt from charges of bigotry, the bigotry of Christophobia becomes clearer. Its most distinguishing characteristic is to assume that Christians have the worst of all possible motives. They do not oppose same-sex marriage because they think men and women are different and children deserve a mom and a dad, but because they supposedly hate homosexuals as people. They assume that any man who opposes abortion does so because he wants to deprive all women of their rights, not because he may have a legitimate concern about taking a life. They assume Catholics want to keep women out of the priesthood not because of theological concerns about Christ's intentions toward his disciples, but simply because the men who run the church hate women. Little a Christian can say or do can change their minds. It is a classic case of stereotypical prejudice wherein minds are already made up and no amount of evidence to the contrary can change them.

The intolerance toward Christianity is driven not merely by policy disagreements, but by a general bias against Christianity *as a religion*. When *New York Times* columnist Frank Bruni associated Christianity with bigotry in an opinion piece, he did so because he truly believes Christians hold outdated and erroneous prejudices in general.[33] He thinks Christians are stuck in the past. They need to discard their outdated views, "much as they've jettisoned other aspects of their faith's history (like slavery), rightly bowing to the enlightenments of modernity." It is not enough to leave

Christians alone to believe as they please. They must be made to see the error of their ways and to convert. Their influence on society must be neutralized and at best eradicated. Not only liberal commentators but high-ranking Democrats hold this view of religion. Hillary Clinton told attendees at the Women in the World Summit in April 2015 that "deep-seated cultural codes, religious beliefs and structural biases have to be changed" in order to give women access to "reproductive health care and safe childbirth."[34] How this change should occur, she did not say. But suffice it to say that if America's most prominent Democrat in 2015 next to the president believes people of faith must be made to give up their most sacred convictions, we are in new political territory indeed.

The prejudice against Christians today contrasts with how Muslims are treated. Progressive liberals routinely advise Americans not to judge all Muslims by the action of a few lunatic terrorists. But they are not so careful about judging Christians. They will quickly lump all Christians together when some fringe Christian group or person says or does something outrageous. Because Muslims are considered an oppressed minority—and too few in number to threaten the sexual liberties of progressive liberals— they are given a pass when they discriminate against women and gays. When, for example, a Muslim baker in Dearborn, Michigan, refused to bake a cake for a gay wedding, there was no outcry from the gay community against that baker. Yet when Christian bakery owners in Oregon did the same, they were not only made to pay damages of $135,000 but held up by gay activists as a prime example of religious bigotry. When a baker in Colorado refused to bake a cake for an *opponent* of gay marriage, she was exonerated by the state's Civil Rights Commission. The baker, it determined, was only upholding a policy against displaying "derogatory language and imagery" on its cakes.[35]

What is the defense for the double standard? Progressives usually argue that because Christians are still a dominant majority—

and thus by definition the oppressors—they cannot be victims. It is not ideologically allowed. But there is a problem with this argument. The Christians being fined and coerced are not the majority but a distinct minority living in jurisdictions controlled by progressives. Now that the Supreme Court says gay marriage is the law of the land, does that mean that Christian dissenters will be accorded the same rights of dissent as a minority? It is not likely. Clerks who refuse to issue gay marriage licenses may be fired or jailed.[36] As public opinion on same-sex marriage changes, it is not gay activists who will be on the defensive, but Christians.

Another defense is that Christians purportedly deserve their ill treatment. Gay people have had to endure humiliation for centuries at the hands of Christians, the thinking goes; so Christians have no right to complain if LGBT people return the offense. No doubt gay people have felt humiliated by egregious forms of discrimination, but there is no evidence that the Christian bakers who were fined for refusing to bake a wedding cake for a gay couple had ever engaged in any anti-gay activities. So why hold them accountable for what other people have done in the past? The issue today is not how gay people have been mistreated in history but whether the state should officially recognize gay marriage. Moreover, if taking offense is the only standard for providing special protection, why are the feelings of Christians not defended as well? After all, the Oregon bakers were not only publically humiliated by authorities but boycotted. They were forced to close their shop and move their business into their home, severely affecting their livelihood as well. Why is their humiliation not an issue? In bringing the suit against the bakers, the gay couple argued such dubious emotional and mental damages as "excessive sleep," feeling "mentally raped," and even a "resumption of smoking habit."[37] Presumably this kind of hypersensitivity is supposed to attract sympathy, as if failing to have a cake baked upon demand is of the same moral order as a woman being refused employment solely because she is woman. In the public harm department, it would seem to me that nearly losing one's business and livelihood is a lot more distressing than losing sleep. There is an "eye for an eye" kind of logic to this way of thinking, but vengeance is hardly a laudable motive in public morality.

The true liberal position would be to let the bakers bake what they want for anyone they want, and to settle the matter of giving offense by letting everyone make their own free choice to shop or not to shop there. Instead, the double standard of illiberal intolerance prevails. Despite all the flouted taboos against bigotry, there is one very profound exception: bigotry against Christians, especially Catholics and evangelical Christians. It is not even recognized as such, which is what makes it particularly dangerous. Without the slightest bit of self-awareness, or even irony, progressive liberals today regularly make negative stereotypes of Christians that, if they were directed against blacks, would make a white supremacist smile.

As bad as the situation is, we must not overstate the case. There is no widespread campaign in America today to criminalize Christianity, as Mike Huckabee has argued.[38] There is open hostility to Christians in progressive liberal circles, but millions of Americans worship every day unmolested by the government or activist groups. It would be more accurate to say that because of the legal successes of the progressive left in recent years, some Christians are being forced under penalty of law to curb their public expressions of faith in the marketplace and civil society. It is not only that the political space in which Christians have traditionally operated in general is shrinking. It is also, and more importantly, that the *social* space for acting on one's religious convictions is getting smaller. Notwithstanding that only a minority of Christians is affected, the implications for all Christians are huge. They could, in the future, find themselves at the opposite end of the "separation of church and state" debate, not unlike what James Madison experienced in his defense of the Baptists against the Anglican-controlled colonial state of Virginia. They faced a government back then that not only imposed penalties on dissenters but decided what was and was not an appropriate form of religious expression in the "public" square.[39]

Now that the Supreme Court has ruled in favor of same-sex marriage, Christians fear the worst. They worry not only that the tax-exempt status of their churches will be challenged, but that they will now be open to civil suits forcing their ministers to participate in gay marriages against their conscience. Such a suit is already underway in the United Kingdom,[40] and it will likely not be long before similar lawsuits start surfacing in the United States. But as they do, progressives should remember one thing: freedom of the press and freedom of religious expression were put together in the First Amendment for a reason. The writers of the Constitution, most assuredly Madison himself, understood that these freedoms are two sides of the same coin. Suppress one and you open up the door to suppressing the other. It is a slippery slope indeed, and one that liberals should embark on with trepidation.

### THE ZERO-TOLERANCE CULTURE

One of the greatest achievements in American history is that we no longer openly tolerate racism. The speed with which Los Angeles Clippers owner Donald Sterling was roundly condemned in 2014 for racist remarks is something we should be proud of.[41] Diminishing racism was a hard battle fought by many people, but it was won by Americans drawing a line in the sand. Not only was the cause noble, so too was the courage required to draw that line. The evils of racism and racial bigotry were so great that the government was justified in enacting broad measures to eradicate them.

But there is a catch. Intolerance is a weapon that can be wielded for good or ill, just as a gun can be. It is not only the cause that justifies the means but the actual methods used. The fact that intolerance is at the heart of the very thing we are trying to combat in racism means it has a double-sided nature. For the civil rights leader, being intolerant of racism and bigotry was necessary to defeat the intolerance that is endemic to racism and bigotry. But, as we have seen repeatedly in the debate over same-sex marriage and other moral issues, when the methods deployed against someone or some cause are inappropriate, intolerance is no longer noble. It is mendacious.

Take, for example, the zero-tolerance culture in our schools and other parts of society. It provides a litany of examples of otherwise reasonable people feeling compelled to do unreasonable things. Children are suspended from school for pointing their fingers like a gun,[42] using an imaginary bow and arrow on the playground,[43] or chewing their Pop-Tarts into the shape of a gun.[44] Seven high school students are arrested for engaging in a harmless end-of-the-year water balloon fight. A student is slammed down on the sidewalk and hospitalized for an injury, and a parent standing nearby and complaining about the excessive use of force is threatened with a stun gun and arrested for trespassing.[45] A high school student called by a drunken friend to drive her home is suspended from school along with everyone else even though she is entirely sober.[46] So-called "free-range children" who are allowed to walk home by themselves from the playground are picked up by police, and their parents are investigated by Child Protective Services. Only decades ago their "offense" was the norm for most American families.[47]

One of the most notorious examples of the zero-tolerance attitude is the campaign to fight the so-called "rape culture" on college campuses. The understandable desire to coax victims of rape to come forth and testify has in some cases turned into witch hunts. University administrators are now judge and jury in alleged rape cases. They take sexual disputes between students that otherwise would not rise to the level of filing criminal charges and turn them over to campus tribunals for adjudication. Normal rules for judging evidence are discarded, and it is widely assumed, because of the narrative that women underreport instances of rape, that a victim's word and feelings trump any other evidence provided either by the alleged perpetrator or by witnesses. The most egregious example of this mentality is a story published by *Rolling Stone* magazine about an alleged rape at the University of Virginia, which turned out to be false.[48] But there are many other instances as well.[49] They point to a troubling willingness to suspend the most basic principles of evidence and even justice in order to make a political point.

It is no accident that the zero-tolerance culture thrives on political correctness. The instinct to constrict boundaries of permissible behavior is becoming rampant. So, too, is the view that no part of private human behavior is too small to escape the social control of busybody administrators and politicians. Once you decide that society or "culture" is to blame for a social problem, as opposed to the actual people who may or may not have committed the offense, you can take all sorts of shortcuts. You can also set yourself to the task of completely trying to control the environments in which all these bad things happen. Instead of going after actual criminals with guns, you go after all guns. Instead of punishing the participants in a fight, you arrest everyone in sight. Instead of seeing a child pointing his finger like a gun as just being a child, you suspend him from school. It is all quite senseless and much too focused on the feelings of the authorities rather than the impact on the alleged victims. It is, oddly, the same kind of super-strictness that overbearing teachers used to maintain discipline in the schools of yesteryear, only then it was about building character and not, as today, about legitimizing a self-preening ideology.

Most people think the biggest problem with the zero-tolerance culture is that it lacks common sense. That is of course true. If only school and state administrators were more reasonable, there would be fewer instances of really stupid behavior. But I worry about a larger problem—namely, the lessons it is teaching our children. Throwing a child out of school for playing with cookies or treating a water balloon fight as if it were a terrorist attack is in effect saying that taking injudicious, unfair, and even extreme measures, supposedly for the right cause, is a good thing. It sanctions not only the excessive use of force but a mendacity of purpose, which is surely at work when one cooks up charges or exaggerates threats that would be dismissed by any sensible person. Above all, the zero-tolerance culture acculturates every-one—students and parents alike—to the abuse of power. It sends the message that people's rights can easily be overturned if the authorities can appeal to some socially acceptable cause—whether it is stopping gun violence, stamping out teenage drunkenness, or combating rape on campus.

In effect, zero tolerance is no different than any kind of mob-sanctioned punishment. Because the cause is deemed unassailable, due process can be ignored, because prosecutors claim it is not needed. The cause is simply too great to worry about the incon-sequential details of getting the facts. It is actually worse than that. In campus investigations of rape cases, being concerned about actual evidence is sometimes equated with being intentionally in-different to the victim of the rape. The ethos of summary justice, which has long been a characteristic of the hard left, is the norm, and it can be applied sometimes in the most trivial of cases.

Any reasonable person opposes gun violence in schools, rape, or rampant drunkenness among teenage high school students. And we must surely be sensitive to the very real fact that rape victims are often too intimidated to come forward. Conserva-tives object not to the purpose of the zero-tolerance culture—to prevent violence and other crimes—but to the lack of perspec-tive and common sense about how to achieve it. The excessive and arbitrary methods used not only do not work,[50] they spread a pernicious authoritarian culture that devalues fairness and respect for basic rights. Whether by the school principal who suspends a student for some innocent gesture or the college bureaucrat who railroads an innocent student out of school on a trumped-up rape charge, unfairness and injustice are being held up as public virtues.

Progressives may think they are doing "the Lord's work" for a good cause, but they are, in fact, making a Faustian pact with the spirit of intolerance—the very thing they insist they want to stop.

### AUTHORITARIAN COOL

When actor Sean Penn told CNN's Piers Morgan in 2013 that Tea Party favorite Ted Cruz, a Republican senator from Texas, should be hospitalized in a mental institution, even the famously liberal Morgan was shocked. "Actually have him committed?" he asked. Penn seemed nonplussed and simply said, "I think it's a good idea."[51] When Susan Sarandon and one of the actors on *Real Housewives of New Jersey* found out that a teacher at a Catholic school posted a remark critical of sexual liberationist Dan Savage on her private Facebook page, they tried to have her fired.[52] In a 2015 *Playboy Magazine* article, rapper Azealia Banks said she hated "fat white Americans" and "these racist conservative white people who live on farms."[53] Actress Janeane Garofalo compared the Bush administration to Adolf Hitler's regime[54] and, echoing the antics of Jane Fonda during the Vietnam War, called Iraqi saboteurs of U.S. reconstruction efforts the "anti-occupation resistance."[55]

What is remarkable about these statements is not that celebrities from the entertainment industry are making them. There is nothing new about actors leaning to the far left in their politics. Musicians like Carlos Santana have sported Che Guevara t-shirts for decades. Pete Seeger, Woody Guthrie, and the American folk music movement were steeped in radical politics in the 1930s and 1940s; Seeger was an unrepentant Stalinist until 1995. Hollywood always had a soft spot for radical politics, going back to the days of Paul Robeson and Charlie Chaplin and even to the Communist Party's attempts to infiltrate the movie industry in the 1930s.

What is new is how mendacious these people are. A threat of coercion and in some cases even violence is overtly suggested or implied by what they say. In Penn's and Sarandon's cases, it is overt, with Penn literally suggesting that Cruz be committed to an insane asylum. Garofalo and Banks describe their enemies in such vicious ways that no one should really care if the subjects of their scorn are imprisoned or even killed. These are not statements of mere disagreement, as in "so-and-so conservative has misguided views of race" or "the Iraq War was a mistake." Rather, they are the words of bullies, calling someone out to a fight. While it is true that the far right is no stranger to this kind of enemy-mongering, that is no excuse for liberal entertainers to use their popularity to incite violence or its equivalent. They are the popular culture's most important identifiers of what is fashionable, and they are blaring over a very loud cultural loudspeaker that their brand of authoritarianism is "cool."

Few if any of these actors have suffered any rebuke or ostracism from the media or their colleagues. After Penn made his remark about Cruz on CNN, he was invited on respectable TV shows to explain his views. He was questioned deferentially as if he were the pop cultural equivalent of Henry Kissinger. Outrageous statements against conservatives made by actors and actresses at celebrity events such as the Oscars are often a boon for their careers, providing them with far more attention in the media than their artistic performances would ever attract. Conservative entertainers such as Dennis Miller, Adam Carolla, and Chuck Norris may be ostracized in Hollywood, but radical activists like Susan Sarandon, Tim Robbins, Danny Glover, and Martin Sheen receive nothing but accolades from the industry and the media.

In the tribal skirmishes of the culture wars, it matters a great deal which side the country's main cultural identifiers are on. They are the ones who get to decide how fashion serves politics. They are the ones who signal to their fans what is socially acceptable and what is not. This is especially the case with young people. If you are a young, apolitical person and your favorite entertainer is in favor of same-sex marriage, even if you are religious, you will be more tempted to listen to him or her than to Cardinal Timothy Dolan. The perception may be that the Catholic Church is old-school authoritarian, but, ironically, the mentality represented by Penn and Sarandon is even more authoritarian. Instead of viewing Pope Francis as a hero, they fancy a mass murderer like Che Guevara.

*National Review* columnist John Fund tells a story of a conversation he once had with John P. Roche, a former speechwriter for Hubert Humphrey. Roche explained that one of the reasons the communists were successful in the 1930s was because they had wrapped their ideology in the trappings of American traditions. They tried to appear to be all-American. "If authoritarianism of the right or left ever comes to America," Roche insisted, "it will come surrounded by patriotism and show business. . . . It will be made fashionable by talented people like Pete Seeger."[56]

It may sound like Roche is describing someone like Donald Trump, who mixes entertainment with politics. But he could be speaking of Penn and Sarandon too. Theirs is the popular ethos of authoritarian cool.

### THE NEW RULING CLASS

American liberalism's drift toward illiberalism would not be so widespread were it not for a simple fact: it enjoys the support of America's most powerful and influential people. The United States is a diverse country, but it does have a ruling class—one that not only is new in historical terms but whose members are part of a larger upper class (defined by income and cultural habits). Its members go by many names. *New York Times* commentator David Brooks calls them "bourgeois bohemians," meaning wealthy Baby Boomers who work hard to get rich but who still want to think of themselves as being on the cutting edge of bohemian culture.[57] Political scientist Charles Murray describes the upper class as the new "cognitive elite," which he defines as highly intelligent people dominating the professions and the business world.[58] Social scientists have argued for decades that the American economy favors people who work with their minds instead of their hands; professor and former Labor Secretary Robert Reich called them "symbolic analysts."[59]

Inside a large social class of executives, top media figures, judges, political leaders, and their allies in the entertainment industry and universities is a subset of elites. It is not a mass of corporate CEOs, politicians, lawyers, or businessmen who number in the millions. Rather, it is, as Murray points out in *Coming Apart: The State of White America, 1960–2010* (2012), a much smaller group that, because of its members' education and positions, exercises influence far in excess of its numbers. Murray estimates the "broader elite" makes up only about 5 percent of adults who are at least 25 years of age and are the most successful, work in the professions, and hold managerial positions. A smaller group, which Murray calls a "narrow elite," has the most influence on the culture, politics, and the economy. It numbers fewer than a hundred thousand people, perhaps as low as ten thousand.[60] It is this group that provides the social foundation for America's ruling class.

The power of the ruling class is not mainly in wealth; as a class it is well-off, but it does not always include the richest people in America. What makes the new ruling class different is that old money matters little. Its ranks are younger and more highly educated and culturally homogenous than America's ruling elites of the mid-20th century and earlier. It can be called a class because its members share similar income levels and values. For the most part, its members think alike. They live in the same kinds of places, eat and dress alike, watch the same movies, read the same blogs and news sites, and listen to the same radio programs (*All Things Considered*, not *The Rush Limbaugh Show*). They even share similar habits with respect to child rearing and work, and dwell primarily in large urban areas.

Not everyone in today's ruling class is politically liberal. There are liberals as well as conservatives in this narrow elite group. But a majority of the new ruling class do see themselves as leaning liberal, especially on cultural issues. This is often a function of education. Many attended America's elite universities, which are hotbeds of progressive liberalism. Successful businesspeople can come from any educational background—or even have no formal higher education at all—but America's professions and even its corporate boardrooms are increasingly dominated by people from America's "better" schools. The result is a high correlation between elite education and wealth. Murray observes that 31 percent of Wesleyan University graduates, for example, live in what he calls "Superzips"—the wealthiest zip codes in America based on median family income and education—and 65 percent live in zip codes at the 80th percentile or higher.[61]

The new ruling class is formidable. Its members include not only the wealthy, smart, and well-connected but also highly influential (though less well paid) journalists, academics, and educators. They are leaders of institutions that shape America's popular, political, and legal cultures. They produce and write the TV shows, movies, and commercials we watch; they own and control most of the network and cable news programs and blog sites that give us the news; they make the high-technology products that spur our cultural trends; they have grown in numbers in the state and federal courts that almost singlehandedly have delivered the gay rights revolution in America; and they currently have an ally in the White House.

This ruling class is like an aristocracy, insofar as it is significantly richer, more sophisticated, and more privileged than most Americans. It cultivates outward cultural signs of sophistication to distinguish itself from the lower classes. For all the talk of diversity, it is a socially and culturally homogenous group. Its members intermarry (think of Chicago lawyer Michelle LaVaughn Robinson marrying lawyer Barack Obama, whom she met at the law firm Sidley Austin LLP in Chicago). They isolate themselves in wealthy neighborhoods, walled off from the poor people they claim to champion. They are culturally insular in that they believe that because of their wealth and positions they are quite simply better than everyone else.

But there is a difference. Unlike a landed aristocracy, the new ruling class is built on a creed of ruthless meritocracy. Above all, its members want to succeed, get rich, and be seen as superior to everyone else. The desire to stand out explains some rather odd contradictions. For example, America's wealthy urban elites fashion themselves as hip advocates of equality. But their homes and lifestyles reveal the aspirations of the rich and famous. Their consumption habits are as conspicuous as any nouveau riche suburbanite in the 1980s, provided they display the correct cultural values. These connoisseurs of culture live in $75 million penthouses with paintings by Degas and Warhol covering the walls, and they are willing to spend lots of cash—even $100,000 on a Tesla electric car—to do their green bit for the environment. But still they see themselves as hard-bitten minimalists, critics of capitalist consumption, and defenders of the little guy.

As a group they have no officially recognized social privileges. They are not noblemen with official ranks or rights. They are legally no different from anyone else. But they are privileged people nonetheless. They exercise their supersized influence through very specific institutions, organizations, associations, and professions.

Among these are America's changing corporations. The most influential are Apple, Starbucks, Eli Lilly, Walmart, and Yelp, which adopt a high profile in supporting liberal causes. In addition there are the captains and young billionaires of Silicon Valley and the high-tech industry who support the Democratic Party and its progressive and libertarian causes. Powerful companies in the health care and alternative energy industries (Blue Cross & Blue Shield, General Electric) increasingly rely on government support or subsidies. Some of these are huge empires built by entrepreneurs who have leveraged government funding for alternative energy and other causes. Los Angeles billionaire Elon Musk, for example, had accepted $4.9 billion in government subsidies by 2015 to support his Tesla, Solar City, and SpaceX enterprises.[62] America's old mainline corporations are changing as well. Signaling a major cultural shift, AT&T and Levi Strauss & Co. came out in support of the Supreme Court's legalization of gay marriage—AT&T, for example, turned its blue logo into a rainbow for an hour after the ruling was announced.[63] Corporations such as Mars, General Mills, Dannon, Kellogg, and Nestlé are now full-fledged advocates for action on climate change.[64] America's corporate world is increasingly liberal, seeing huge markets in siding with culturally liberal causes.

It is no accident that entrepreneurs like Musk are supporters of the Democratic Party. They benefit from the government subsidies the Democrats help provide. Corporations and their employees still give more money to Republicans than Democrats,[65] but super-rich CEOs increasingly have become the most important donors to the Democratic Party.[66] Yet the issue is not the amount of money donated; in total amounts Democrats actually raised and spent more money than Republicans in the 2008 and 2012 presidential election cycles.[67] Rather it is the influence of those to whom the money is given. The Koch Brothers and their allies donate millions of dollars to conservative causes,[68] but they do not enjoy nearly the influence of pro-Democrat billionaires like Thomas Steyer and George Soros. The latter's causes are echoed loudly by the institutions of the new ruling class, including the White House, the federal government, the media, the universities and unions, many of the courts, nongovernmental organizations, and even international organizations like the United Nations and the annual gatherings at Davos. It is the synergy of these interlocking players that makes them predominant. Their money goes a very long way not only because they often work together, but because they control the commanding heights of American popular and political culture.

If the Democratic Party is the political home of the new

ruling class, how did the GOP muster enough votes to retake Congress between 2012 and 2014? There are two explanations. One is that the ruling class is more culturally and economically monolithic than politically uniform; thus while a majority would identify themselves as progressive or moderately liberal, a sizeable minority is apolitical (and stays out of politics) or even Republican. Second, as the 2014 election maps for Congress show,[69] there are still large swaths of America—small towns, rural areas, and suburbs, primarily in the South and Midwest—whose residents are outsiders to the ruling class but who can still muster millions of votes. In local and state elections they can even run up huge majorities, which are important locally but which also are irrelevant in the Electoral College sweepstakes of presidential elections. The difference is that despite their power base in certain states and (currently, at least) the U.S. Congress, non-liberal elites are out of sync with the increasing liberalization of America's major institutions. Even though they can dominate locally, they are losing their political advantage nationally as the country becomes demographically more diverse, more urban, and politically more liberal.

A feature of this changing political landscape is the leftward drift of the Democratic Party. Gallup's 2014 analysis found more Democrats than ever self-identifying as liberal, increasing from 29 percent in 2000 to 43 percent in 2013.[70] According to Gallup, "These changes are a telling indicator of the shift in the Democratic Party from a party that was more ideologically diverse to one that is increasingly dominated by those from the left end of the ideological spectrum."[71] The trend appears to match a similar swing to the left among the American electorate in the presidential elections of 2008 and 2012.[72] Therefore, unlike in the 1990s, when "liberal" was a dirty word, today it and its stand-in, "progressive," are quite popular, especially with Democrats. As the primary outlet for liberal politics in America, the Democratic Party provides a commanding power base for the new progressivism.

As powerful as the Democratic Party is, it is not the new progressivism's only power base. Among the Democrats' most influential supporters is a vast network of sympathetic and well-funded nonprofit private groups, many of which are subsidized by government. The biggest players by far are public employee and teachers' unions. Between 1989 and 2012, ten of the fifteen largest contributors to federal campaigns were unions, and studies show not a single one gave primarily to Republicans.[73] According to the Center for Responsive Politics, seven of the top ten political contributors from 2002 through 2014 were labor unions;[74] and nearly all their money went to Democrats. In addition, there are groups like Planned Parenthood, which annually spends about $500 million or so in funding from federal and state governments,[75] and environmental organizations such as Defenders of Wildlife, the Sierra Club, and the League of Conservation Voters, which not only lobby for environmental causes but target Republicans in elections.[76] These groups not only receive federal grants but benefit from the lesser-known practice of having their legal fees reimbursed when they successfully sue the federal government. There are also community activist groups that advance liberal causes and become involved in political agitation. The best known, the now defunct Association of Community Organizations for Reform Now (ACORN), had received an estimated $53 million in federal funds from 1994 onward, according to a 2010 congressional committee report.[77] It received over $5.6 million from just one union, the Service Employees International Union,[78] and it had extensive contracts with numerous local and state governments.[79]

The relationships among such groups are highly symbiotic. They champion Democratic politicians who, once in office, help funnel governmental funds their way. The federal grants they receive on the surface appear to fund public service or educational activities, but they nearly always support causes championed by the Democratic Party. Local community organizer groups often are hotbeds of radical politics. With the advantage given them by government subsidies and grants, they are very serious drivers of the Democratic Party's leftward tilt.

If the Democratic Party is the key political power base and mouthpiece of the ruling class, its megaphone is the mainstream media. Some people still want to deny that the media has a liberal bias, but they do so in the face of overwhelming evidence. A 2004 survey of journalists and media executives by the Pew Research Center for the People and the Press, in association with the Project for Excellence in Journalism and the Committee of Concerned Journalists, found that nearly five times as many national journalists identified themselves as liberal (34 percent) than as conservative (7 percent).[80] If that gap means nothing, then facts mean nothing.

As important as it is, bias is not the most important factor in the media's support for liberal causes. It is rather the monolithic discipline with which it reflects and relays the agenda of the Democratic Party and its allies in civil society. This would not be possible were it not for the interlocking personal relationships that exist between the media and Democratic politicians. The mainstream media cycles Democratic operatives in and out of its ranks regularly. For example, David Axelrod, after leaving his position as a Senior White House Advisor for Obama, became a senior political analyst for NBC News and MSNBC. Clinton operative George Stephanopoulos became a regular at ABC News. There are other cozy relationships between government officials and sympathetic friends in the media. Former White House press secretary Jay Carney, previously Joe Biden's spokesman, came from *Time*, where during almost two decades of reporting he had covered the White House. Carney is married to Claire Shipman, senior national correspondent for ABC's *Good Morning America*. Ben Rhodes, Obama's deputy national security advisor, is the brother of David Rhodes, the president and supervisor of all CBS News shows. NBC *Today Show* co-anchor Samantha Guthrie married long-time Democratic political and communications consultant

Michael Feldman, who had worked on both Bill Clinton's and Al Gore's campaign staffs, among others. The more conservative Fox News has its share of former Republican officials on board, but as influential as it is, it is still overshadowed by the influence of TV's network news outlets.

The mainstream media may lean heavily left, but that is not exactly the case for another influential lever of the ruling class— the legal profession. While it is undoubtedly true that law schools at Berkeley, Columbia, and New York University are very liberal, those at Harvard and Yale have both liberal and conservative professors. Prominent schools such as the University of Virginia and the University of Chicago have been more conservative than liberal.

America's courts are also a mixed political bag. There are very liberal district courts such as the Ninth Circuit Court in California and relatively conservative ones like the Fifth Circuit Court in Texas. Nevertheless, recently the courts have been moving in a more progressive direction. As of mid–2015, courts in twenty-five states had ruled in favor of same-sex marriage after Justice Anthony Kennedy, normally called a conservative, wrote the majority Supreme Court opinion for *Windsor v. United States* (2013), striking down the federal Defense of Marriage Act. Then came the Supreme Court rulings on Obamacare and same-sex marriage in June 2015.

Part of the reason for the shift is public opinion; as it moved left, so did the courts. But another critically important underlying factor is that most judges have been appointed by Democrats. As of December 2014, according to the circuit court websites, the majority of justices on nine of the thirteen circuit courts were appointed by a Democratic president.[81] Of the 174 justices serving in mid–2015 on these circuit courts, 56 percent were appointed by Democrats and 44 percent by Republicans.[82] Sixty-nine percent of the current judges on the very liberal Ninth Circuit Court, the largest circuit court covering cases in California, Washington,

Oregon, and eight other Western states (representing one-fifth of the U.S. population), were appointed by Democrats.[83] Of course, to conservatives' consternation, some Republicans in Congress have played a role, affirming many of these appointees.

America's courts and legal profession may play in both political camps, but another actor in the drama of ruling-class politics does not. America's academic class is consistently liberal. It not only leans liberal but is often far to the left of mainstream liberalism. In his 2013 book, *Why Are Professors Liberal and Why Do Conservatives Care?*, sociologist Neil Gross reports that professors are "about three times more liberal on average" than adults in America, with 50 percent describing themselves as "left or liberal."[84] This is important because the academic class operates as the avant-garde of ideas for the new ruling class. They provide not only a veneer of sophistication but reams of "peer-reviewed" research to back up progressive public policy recommendations.

This is not to say that all of America's universities and professors are progressive. You can find many institutions of higher learning in the South and Midwest that are not, but their professors are not as influential as those at elite universities. They are not the ones the media or professional institutions turn to for their ideas and to substantiate their prejudices. The impact of progressively liberal professors at Ivy League and other elite universities is much higher than those from conservative schools like Hillsdale College or Grove City College. Elite schools supply most of the talent sought by the highest echelons of the professions, corporations, the courts, and government. And many cabinet officials and presidential political appointees leave Washington to take endowed chairs or professorships and chancellorships at major universities. Showing once again the power of synergy, major news outlets defer to them, giving them an outlet for their views about everything from politics to climate change.

Whereas academics are the avant-garde of the new ruling class, the entertainment industry acts as its public relations firm.

As mentioned earlier, there is nothing new about Hollywood liberals. But as was the case with the media, it is not the liberalism per se but the new aggressive discipline of staying on a progressive message that counts. Movies and TV shows are remarkably on point regarding the major new cultural trends in America, especially regarding sexual politics. The more effective ones do not preach or browbeat the audience into submission. Instead they seduce them with well-crafted plot lines and finely drawn characters that humanize the cause, making it appear as if it has nothing to do with politics. Recent shifts of public opinion in favor of same-sex marriage would have been impossible without the positive portrayals of gay people by the entertainment industry. Along with the liberal courts and the Democratic Party, it has given America a new cultural majority that simply did not exist ten years ago.

A ruling class is a complex thing, and I am well aware of the problems associated with trying to identify any social class. There are exceptions and complexities, and even to use the word "ruling" is a bit of an overstatement, insofar as leading influences in society do not always exercise their power through administrative directives and the passing of laws. But the people I have described here are very powerful and influential—of that there can be no doubt. And most lean to the progressive left in cultural values, while there are more divisions over government spending, taxes, and other issues. They may not have a full-blown class consciousness, but a majority of them do share many values. They are not only the captains of America's new economy and America's most powerful political elite; they also are increasingly its main cultural identifiers. They are successful, connected, and cool, and if they say something as contentious as same-sex marriage is okay, then many Americans, not wanting to be tarred as old-fashioned, stand up and listen.

And here is precisely the danger. Because the ruling class is so unconsciously homogenous, it is completely unaware of its own motivations and foibles. Because it is so smug, it cannot imagine anything outside its bubble of self-constructed reality to be even remotely true. Because it is so successful and rich it cannot understand the complexities of social and economic inequality in America today, which is being caused in part by cultural insularities of a progressive upper class (and not by something as inconsequential as a too-low minimum wage). In all this, the liberal majority of the new ruling class is playing the decisive sociological role in the rise of illiberal liberalism in America. It is mainstreaming the radical left's politics of intolerance as a socially acceptable practice, normalizing authoritarian political tactics in a "winner-take-all" mentality, and corrupting the cause of equality by marrying its cultural elitism with an economy-killing populism. It is an old story. Liberal aristocrats pretend to align themselves with the people, not to raise them up in society but to keep them in their place, so that all the while they can accumulate wealth and concentrate on their real enemies—their cultural and economic rivals in the middle and upper classes.

To be fair, not every liberal wants to go in this direction. There are Democrats such as Congressmen John K. Delaney of Maryland, who despairs of his party's attack on free trade,[85] and Ron Kind of Wisconsin, who is "tired of the politics of polarization."[86] There are moderate Democratic activist groups like the Third Way[87] that cringe at the party's left-wing populism and call for compromise. There are liberal journalists and commentators such as Juan Williams, Kirsten Powers, and Julie Roginsky who bridle at the repression of free speech on college campuses. And there are scholars at liberal-leaning universities and think tanks such as the Brookings Institution who are far less interested in scoring ideological points than in finding commonsense solutions to our nation's problems.

Yet these people are swimming upstream against very powerful currents. As their party drifts leftwards they are finding less political space in which to operate. For example, in 2015, after members of the Third Way wrote an op-ed criticizing liberal populism, they were barraged with criticism from liberals—to the point that MoveOn.org and the Progressive Campaign Committee urged members of Congress to break off ties with the Third Way.[88] Hillary Clinton's attempt to curry favor with the left wing of her party is also not a good sign. It shows where the energy and power base of the Democratic Party lie. There is precious little room for moderate liberals to maneuver in today's progressive circles, where the word "radical" has come to mean its opposite—anything practiced or believed by Americans for most of their history.

# FIVE

# Promethean Government Unbound

*I am sick and tired of people who say that if you debate and you disagree with this administration somehow you're not patriotic. We should stand up and say, "We are Americans and we have a right to debate and disagree with any administration."*[1]

This well-known utterance by Hillary Clinton from 2003 raises a fundamental question for progressives: Does it also apply to conservatives who dissent when they are not in power? The answer is apparently not. The number of instances of government agencies abusing their authority to coerce people with whom they disagree once they are in the hands of progressives is growing.

The most widespread and brazen of these abuses in recent years has been by the Internal Revenue Service. On May 10, 2013, IRS Director of Exempt Organizations Lois Lerner admitted that certain organizations were targeted for their political beliefs. We later learned that almost all were conservative. At one point Lerner shared confidential taxpayer information with the Department of Justice,[2] perhaps in hopes it would open criminal investigations into some of the nonprofit organizations. Subsequent revelations showed IRS officials eyeing conservative groups as early as 2010;[3] the cases apparently were deemed to be newsworthy, offering the opportunity to reap political kudos for the agency.[4] As if this were not enough, the IRS even leaked the donor list of a conservative group, the National Organization for Marriage, for which it was forced to pay damages of $50,000.[5]

These abuses all happened before the 2012 presidential election, raising the specter of the IRS being used to sway its outcome. IRS commissioners have lost their jobs over the scandal, but as of this writing no criminal charges have been brought against any IRS official.[6] The Obama administration showed itself to be far more interested in shielding the IRS than getting to the bottom of what happened. Lerner's e-mails were lost and then found. At every step of the way the administration stonewalled congressional investigations. On March 31, 2015, the Department of Justice announced it would not pursue criminal contempt charges against Lerner. It ruled that she had not waived her Fifth Amendment rights, even though in a congressional hearing she publicly claimed she was innocent of any wrongdoing.

IRS power has been abused before. Both the Johnson and Nixon administrations used it to target their political enemies.[7] John F. Kennedy authorized the Ideological Organizations Project at the IRS to investigate right-wing groups, and Richard Nixon approved a secret IRS Special Services Staff to harass his political opponents with audits.[8] Those scandals provoked a backlash and established a consensus that IRS abuses would not be tolerated. This consensus is now dead. The Obama administration and its allies in Congress ran political cover for Lerner and the IRS. The investigation was politicized, ironically, by accusing every congressional critic of the IRS abuse of having political motivations. Even the Secret Service has been politicized under President Obama. In 2015, it was revealed that the Secret Service leaked unflattering information about a congressional critic, Representative Jason Chaffetz, the Republican chairman of the House Committee on Oversight and Government Reform.[9] With the old taboo broken, old-style corruption returned with a vengeance, with the sympathy—if not outright backing—of a compliant media, which decidedly was not the case during the Nixon years.

There are two causes for such an abuse of power. First, a president and political appointees must be willing to commit it. Second, a sympathetic bureaucratic class must be willing to cooperate and help cover it up. The IRS scandal involved both. The degree to which federal employees were complicit is breathtaking. Most belong to unions, which historically and currently favor the Democrats. Between 1989 and 2012, two-thirds of political donations by IRS employees went to Democrats.[10] All sorts of laws prohibit government employees from using their positions for partisan purposes, but the actions of Lerner and others show they do not work. They use their shadowy power to single out political enemies for special scrutiny, while giving a pass to organizations friendly to the administration they favor politically.

As bad as the federal government can be in abusing its power, state and local governments can be worse. Consider the case of the Democrat district attorney of Milwaukee County, Wisconsin, John Chisholm. Chafing at the victories of Republican Governor Scott Walker in negotiations with government employee unions, Chisolm teamed up with the state's Government Accountability Board to launch a "John Doe" investigation into alleged unlawful coordination between Walker's campaign and private conservative groups. "John Doe" refers to a highly unusual Wisconsin law that permits officials to conduct extensive investigations—fishing expeditions, really—in absolute secrecy, even keeping the target of the inquiry undisclosed. Such investigations dispense with the ordinary procedure of presenting evidence to a grand jury, which essentially means that no hard evidence is necessary to start an investigation.

In his zeal to nail Walker, Chisholm got a sympathetic judge to order early morning paramilitary-style raids on citizens' homes. One of the targets was Cindy Archer, the lead architect of a grassroots campaign to limit costly public employee benefits.[11] One morning she woke to her dogs barking and a loud pounding at her door. She looked outside and saw policemen with guns, body armor, and a battering ram. Not taking time to get dressed, she opened the door while begging the police not to shoot her dogs. Armed agents rushed past her and into the bathroom where her partner was taking a shower. When she objected to the search, one of the policemen became furious. "He towered over me with his finger in my face," she said, "and yelled like a drill sergeant that I either do it his way or he would handcuff me." After they were done with their search, which Cindy said left "her dead mother's belongings strewn across the basement in a most disrespectful way," they left carrying only a cell phone and a laptop.

Cindy was not alone. In another raid, a woman reported that, "People came pouring in. For a second I thought it was a home invasion. It was terrifying. They were yelling and running, into every room in the house. One of them was in my face, yelling at me over and over and over again."[12] After it was over a policeman warned her not to call a lawyer. John Doe investigations are secret, she was told. No one was to be told about the raid—not even her mother, father, or closest friends. Even though neighbors witnessed what happened, the victims of the raids were still bound by the secrecy "code" not to discuss them.

The Wisconsin raids did not stand up in a court of law. In July 2015, the Wisconsin Supreme Court ruled against the prosecutor for trampling citizens' rights. "It is utterly clear," wrote the justices in the majority opinion, "that the special prosecutor has employed theories of law that do not exist in order to investigate citizens who were wholly innocent of any wrongdoing," and who have a "fundamental right . . . to engage in lawful political activity . . . free from the fear of the tyrannical retribution of arbitrary or capricious governmental prosecution."[13]

How could such abuse happen? First a badly framed law that casually and quietly dismisses checks on prosecutorial abuse is passed. In the Wisconsin case, the requirements for a grand jury, the legal need for hard evidence, and the public's right to know about due process were dropped. The problem is compounded by setting up so-called accountability boards, which heavily implies that certain politically charged views are worthy of state oversight. Add to the mix a prosecutor willing to abuse his power in a political vendetta, and voilà: the near-perfect case of prosecutorial misbehavior enabled and encouraged by a legal system corrupted by illiberal attitudes about politics and the rule of law.

A conclusion is inescapable: organizations and institutions like the IRS and the Milwaukee district attorney's office are misused because they can be, and because the people in charge think they can get away with it. There is little scrutiny, no transparency, and weak due process. It is just the secret workings of officials in power abusing the rights of citizens they are supposed to serve.

## THE WAR ON DISSENT

Prosecutorial abuse directed against those who dissent is growing in this country. As the IRS scandals show, government agencies are being used to try to suppress freedom of opinion, speech, and expression for a very specific reason: the people in power want to transform both the American system and the American culture, turning them into something they have never been before.

The war on dissent has many fronts. The abuse of power by governmental agencies with investigative powers is only one. A far more pervasive campaign against dissent is taking place as part of America's culture wars. In courts and town legislatures across America legal battles are being waged over same-sex marriage and other sexual and gender "rights."

Even before the Supreme Court ruling in *Obergefell v. Hodges*, government officials were cracking down on dissent against gay marriage. In 2014, after the Ninth U.S. Circuit Court of Appeals struck down Idaho's constitutional amendment defining marriage as the union of a man and a woman, officials from the town of Coeur d'Alene told two resident ordained ministers, Donald and Evelyn Knapp, they must perform same-sex weddings or face fines and jail time.[14] In Houston, Texas, the lesbian mayor subpoenaed five pastors for "all speeches, presentations, or sermons" related to homosexuality and gender identity.[15] Oregon officials ordered the owners of a bakery to pay $135,000 in damages to a gay couple for declining to bake their wedding cake, and a state labor commissioner issued a "cease and desist" order that equated their statement of continued fidelity to their religious views with the intent to commit discrimination in the future.[16] The City of Oakland, California, told its employees they would be fired if they set up a Christian employees association, even though a group for gay employees had been created.[17] The Ninth Circuit Court, which covers California, was already on record ruling that municipal agencies can censor the terms "natural family," "marriage" and "family values" as "hate speech."[18]

Even the U.S. Navy is policing attitudes about gay marriage. Chaplain Wesley Modder, who had served for twenty years in good standing, was relieved of his duties, removed from the promotion list, and facing expulsion procedures after a gay subordinate got others to complain about his private counseling on homosexuality.[19] His superior officer had decided Modder's religious views imperiled "unit cohesion" and "military preparedness."[20] Even though he was later exonerated, this shows the pressure to conform to the new agenda.[21]

All of these examples have one thing in common: people in authority using their power to silence, punish, or criminalize those who hold differing views on homosexuality and same-sex marriage. Any argument against gay marriage, religious or otherwise, is not merely dismissed, it is expressly prohibited. These are not instances of public boycotts by private citizens or grassroots campaigns in which people have a right to say whatever they think—a right that can work both ways, for and against same-sex marriage. They are actions that take aim at a type of expression singled out for constitutional protection—namely, religious belief—in the

First Amendment of the Constitution. Perhaps if there were evidence of blanket discrimination against gay people, an argument could be made that religion is being used as an excuse to discriminate. But there is no such evidence in these cases. The Christians involved are merely asking not to be forced to participate in a public activity that violates their religious conscience.

The constitutional protections of religious liberty and free speech are not mere technicalities. They are not rules that can be negotiated away out of expedience or in response to changes of opinion. They are fundamental, permanent, and unalienable rights. For both freedom of speech and religion, the issue ultimately is one of compulsion—whether liberal democratic societies have the authority to force people to alter or deny their deepest convictions, religious or otherwise. As *National Affairs* editor Yuval Levin observes:

> They [religious people censored by law] are . . . more like religious believers under compulsion in a society with an established church than like believers denied the freedom to exercise their religion. Liberals are in this respect right to say they're not trying to kill religious liberty. They're trying to take it back to something like the form it had in the Anglo-American world when [it] had a formal state religion—except now the state religion is supposed to be progressive liberalism.[22]

In other words, in the mind of the same-sex activist, if you are a religious person who objects to same-sex marriage, you may attend your church service and pray when and wherever you like, but you must keep quiet on the subject of same-sex marriage in the public domain. You are in this respect somewhat religiously free, insofar as no one is physically shutting down your church; but the political space in which you can express yourself is circumscribed and regulated by the state. Just as in the days of colonial America, you can be fired from your job, fined, or even jailed if you cross a certain line.

It makes no difference that the new rules are not imposed in the name of a formally established church. The effect is the same. People of religious convictions—in colonial days it was largely Baptists fighting the Anglican establishment—face discrimination. Nor does it make a difference that the beneficiaries of the changing laws, homosexuals, are thought to be minorities, while the "discriminators" are presumed to be an oppressing majority. Rights may be thought to only protect small minorities, but in reality they are for everyone to possess equally. If surveys are correct in estimating that 60 percent of Americans support gay marriage, it is hard for same-sex marriage proponents to argue that Christians are calling the shots in popular culture.[23]

It matters a great deal to a liberal democracy that the technicalities of the law are observed. When the Coeur d'Alene officials decided a for-profit chapel was a "public accommodation" so they had the "right" to prosecute its pastors, they ignored not only the spirit but the letter of the Constitution. The issue of religious free speech is not defined by the brick and mortar of a building or an entity's tax status, whether it is a church or a chapel, but by the rights of the people who occupy it. By the same token, when the City of Houston was faced with a lawsuit demanding a referendum on its equal rights ordinance, it should have determined whether there were enough signatures on the referendum request to hold such a ballot. Instead it chose to prejudge the whole affair by deciding the issue ahead of time. It is in such seemingly small matters that tyranny creeps up on a free people. Desensitized by thousands of tiny violations, they get used to the exploitation of due process for political gain.

The war on religious dissent also involves very sloppy thinking. There is a huge difference, for example, between a real bigot who means to do gays actual harm and a business owner who does not want to be forced to participate in ceremonies that make her uncomfortable for reasons of conscience, such as the grandmother who owns Arlene's Flowers in Washington State.[24] Organizations that oppose calling gay civil unions "same-sex marriage" are not advocating discrimination against gay persons. Tony Perkins of the Family Research Council, which the Southern Poverty Law Center has tarred as a "hate group," explains: "Christians would never deny people [a seat in a restaurant or a room at a hotel], but being forced to participate in a ceremony that violates religious beliefs is completely un-American and uncivil." Moreover, he adds, religious freedom restoration acts "are not intended to nor have they ever been used to deny anyone non-religious goods or services."[25]

The mistake is to ignore the difference between being forced to participate in social rituals like wedding ceremonies and refusing to serve any gay person in a business setting. The former involves violating a legitimate right of religious freedom. The state long ago recognized, largely in the interest of religious diversity, that certain acts involving religious conscience should not be made compulsive. We would no more expect the City of Houston to demand that rabbis perform Christian weddings for Baptists than to insist that an Episcopal priest marry a Muslim couple in an Islamic ceremony. It is obvious that religious scruples are involved and the government has no compelling interest in forcing people to violate them. It would be a very different story if a baker refused to sell any gay person a cupcake or a generic wedding cake from a display case. That would be an example of outright discrimination, and whether it now is illegal or not, it should not be endorsed as a matter of public ethics. The fact is that the Oregon bakers who were ordered to pay damages to a gay couple had served them as regular customers of their shop in the past.[26]

The principle behind the various religious freedom acts has always been to *prohibit* the government from substantially burdening religious exercise unless it can show a compelling interest in doing so. Even then, it must be done in the least restrictive way possible. In addition to the deference to religious freedom there is also the presumption that protections apply to individuals as well as organizations, be they schools, charities, or businesses. The law does not establish any particular view on religion, but it does allow someone or some entity the right to use religious conviction as a defense in court if they are sued, provided such convictions are exercised in good conscience. It is quite wrong to assume that religious freedom laws are intended to discriminate against gay people. It is the opposite: they are meant as a last-ditch defense of people who feel the public, and the law, are moving against them solely because of their religion.

Sadly, it seems the rise of coercion in the name of gay rights has less to do with eliminating discrimination than with establishing a new state-sanctioned public morality regarding sexual and gender affairs. There is no room for individual dissent. If it were otherwise the gay activist community would settle for prohibiting overt discrimination. Instead they have pressed for positive new legal norms in which there is virtually no room for dissent. If the issue were truly about overt discrimination—refusing any restaurant service or housing, for example, which seldom occurs and is already loudly condemned—then they should be happy to let the Religious Freedom Restoration Act in Indiana and similar laws stand. Some gay activists are indeed willing to do that, but the more militant ones are not. The fear in religious communities is that they will not stop until they have achieved state regulation of all public utterances on the issue of sexual morality, whether at the public lectern, in the workplace, in the pulpit, or even in private conversations.

As Mr. Levin suggests, the true danger in oppressing religious liberty is larger than religion. If the government can suppress the most cherished private convictions of religious people, it can do the same to non-religious people. Once this line is crossed, there is no going back. Practically anything can be justified as a "compelling government interest" provided the authorities in charge can mount a reasonably convincing legal argument to sustain it. Activists may feel comfortable because they and their allies are now in charge. They may take comfort that public opinion is moving their way. But if anyone should know what it is like when that is not the case, when the public is against you, it should be gay people, who have suffered discrimination of a kind far worse than having one Christian photographer decline to participate in a ceremony.

The true test of a liberal order is indeed how it treats its minorities and others who do not enjoy popular favor. That is true not just sometimes, but always, and it is true for everyone in society, not just for those who claim an oppressed status. Progressive liberals are right to demand that gay people should not be singled out for harassment or official condemnation. But what happens when the tide of popular opinion turns the other way? What happens when the "oppressed" become the "oppressors"? As the public grows more accepting of gay people, not only are outright bigots put in the dock, but so too are people who simply have a different belief about the long-established institution of marriage. It is in such circumstances, when popular opinion is on your side, that the greatest temptation exists to press your advantage unfairly.

### GOING AFTER CLIMATE DENIERS

Although the highly charged issues of sexual politics are the most likely to elicit illiberal responses from progressive liberals, these are not the only issues that have that effect. The issue of climate change sparks similar outbursts. As with other progressive causes, government officials are all too happy to use their authority to intimidate and silence people who disagree with their views of global warming. It is supposedly all about the "science." In reality it is about controlling the outcome of a policy debate.

Consider the case of U.S. Representative Raúl Grijalva from the Third District of Arizona. A ranking member of the House Committee on Natural Resources, in 2015 he demanded from universities the financial records of certain professors who held skeptical views of catastrophic climate change.[27] One was Professor David Legates of the University of Delaware, the former state climatologist, who co-authored a paper with Harvard-Smithsonian Center for Astrophysics researcher Willie Soon that predicted only a one-degree temperature rise from 2001 to 2100, which runs counter to other more alarmist reports. Grijalva's demand for information about funding sources did not go over well with the universities. Though Arizona State University provided most of the information Grijalva requested, it reminded him of the principle of academic freedom. The University of Delaware turned over general information about its funding policies but refused to provide details about Legates's funding; it chose "not to act in a manner inconsistent with its governing principles and contractual commitments."[28]

Grijalva is not the only member of Congress to use his power to intimidate ideological enemies. Senator Sheldon Whitehouse, a Democrat from Rhode Island, has suggested that racketeering laws should be used to go after the fossil fuel industry and climate change "deniers" in the scientific community whose research it funds.[29] In other words, he advocates that the civil discovery powers of the Racketeer Influenced and Corrupt Organizations (RICO) Act be used to investigate whether the fossil fuel industry "has crossed the same line" tobacco companies did in falsifying scientific research. That's right: he believes scientists who question climate change orthodoxy, and who received funding from an oil company for research, should be prosecuted for racketeering. Completely legal activities on the part of oil companies such as lobbying, donating to political campaigns, or conducting media operations, could be used as evidence of racketeering. Showing that Whitehouse was not alone in this idea, twenty climate scientists from several universities and research centers endorsed using RICO investigations against the fossil fuel industry and its supporters.[30]

This is truly Orwellian. Put aside the mistake involved in using RICO laws to go after the tobacco industry. Even if you
accept that it was legitimate in that case, the indisputable health
dangers of smoking are in a different class than the health dangers
of climate change. Moreover, tobacco companies were caught
falsifying the facts. That is a far cry from a scientist raising legitimate questions about why predictions based on climate change
modeling are not matched by actual data. Most of the cases of data
falsification, in fact, involve people on the *pro*-global warming
side of the debate, not those who question it.[31] Would Whitehouse suggest an investigation of them? The government should
not tell scientists what they should or should not say on pain of
facing criminal charges. Any law can be stretched for political
purposes and for good or ill. But Whitehouse's attempt to twist a
law intended to catch mafia criminals and murderers into a vendetta against scientific researchers is scandalous.

It would be one thing if Grijalva and Whitehouse were marginal figures representing only the fringe of liberal politics. But
that is not the case. They are the vanguard of a growing movement inside liberal environmentalism to effectively criminalize
dissent against climate change correctness. The office of the attorney general of the State of New York, for example, has launched
a sweeping probe of Exxon Mobil to determine whether it hid
the risks of climate change from investors.[32] Using a broad interpretation of the state's consumer protection and securities laws,
the attorney general is investigating a leading coal company, Pea-
body Energy, for the same reason. As with RICO investigations,
the idea is that these companies are supposedly damaging public
health and safety by, in the words of Harvard University professor and activist Naomi Oreskes, "fomenting disinformation" that
undermines public support for such climate change initiatives as a
carbon tax. The intent could not be clearer: the state should suppress any questions about the reliability of climate change findings or data. In other words, a court should be invited to silence

one side of a public policy debate. A similar move is afoot at the United Nations, where environmental activists, in the name of "climate justice," are seeking the creation of an international tribunal to punish nations for not adequately controlling carbon emissions.[33]

Hoover Institution Fellow Thomas Sowell reminds us that there was a time when Southern politicians employed similar harassment tactics against the National Association for the Advancement of Colored People (NAACP).[34] As in the days when the Southern press targeted civil rights groups for their funding sources in the North, the press today runs stories about climate change "deniers" whose research is funded in part by the oil industry.[35] The implication is the same: people are supposedly being bought by special interest money. Activists cannot bring themselves to believe that climate change "denying" scientists actually believe what their scholarly research shows.

## BENDING THE CONSTITUTION INTO LINE

Despite debating the meaning of the U.S. Constitution for more than 225 years, Americans always have taken that constitution seriously. They parry and thrust over whether it is "living" or not, and legal scholars endlessly parse the meaning of certain phrases and words.[36] But for most of U.S. history there has been a fairly consistent consensus that the Constitution is a document that establishes limits on what the federal government could and could not do. Unlike many others around the world, the American Constitution makes quite clear that the actual powers of the federal government are limited—they are "enumerated" or reckoned in ways that indicate government power is bound by certain rules and principles.

Today's illiberal liberals do not agree. They view close adherence to the Constitution, as *Washington Post* columnist Harold Meyerson describes it, to be a "fetish" of the Republican right.[37] They adhere to what is, in their minds, a higher calling. They believe in social justice, about which the Constitution is completely silent. They have faith not in the words on an old parchment but in their own vision of a new democratic order of their own making. They have supreme confidence in themselves. As candidate Obama once declared, they are the "ones" they have been waiting for.[38]

No better example of this dismissive view of the Constitution exists than the Obama administration's regular abuse of executive authority. It is not as if President Obama tried to hide his views. He quite openly asserted his right to issue executive orders as a means to achieve policy objectives unattainable through congressional legislation. In 2014, during a cabinet meeting, he said: "We're not just going to be waiting for legislation in order to make sure that we're providing Americans the kind of help they need. I've got a pen and I've got a phone. . . . And I can use that pen to sign executive orders and take executive actions and administrative actions that move the ball forward."[39] It could not be clearer that he desires to expand executive authority far beyond executing the laws or even interpreting them. He wants instead to decree the equivalent of law by executive fiat.

His attempts fall into three categories: (1) unilateral executive actions that are unambiguously unlawful and unconstitutional; (2) measures that may be constitutionally questionable but are abusive; and (3) aggressive lawsuits to target private citizens who oppose the administration's agenda.[40]

Let's take the first, the abuse of executive authority. The most notorious case is an executive memorandum in 2014 extending amnesty to four to five million illegal aliens. Although Obama previously said that such an action would be unconstitutional— and that immigration law was rightly a matter for Congress to settle[41]—he ordered that immigrants who had been in the U.S. illegally for more than five years and whose children are citizens or lawful permanent residents could seek relief from deportation and get work permits. The measure has received numerous rebukes from the courts. In May 2015, for example, the U.S. Fifth Circuit Court of Appeals denied a Justice Department request to allow Obama's immigration actions to go into effect pending appeal.[42]

Most of the court decisions have largely been about procedural issues, but they suggest that Obama's executive action was unconstitutional. The 2-to-1 majority ruling by the Fifth Circuit Court said as much: "Because the government is unlikely to succeed on the merits of its appeal of the injunction, we deny the motion for stay and the request to narrow the scope of the injunction."[43] Texas Attorney General Ken Paxton, whose office was involved in the federal appeals case, agreed:

> Telling illegal aliens that they are now lawfully present in this country, and awarding them with valuable government benefits, is a drastic change in immigration policy. The President's attempt to do this by himself, without a law passed by Congress and without any input from the states, is a remarkable violation of the U.S. Constitution.[44]

In November 2015, the Fifth Circuit Court again blocked implementation of the Obama administration's executive orders on immigration.[45] A final decision awaits the Supreme Court.

Other unconstitutional actions include the administration's 2013 temporary suspension of the employer mandate in its own health care law; the 2012 "recess" appointments to avoid the Senate confirmation process while the Senate was still in session; and the Department of Labor telling federal agencies, during the government shutdown debates of 2012, that they did not have to give a sixty-day notice of layoffs.[46] That same year the Department of Health and Human Services suspended a well-established work requirement for welfare benefits that President Bill Clinton had signed into law. Secretary Kathleen Sebelius claimed she was merely exercising her waiver authority, but the law explicitly states that waivers "shall not affect the applicability of section 407 [establishing the work requirement] to the State."[47]

The willingness to push the boundaries of executive authority extends beyond these cases. It is also reflected in the implementation of the Affordable Care Act (ACA), known as Obamacare. The most egregious example is the ACA's mandate that small companies must provide their employees with contraception insurance coverage even if the owners object on religious grounds. The company Hobby Lobby sued the government over this measure, insisting that the mandate violated its owners' right to religious freedom. The administration fought back hard but lost its case in the Supreme Court, which agreed with Hobby Lobby that the government had violated the Religious Freedom Restoration Act as it applies to regulations written by the Department of Health and Human Services to implement the ACA.[48]

There are other cases contesting the contraception mandate. They include a suit brought by a Catholic order of nuns who take care of the elderly, the Little Sisters of the Poor. The Supreme Court in late 2013 issued a temporary stay on the mandate's implementation by the Little Sisters, sending it back to circuit court. But their appeal before the Tenth Circuit Court was denied in 2015, which would force the Little Sisters to provide contraceptives and abortion services or pay a $2.5 million fine for each facility they operate.[49] On July 23, 2015, the Little Sisters of the Poor appealed the Tenth Circuit's decision to the Supreme Court.[50] Some lower courts have ruled against other complainants over the mandate on technical grounds regarding seeking an exemption, but the Supreme Court ruling in the Hobby Lobby case on the mandate's unconstitutionality still stands. Moreover, on September 17, 2015, the Eighth Circuit Court determined that the Affordable Care Act unjustly burdens religiously affiliated employers, such as Christian colleges.[51]

Despite setbacks in the courts, the Obama administration has doubled down on its campaign to push the boundaries of executive authority. In 2014, Obama issued Executive Order 13672,[52] prohibiting discriminatory practices based on sexual orientation or gender identity in any hiring by the federal government or by its contractors with over fifty employees. Contractors could include, for example, nongovernmental organizations (NGOs), faith-based organizations, and religious organizations providing U.S. humanitarian relief.

Besides issuing executive orders and less formal executive guidance, sometimes in the form of a letter, the Obama administration has stretched its authority by making broad assertions about executive prosecutorial discretion. This method was used to justify Obama's decision on immigration amnesty. It was also used when the administration refused to uphold and defend the Defense of Marriage Act, a decision that flew in the face of the longstanding practice to defend existing laws, provided constitutional arguments in their favor were "reasonable." Other prosecutorial stretches include: 1) the Justice Department's refusal in 2009 to bring certain kinds of illegal drug use cases to court even when they violated federal law; 2) the Justice Department's abuse of the Voting Rights Act to intimidate the state of Florida, which sought to remove fraudulent voters from its voting lists; and 3) the use of dubious "guidance" communications such as a "Dear Colleague" letter by the Department of Education to change the legal standards for assessing evidence in sexual assault cases on campuses.[53]

There is nothing new about a president's assertion of executive authority.[54] Chief executives have raised constitutional questions about legislation ever since President James Monroe issued the first signing statement in 1822. In 1986 the Supreme Court stated in *Bowsher v. Synar* that "interpreting a law enacted by Congress to implement the legislative mandate is the very essence of 'execution' of the law."[55] There can be no doubt that under the constitutional authority of the executive, presidents have broad discretionary powers. They have issued executive orders not only to execute the law but to exercise presidential prerogatives to conduct foreign policy, protect national security, and fulfill specific obligations mandated by the Constitution.

Yet as the Supreme Court reminded us in its ruling on the Jerusalem birthplace passport case, "whether the realm is foreign or domestic, it is still the Legislative Branch, not the Executive Branch, that makes the law."[56] It is one thing for a president to use the executive's constitutional prerogatives to exercise authority well within its rights. It is another altogether to use that power to cherry-pick which laws to enforce. Past presidents used signing statements regularly to suggest legislation but also to preserve the constitutional privileges of the president regarding legislation. According to the Constitution, these privileges allow the president "from time to time . . . [to] recommend" for Congress's "consideration such Measures as he shall judge necessary and expedient."[57] Privileges also pertain to the constitutional powers of the commander in chief. Nevertheless, very few presidents have tried to use executive authority to override specific legislation or as a pretext not to enforce provisions of laws with which they disagreed as a matter of policy.[58]

It is also true that past presidents issued numerous executive orders. But they were normally well within the constitutional prerogatives of the executive or issued on authority delegated to the president by statute. They include such examples as President George W. Bush's EO 13484, amending the order of succession in the Department of Agriculture, or EO 13464, blocking property transactions to Burma. The novelty of President Obama's approach to executive authority has not been in the number of executive orders he issued, but rather his use of them and other less formal means to bypass specific provisions of laws with which his party and his supporters disagreed.

Another issue raised by President Obama's executive actions involves the "take care" clause in Article II, Section Three, of the Constitution. It states that the president "shall take Care that the Laws be faithfully executed." Although the president does have wide discretion in deciding how to execute laws, he does not have the authority to implement the equivalent of new laws or to amend or effectively repeal existing laws. As the Supreme Court ruled in *Clinton v. City of New York* (1998), "[o]nce a bill becomes law, it can only be repealed or amended through another, independent legislative enactment."[59] Moreover, although the president has discretion to set law enforcement priorities and even to refuse to enforce a law against a particular individual or small group of people, he does not have the authority to exempt entire categories of lawbreakers from existing law. Thus, even if the president personally disagrees with a certain law, he is obligated by the oath of his office to enforce it "faithfully."

Apart from legal issues, the Obama administration has shown a willingness to use aggressive federal action to advance its cultural agenda. This was clear in the administration's regulations written to implement the ACA contraception mandate, and in its efforts to change education policy through tendentious regulatory interpretations of the law. Another example occurred around the time Houston voters overwhelmingly rejected a referendum to allow transgendered men to share women's public bathrooms. The U.S. Department of Education threatened an Illinois school district with sanctions for not allowing a transgendered male student to shower and change in a girl's locker room.[60] The school district already had made efforts to comply with other federal government demands, including allowing students to use the bathroom of the gender with which they identify. But the federal Education Department concluded that there was a "preponderance of evidence" that the school district failed to comply with Title IX of the Education Amendments of 1972, a law prohibiting sex discrimination in education programs. Not only was the Obama administration trying to force local school districts to apply Title IX to a purpose for which it was not intended—namely, to advance transgender identity claims instead of protecting women and girls from discrimination. It was doing so in a way that discriminates against women and girls by depriving them of a most basic right— the right to privacy.

Lawyers can sort out whether President Obama's acts were strictly constitutional or not, but one thing stands out: his expansion of executive authority goes beyond any concern for protecting the constitutional privileges of his office. It appears to be driven by a desire to achieve by executive fiat what cannot be obtained through the regular legislative process. The same is true for how Obama handled the Iran nuclear deal to bypass the Senate's treaty powers. This is dangerous. At best it represents a cavalier attitude about the Constitution and the law. At worst it could be an abuse of power not seen since the days of Lyndon Johnson and Richard Nixon.

## THE ILLIBERAL RULE OF THE COURTS

Like the expansion of executive authority, judicial activism has been around a very long time.[61] Some conservatives believe it started with *Marbury v. Madison*, in which the Supreme Court established the practice of judicial review. Since at least the Civil War, courts have been playing legislature and nullifying or restricting rights in the Constitution.[62] We may think that the court ruling establishing the "exclusionary rule" on illegally seized evidence is new, but it is not. It was created in 1914 by the Supreme Court decision in *Weeks v. United States*. It was in 1934, in the case of *Home Building & Loan Association v. Blaisdell*, that the Supreme Court overturned the literal meaning of the Constitution's "contract clause" by creating exceptions due to economic hardship. Although the Supreme Court has recognized that "each branch of the Government has the duty initially to interpret the Constitution for itself, and that its interpretation of its powers is due great respect from the other branches,"[63] it also has referred to itself as the "ultimate expositor of the constitutional text."[64]

Judicial activism may not be new, but it has been growing. The upswing started in the 1960s, and by the 1990s cases of judicial activism had become commonplace. Courts not only played legislature, nullified rights, abused precedent, and contorted texts, but sometimes were even downright dishonest in interpreting evidence and the law.[65] It is hard to say whether the number of court cases involving liberal activist judges grew under President Obama, but his administration definitely packed the courts with liberal judges. As Elizabeth Slattery of The Heritage Foundation points out, by early 2015, the Senate had already confirmed more than twice as many judicial nominees in Obama's second term as it had in all of President George W. Bush's second term.[66] It is a safe bet that Obama is not appointing "originalist" judges who seek to abide by the original meaning of the Constitution, but rather those who share his activist constitutional philosophy.

What cannot be disputed is the fact that U.S. courts are highly involved in establishing social and cultural policies in America. They use renderings on the law, especially on highly controversial cultural issues like abortion and same-sex marriage, to break new policy ground. The Supreme Court's 2015 ruling on same-sex marriage was in line with this trend. As of mid–2015, when that ruling came down, twenty-five states had already been forced by the courts to allow same-sex marriage. In each case the court had overturned a state constitutional amendment or a referendum approved by voters in a constitutionally legitimate democratic process. Although the decisions were often justified on technical matters of the law, they also likely expressed the policy preferences of some of the judges.

It may be obvious that Congress is the lawmaking body in this country. But it is not so obvious when it comes to defining minority rights. After all, as a matter of precedent, the courts played a significant role in granting civil rights to African-Americans. Congress played a role too with the passing of voting rights legislation; but the role of the courts in establishing civil rights is now obviously the vanguard in creating new rights for other minorities.

There are numerous problems with this approach. Court rulings on the civil rights of black people were not about creating new rights. Nor were the courts discovering these rights at the far speculative edges of broad interpretations of the law (as has been done in the case of abortion and same-sex marriage). They were, rather, legalizing core political-civil rights that had wrongly been denied to blacks from the very beginning of the republic. The Constitution is utterly silent on the matter of marriage rights. As a matter of fact, as it is not enumerated as a specific right in the Constitution, it should fall under the Ninth Amendment, which states that "[t]he enumeration in the Constitution, of certain rights, shall not be construed to deny or disparage others retained by the people." Though gay marriage activists may argue that same-sex marriage exists as one of these "other" rights, that is patently untrue. Instead, the Supreme Court's ruling looked to the Fourteenth Amendment to establish gay marriage as a new constitutional right.

When gay activists seek official recognition of their unions as marriages, they are not only seeking to change the definition of marriage for themselves but for everyone else as well. They are not seeking to gain "access" to something that remains unchanged, but demanding the transformation of marriage as an institution. Thus the issue is not equality but, as Justice John Roberts explained in his dissenting opinion on the *Obergefell* ruling,[67] the right to mandate an institutional change for everyone in society. If it were truly about equality—about joining an institution as an equal—the definition of marriage would be left alone. But that is a logical impossibility. For something to be equal to something else, the two things must be of a like character. The whole point of the same-sex marriage demand is to make two different things—marriages between men and women and the unions of same-sex couples—appear to be the same, when in fact, by the very fact that men and women are different, they cannot be.

While it is true that courts overturn laws all the time, it is also true that most of the time they do so only when there is a clear and compelling case based on precedent. The Supreme Court's ruling on same-sex marriage in 2015 did not respect precedents regarding due process or equal protection.[68] Instead it boldly proclaimed the existence of a new right that Justice Anthony Kennedy and others discovered (one wonders where it had been hiding all this time!). Neither a compelling government interest nor the argument that gays were a suspect class facing discrimination is advanced as the rationale for legalizing gay marriage; if the court had done so, it would have at least been in the ballpark of past precedents. Instead Kennedy and the other four justices simply asserted that gays should enjoy equal access to marriage because not doing so would be an affront to their dignity. A new fundamental right is thus concocted, not because the state has a compelling interest in protecting it, or because gays are being discriminated against as a class of persons, but simply because homosexuals who wish to marry feel offended without it.

The Supreme Court decision on gay marriage is an affront to the principle of democratic self-government. Kennedy and the other justices may believe they were merely delivering what the people wanted, based perhaps on their reading of opinion polls. But since when do opinion polls trump the constitutional expression of the will of the people in passing actual laws and referenda? Is the high court's interpretation of surveys of popular opinion a legitimate reason to overturn democratic votes that over the past ten years showed a 60.93 percent to 39.07 percent majority against gay marriage when the issue was placed on the ballot?[69]

The Supreme Court's 2015 ruling reveals a startling disregard for judicial restraint and precedent. The majority's motive for finding a way to follow what it thought was the tide of public opinion also lay behind the court's decision to uphold the constitutionality of health care exchanges in Obamacare. Like Justice Kennedy, Chief Justice John Roberts seemed enthralled by an extrajudicial metanarrative—deciding what Congress "really" intended in its health care law. Either way, the high court was stretching not only the law but the actual meaning of words (in Roberts' case, the meaning of "the states") to get to a politically preferred decision. It is a thoroughly postmodern way of doing things. It is what you would expect from a court inspired by radical multicultural lawyers, not John Marshall or Oliver Wendell Holmes, Jr. It allows assumed narratives to crowd out facts and uses elaborate, novel interpretations to change the way we perceive things. In the process, since the high court cannot seem to restrain itself, legal fiat replaces republican democracy. It overturns the will of the people and confers on the court the right to transform fundamental civil institutions without so much as a bow to the democratic process.

In the end, judicial activism is harmful not only to constitutional government but to democratic self-governance. When judges try to ram through their policy preferences by contorting texts, abusing precedents, and making up new constitutional rights, they undermine the credibility of both the Constitution and democracy. The same thing happens if courts, with no basis in the Constitution, overturn democratically enacted state constitutional amendments, laws, and referenda. Laws should be nullified in rare cases and only when they clearly violate rights, rules, or procedures delineated in the Constitution and its amendments. We should remember that the civil rights movement succeeded because Congress (through the Voting Rights Act) and the courts moved in tandem. If new rights are to be recognized and enumerated beyond those in the Bill of Rights, or in addition to those already clearly established and agreed upon by existing precedent, they should be decided through the democratic process, not by judicial fiat.

### THOUGHT CRIMES REVISITED: THE CASE OF HATE CRIMES

Intolerance and illiberalism, nakedly defined as abstractions or principles, are seldom if ever outwardly embraced by progressives. None but the most extreme will argue that intolerance and censorship are good things in themselves. Normally the preferred course is more subtle. Instead of openly arresting people who say

the wrong things, the new purveyors of intolerance try to subli-
mate their prohibitions on speech, expression, and thought into
more popularly accepted channels. Something must be done to
make these prohibitions more palatable, because there is still a
great deal of respect in America for freedom of thought, speech,
and expression.

How to do that? The answer is quite simple: change the subject. Shift the gaze away from the sanctity of speech to something
more wholesome—to the feelings of minorities, for example, or
to the supposed desire to live in more diverse communities. One
of the most popular strategies is to carve out a special category
of speech that, in theory at least, leaves the rest of free speech
alone. If this can be done, speech can be regulated and criminalized without involving a direct assault on the First Amendment.

A prime example of parsing good speech from bad is the
notorious notion of "hate speech," which involves designating
certain kinds of remarks, gestures, expressions, and writings as intentionally hateful and thus worthy of regulation and even criminalization.[70] Attempts to prohibit hate speech and hate crimes
have been around for years in the United States. Appropriate efforts to condemn symbolic acts of violence such as cross burnings
by the Ku Klux Klan have expanded over the years to include
all sorts of alleged speech and thought crimes. Today a public
statement against illegal immigration or same-sex marriage can be
labeled hate speech. The Southern Poverty Law Center routinely
includes pro-family groups in its list of "hate" groups based solely
on their opposition to same-sex marriage.[71]

By and large America's upper courts have not looked favor-
ably on campaigns to criminalize speech. When such cases have
come before the Supreme Court, it has ruled in favor of free
speech. Nevertheless, proponents of hate speech restrictions are
not giving up. The movement has grown in recent years, particularly as the values and ideologies of identity politics became
acceptable to more Americans.

There are two types of threatening or defamatory speech that can potentially be restricted by the law. One is any speech, gesture, or conduct that is intended to incite, and is likely to incite, imminent lawless action such as violence. The second includes certain classes of speech, such as obscenity and libelous words, which can be limited. They were not considered to rise to the level of First Amendment protected speech. Oliver Wendell Holmes added a twist to the theme of prohibited speech in 1919 when he argued in *Schenck v. United States* that "falsely shouting fire in a crowded theater" was prohibited.[72] The circumstances for restricting speech were expanded somewhat, but the main purpose of preventing physical harm was retained.

Every attempt to curb free speech in America has run up against the First Amendment, which provides clearly that "Congress shall make no law . . . abridging the freedom of speech, or of the press. . . ." Yet the First Amendment is not the only obstacle. There is also the tendency in American jurisprudence to observe what is called the "strict scrutiny" test of the law. The least restrictive means available should be used to pursue a certain end. In addition, laws should be narrowly tailored to deal with conduct that pertains to a relevant end.[73] When it comes to connecting intentions and actions, the law should focus on what can clearly be discerned. It must also be very careful not to allow extraneous factors to cloud judgment about whether a crime was committed. Criminal intent has always mattered in determining if a crime was premeditated.

All this started to change with the rise of radical multiculturalism. Under its influence the ideas of hate speech and hate crimes were invented. Instead of worrying about the violent intent of individuals, hate speech advocates wanted to ban utterances, gestures, conduct, or writing that they deemed prejudicial against a protected individual or group. They were most successful on college campuses, spawning a rash of new speech codes and other imaginative methods to control what people say and think. In the name of diversity certain classes of people—racial minorities, women, and homosexuals—were considered to need protection from offensive language. The shift was not to some heightened awareness of persecution so much as a new focus on generalizing the causes of the persecution. Hate speech no longer focused on the acts of individuals but on whole classes of people who were supposedly to blame, regardless of what individuals in each class might say or believe.

Despite their success on campus, advocates for hate speech restrictions have been rebuffed repeatedly by the courts. One well-known case is the high court's 1977 decision ruling that the City of Skokie, Illinois, violated the First Amendment when it passed a series of ordinances designed to prevent demonstrations by American Nazis without affording strict procedural safeguards. Another case involved a St. Paul, Minnesota, teenager's burning of a makeshift cross on an African-American neighbor's lawn in 1990. He was convicted of violating St. Paul's Bias-Motivated Crime Ordinance, but his conviction was overturned in a 1992 unanimous decision by the Supreme Court on free speech grounds.

As the courts closed the doors on hate speech laws, advocates sought other windows of opportunity. The most successful has been to try to control speech through administrative regulation, such as enlisting the Federal Communications Commission (FCC) to regulate the content of speech on radio, TV, and other broadcast media. The first attempt was the so-called Fairness Doctrine of 1949, whereby political content on the airways would supposedly be balanced by regulation. The Fairness Doctrine has been overturned, but in 1992 Congress directed the National Telecommunications and Information Administration (NTIA) to examine the role of telecommunications in disseminating hate speech as an incitement to hatred and violence. In 1993 the NTIA issued a report titled "The Role of Telecommunications in Hate Crime," in which it argued that a "climate" of hate can be seen as an inducement to violence.[74]

These attempts to regulate free speech directly have been no more successful than attempts to curtail speech through the courts. But that does not mean the hate speech movement has been a failure. Its most significant impact has been on public and political opinion—on expanding the acceptable boundaries for defining what free speech actually is. By the time of the Oklahoma City bombing in 1995, the ground had already been prepared to bring hate speech norms and concepts into popular political discourse. It was then that President Bill Clinton tried to place blame for the Oklahoma attack on the "loud and angry voices of hate," by which he was widely interpreted to mean conservatives and Republicans.[75] Under this new standard, people who had nothing to do with a crime could be held accountable for it, at least indirectly and politically. It was a subtle but important step toward blurring the lines between actions and speech, and between individual culpability and the social "climate" in which crimes are thought to take place. Since the 1990s, under the influence of the radical multicultural movement, the definitions of hate speech have become far more elastic. In 2009, the National Hispanic Media Coalition outlined its definition in a report. It specified four areas as hate speech: false facts, flawed argumentation, divisive language, and dehumanizing metaphors.[76] Hate speech was no longer about the explicit words of individuals meant to incite violence, but a general atmosphere of public opinion that could be construed to encourage violence against certain kinds of people.

There are very serious problems with the concept of hate speech. For one thing, it fails to distinguish between legitimate political content, which is protected by the Constitution, and explicit intentions to commit violence, which are not. Under the new rules, what may clearly be an expression of political opinion could be interpreted as offensive to anyone anywhere, and therefore arbitrarily deemed hateful. No direct threats of harm are even necessary. Certain ideas and opinions are now defined *by their political content* to be the moral equivalent of a threat to do violence and physical harm. The motive of hatred is inferred not from actual words threatening violence but from, for example, what the National Hispanic Media Coalition deems "false facts, flawed argumentation, and divisive language." No distinction is made between threatening someone with real violence and merely disagreeing with the facts and arguments. Nor is allowance made for the possibility that a disagreement over facts and logic may have nothing whatsoever to do with feelings of hatred.

Hating someone and criticizing their arguments or positions are not the same thing. A Christian, for example, may object to gay marriage on religious grounds, but that does not mean he hates any individual gay person any more than a gay person's objection to the traditional definition of marriage means he hates straight people. To assume that all disagreements are grounded in irrational fears is itself irrational. If it were otherwise, we might as well abolish not only our universities but our system of law: both rely on the assumption that people are moral beings with the freedom to make choices. Without that assumption, people honestly could not be held accountable for anything. If it were all about presumed ill motives, especially those mandated by vague social forces, we might as well not bother to learn the facts about anything. Our pursuit of knowledge and justice fundamentally depends on open and honest debate, and to sacrifice that standard is not only to return to pre-liberal standards of controlling knowledge but to slide over into authoritarian methods of thought control.

Another serious flaw is that hate speech laws completely ignore a fundamental principle of American jurisprudence—namely, that a person convicted of a crime must have actual criminal intent. It is ludicrous to argue that saying offensive words alone or simply disagreeing with someone in an argument shows criminal intent. Even in cases where maliciousness was clearly involved, such as the St. Paul case, the Supreme Court has ruled that freedom of speech trumps offensive speech when no physical harm is intended. It also has ruled that criminal intent is required even in cases where violent language is aimed at a specific person. It is not enough, the high court ruled in the 2015 Facebook case of Anthony Elonis, to show that a "reasonable" person could detect a threat from someone's postings.[77] The mental state of the person making a threat must be considered to determine whether the real intent to commit violence existed.

Proponents of hate speech restrictions such as New York University Professor Jeremy Waldron believe that criminal intent to commit violence is irrelevant. All that is required for speech to be categorized as hate speech is that a person's or group's "dignity" is under threat.[78] Put aside the huge difference between offending someone and meaning them physical harm. The bigger problem is that it is left almost entirely to the accuser to determine and apply the standards for defining dignity and therefore establish what is offensive and what is not. The rational give-and-take that one assumes should be part of such determinations—and which necessarily presumes some social consensus on how the speech affects the public good—is short-circuited by giving one side a decided advantage. The problem is compounded by the fact that there can be legitimate disagreements over the political content of speech.

Nor can the determination of hate speech be justified solely on the basis of whether doing so engenders "social peace," as Waldron argues. If this were an unassailable public good in and of itself, we could find any number of authoritarian ways to try to enforce it. But we would be considerably less free and democratic as a result. Authoritarian rulers ban free speech to maintain public order, but even if this extreme case is not what Waldron and other defenders of hate speech have in mind, we must ask where to draw the line. Should the people at the Council on American-Islamic Relations (CAIR) get to decide that any criticism of Sharia law is ipso facto "Islamophobia" and therefore make it legally prohibited? Where is the threat to public order here? Surely it is not from people who object to the religious coercion demanded by Sharia law, but rather from those who use coercion (1) to maintain religious discipline among the faithful and (2) to muzzle those outside the faith who may have religious views of their own. If peace is about justice, there is precious little justice in that.

Not since George Orwell's "thoughtcrimes"—the author's word for unapproved thoughts in his novel *1984*—has there been so little regard for the dangers of controlling free speech. Not only has the bar been lowered from threatening physical violence to merely giving offense, it is now up to those who allege an offense to decide whether the offense was intended. The presumption of guilt is built ideologically into the structure of the political narrative underlying the accusations: Only racial minorities can know what it is like to be discriminated against, so only they can know what hate speech is. Only Muslims get to decide what "Islamophobia" is and what it is not. What is really in the heart of the accused is immaterial, because both meaning and intent are prejudged by a set of proscribed ideological positions and, in some cases, even by the race of the accused.

Whatever this may be, it is not liberal. Liberalism of all kinds, including the more progressive variety adopted by the ACLU in the 20th century, always made freedom of expression and speech a constitutionally protected principle. Not anymore. Today free speech is in progressive liberal circles clearly subordinated to other concerns. Lost are not only a sense of balance and proportion but the principle of mediation. Liberalism has survived all these years because it was flexible. It accepted implicitly the idea that people had different interests as individuals, and that the only way to reconcile those differences was to assume the good faith of everyone equally as individuals. Hate speech theory does not do that. It assumes bad faith on the part of people regardless of their stated intentions, essentially calling them liars if they defend themselves against the current orthodoxy.

Above all, hate speech theory obliterates the ethical responsibility of the individual. Liberal philosopher and lawyer Ronald Dworkin was quite right that, as obnoxious as some hateful speech can be, it is necessary to allow it for no other reason than that trying to ban it will undermine the moral case against discrimination.[79] Ultimately people—individual people—have to make their own moral judgments about how to treat each other with respect and dignity. Having this issue forced on them by law and coercion not only takes away the right of individuals to make that call on their own, it also undermines the moral authority of making the right decision. As John Locke argued in his *Letter Concerning Toleration* (1689),[80] coercion in matters of conscience can undercut the moral legitimacy of the oppressor's cause. One must be free to decide; otherwise the decision is not ethical at all but simply a matter of submission as a way to avoid punishment.

Am I exaggerating the threat to free speech? Most Americans still cherish free speech. They will not give it up lightly. But the trends are not good. Look at what is happening in other countries. Most European countries and Canada have had very strict hate speech laws for quite some time. Most of them are far more intrusive in criminalizing the content of speech and expression than we are used to in the United States. For example, in Sweden a pastor arrested in 2003 was sentenced to one month in prison for delivering a sermon in church critical of homosexuality. The conviction was eventually overturned on free speech grounds, but what opened the door for the prosecution in the first place was a 2002 law that explicitly listed criticism of sexual orientation in church sermons as a criminal act.[81] The abuse happened because the law was written with little or no regard for religious liberty, which may not be surprising in a highly secular country like Sweden, but which should be a scandal in the United States.

One of the unique attributes of being American has been a passionate devotion to free speech. It is one characteristic that sets us apart from other Western countries, where the tradition is far less cherished. As lines get blurred and free speech is cheapened as a mere social fiction by clever intellectuals, we could find ourselves losing one of the most precious birthrights of our historical fight for freedom—the liberty to believe and say what we please about the nature of our government, our politics, and our society.

## THE NOT-SO-GUILTY MINDS OF REGULATORY CRIMINALS: THE CASE OF OVER-CRIMINALIZATION

Lurking in the background of practically every illiberal abuse by government is an assumption: there is precious little the government cannot do to enforce a law that is presumed to be for the public's own good. This is less a developed legal idea than a prejudice affecting one's judgment. It is seen in the actions of the prosecutor who indicts to the hilt over some small infraction, or the well-intentioned lawmaker who believes that people who unintentionally violate some obscure land use or import regulation should be charged with a federal crime. At play more often than not are a lack of common sense and a warped sense of proportion. It is the same blindness about the potential misuse of government that afflicts all occasions of state overreach. It is a recurring feature of illiberal liberalism.

This phenomenon has a name. It is called over-criminalization. It occurs when a businessman is made to spend six years in prison for importing Honduran lobsters in plastic bags rather than cardboard boxes, a rule for exports that even the Honduran government said in an amicus brief was not valid.[82] It happens when the federal government accuses the Gibson guitar company of violating Madagascar's export laws, about which it knew nothing and which were not even written in English. And there is the case of Lawrence Lewis. As Heritage legal expert John Malcolm relates the story,

> [Lewis], who worked his way up from humble beginnings to become the head engineer at a military retirement home, was charged with a felony and pleaded guilty to a misdemeanor for following the procedure he had been

instructed to use (and which had been used for years) to clean up accidental toilet overflows which wound up, unbeknownst to Lewis, in a small creek that flows into the Potomac River.[83]

Over-criminalization has many causes.[84] There has been a dramatic expansion in recent years of the size and scope of the federal criminal code. As the regulatory state grew so, too, did the tendency of Congress either to forget or intentionally fail to include a so-called *mens rea*—"guilty mind"—requirement, without which a person could be sent to jail for doing something he had no idea was a crime. Or sometimes Congress would word laws so carelessly that an overzealous prosecutor could make them mean almost anything. There has been an ever-increasing labyrinth of regulatory crimes that, in the hands of malicious prosecutors and administrators, can ruin a person's life faster than you can say Honduran lobsters.

From a legal point of view there is much wrong about over-criminalization. The crimes of murder, rape, and robbery are moral offenses that, even if you did not read the fine print of the law, you knew were wrong. But today, in the Code of Laws of the United States (the U.S. Code) and the Code of Federal Regulations, there are around 4,500 statutes and another 300,000 or more implementing regulations that can carry potential criminal penalties for violations.[85] There are so many criminal laws and regulations that no one lawyer, let alone average American, can possibly know them all. Not only that, they are so voluminous and far-reaching that practically any one of us, if facing an eager prosecutor, could be charged with a crime of some sort.

The biggest problem is that these laws criminalize activity that is not inherently wrong. It may be against the law in Honduras to export lobsters in plastic bags, but not because some moral offense has been committed. These *malum prohibitum* offenses criminalize acts that do not violate any obvious moral code.[86] To be found guilty of a regulatory law violation today, a defendant need not even know the law exists, much less that his particular activity is actually criminal. For example, a person can be convicted under the Clean Air Act regardless of whether he actually intended to violate the law. There is no room whatsoever for confusion about the law. A technical misstep or mistake can land you in jail.

It is not easy to avoid breaking these types of laws. There are no conveniently accessible and complete lists of all the laws that criminalize regulatory offenses. People can of course read the massive federal code, but without legal counsel it is not easily understood. Frankly, often lawyers are not much help either. U.S. laws and regulations are so vast that not even lawyers are sure of what is legal and what is not. If this system is not explicitly designed for entrapment, it often ends up having the same effect.

### PROMETHEUS AND THE HUBRIS OF GOOD INTENTIONS

We have all heard the proverb that "the road to hell is paved with good intentions." It has been said so often that no one knows for sure who first uttered it. Saint Bernard of Clairvaux said something similar in 1150 when he warned, *"L'enfer est plein de bonnes volontés et désirs"* (Hell is full of good wishes and desires). Doubtless he was not the first to caution against good intentions gone awry. The Greek poet Hesiod, centuries before Saint Bernard, tells of the mythological Prometheus who was punished for stealing fire from Zeus to help mankind. Had he not done so, Hesiod tells humans, "you would easily do work enough in a day to supply you for a full year even without working." But because he disobeyed, Zeus created Pandora and sent her with her box of illnesses as punishments to man. The moral of the story is obvious: Prometheus's good intentions brought suffering. Defy the gods, which in a larger sense means denying the truth about life itself, and the very means to life will be taken from you.

It is not as if mankind has not been warned of well-meaning plans ending up badly. And yet progressive liberals are wholly oblivious to the dangers. They are blind to the potential for governments to abuse their powers in the name of the public good. The Founders of the American republic understood the problem very well, but progressive liberals largely dismiss their concerns. They believe there are precious few good things that government and the law cannot achieve provided there is enough money and political will. That is certainly the view of President Obama. When given the opportunity to use the power of government to advance some progressive liberal cause, he and his allies drive it as far as their powers will allow. Whether it is an activist judge overturning democratic referenda, local governments curbing free speech or religious expression, or an administration ignoring constitutional constraints on the exercise of executive authority, progressive liberals would rather have a victory than worry about the rights they are violating or the terrible precedents they may be setting for future generations.

Conservative critics of liberalism are not keen on ascribing lofty motives to liberals. Many think liberals are quite simply power-hungry hypocrites. But for liberals the misguided judgments derived from trying to do the right thing are precisely the problem, the barrier that blinds them to seeing anything but their own pristine motives. Their flaw is the same one that brought down Prometheus: the hubris of professed good intentions misunderstood as a different kind of wisdom—of pretending to know better than everyone else and believing there is no such thing as accumulated wisdom.

When the dust settles on the debates and all the facts and figures have been analyzed, progressives believe they cannot be wrong. They have a penchant for dismissing criticism as malicious lies and for making excuses when predictions—from lower health care premiums to rising global temperatures and melting ice caps—do not exactly turn out as promised. They have a firm belief that no matter how bungled things may get or how much money is wasted, the goodness of the cause is worth it. Above all, they are willing to turn the truth upside down to advance their causes. There is no such thing as "real" free speech; all speech has to be "contextualized," which is another way of saying free speech exists only when some elite says it does. Intolerance is necessary to further tolerance. Equality requires that the law treat people unequally. Blatant power grabs by government do not violate the Constitution but fulfill it. Certain kinds of scientific research must be criminalized in order to save science itself. It is the old Orwellian tendency of doublethink, bending reality to the point that it is unrecognizable.

This brings me back to Prometheus. We feel sorry for him; he was only trying to help mankind. If only Zeus had understood what a good guy he was, he never would have chained him to that rock and had birds peck out his liver and eat it again and again, every day of the year. But was Prometheus really a good guy? If you assume for a moment, as the Greeks did, that Zeus was a god who truly did know what was best for mankind, then Prometheus was not doing humanity any favors. He was actually betraying it. It was Zeus's job to give mankind fire, not Prometheus's.

This is a hard idea to grasp in our humanistic age, but that is not the point. It is that we should beware of making gods of ourselves. We are as fallible as Prometheus, which only means that we, too, need to be careful not to be guilty of hubris. When we say there are no limits to what we *can* do provided our intentions are good, we are really only saying there are no limits on what we *may* do. We need to take special care not to ascribe to human endeavors, especially those as ubiquitous and compulsory as government and the law, the promise of bringing perfect justice to the world. Only absolute power could ever hope to do that. And as we should know by now, power is the most perfect corrupter of whatever good there is in man.

# SIX

# Bullies, Shaming Rituals, and the Culture of Intolerance

The intolerance of the American left comes in degrees. Its most nuanced form is simply to ignore a contrary point of view as if it does not exist. From there are various gradations ranging from the subtle snub of a conservative at a cocktail party to attempts to use the courts and administrative rules to shut down debate. Among all the varieties of leftist intolerance, however, none stands out quite like the bigotry on America's campuses. It can be breathtakingly nasty—nearly totalitarian in its disregard for human decency—and it occurs at the very places our society entrusts with educating our future leaders. It is often the worst of the worst, and it can involve shaming rituals reminiscent of Hester Prynne's ordeals in *The Scarlet Letter*, or worse, the public denunciations on Chinese campuses during the Cultural Revolution.

## CAMPUS BULLIES

Once bastions of free speech, America's campuses are now among the least free speech–friendly places in the country. Prominent people such as former Secretary of State Condoleezza Rice and former Harvard University president Larry Summers are effectively disinvited from speaking at campus-related events. Speech codes and "trigger warnings" about course or lecture content that could offend someone's sensitivities are prevalent. Administrators impose limits on campus protests and show a pronounced bias against Christian and conservative groups, enforcing a double standard of scrutiny.[1] Rigorous race, gender, and ethnic sorting (identity) exercises are used in sensitivity training programs to expose supposedly innate biases. Even the use of language is controlled: some universities impose a practice of using "preferred gender pronouns" for all students (as in, "Hi, I'm Noelle, I take she/her/hers").[2] In extreme cases professors punish students with political views different from their own, and at least one has forced students to recite an *anti*-American pledge of allegiance in the classroom.[3]

The American university classroom, in the words of former Yale Law School dean Anthony Kronman, has become "intellectually and spiritually frozen."[4] It is a place where a misspoken word can result in administrative proceedings lodged against professors for alleged bias. When it is not students harassing professors, it is professors indoctrinating students. Responding to a 2004 survey for the American Council of Trustees and Alumni and the Connecticut Center for Survey Research & Analysis, almost half of the college students surveyed said their professors frequently injected political comments into their coursework, "even if they have nothing to do with the subject," and almost a third felt they "had to agree with the professor's political views to get a good grade."[5]

Little has changed for the better since that report was published. A 2015 report of the Foundation for Individual Rights in Education (FIRE) finds that policies severely restrict students' right to free speech at over half of the 437 universities it surveyed.[6] Among academics, the pressure to conform is insidious. Psychologists Yoel Inbar and Joris Lammers of Tilburg University in the Netherlands surveyed a representative sample of academics and scholars in social psychology (over 80 percent of whom were in the U.S.). Among their findings, published in the peer-reviewed journal *Perspectives on Psychological Science* in 2012: "In decisions ranging from paper reviews to hiring, many social and personality psychologists said they would discriminate against openly conservative colleagues."[7]

The cause of such closed-mindedness is no great secret. It is a pervasive left-wing bias that has been amply documented.[8] Crowdpac, a nonpartisan firm that analyzes political data going back to 1980, produced a report in 2014 showing that academia is one of the most "liberal" of all America's professions.[9] Ivy League professors gave most of the more than $2 million they donated in the 2014 election cycle to liberal candidates, committees, and causes.[10] There are of course many universities and colleges in America where this leftist bias is less pronounced, especially in the South and Midwest. But the overall trend is unmistakable, particularly at the more elite and influential schools. The American academy leans far to the left.

The strategy of choice for shutting down freedom of thought on campus is the public shaming ritual. By this I mean using some socially acceptable practice to shun the ideas of people with whom one disagrees. These practices include shouting down a speaker and disinviting others after a few students protest, using "diversity" policies to stifle free speech and punish students and professors who do not toe the line, or employing indoctrination methods, under the guise of sensitivity training, to force students and employees to comply with restrictions on the content of speech.[11] Other tactics include ostracizing colleagues who disagree. This is more than mere bias. It is the active use of one's position of power and/or protected sociocultural status to stifle ideas that differ from the perceived dominant views of the prevailing culture.

The campus shout-down is the crudest kind of shaming ritual, but there are subtler ones. Much more effective, in fact, is passive-aggressive bullying through charges of microaggression and trigger warnings. A microaggression may include an innocent remark that gets twisted into meaning an intentional insult. In a set of guidelines established by the University of Wisconsin, a microaggression can be anything from asking an Asian-American where she is from to insisting that the most qualified person should get a job.[12] The former is deemed racist whereas the latter is interpreted to imply that "people of color" get unfair benefits. Trigger warnings are messages tweeted or sent out by text or e-mail to forewarn tender-hearted students that they may be traumatized by, for example, a sculpture of a man in his underwear; according to students at Wellesley College, this scene could be "triggering thoughts regarding sexual assault."[13]

Being accused of a microaggression can be a harrowing experience. Manhattan Institute Fellow Heather Mac Donald relates in *City Journal* how an incident got out of hand at the University of California, Los Angeles, in 2013.[14] Professor Emeritus Val Rust taught a dissertation preparation seminar in which arguments often erupted among students, such as over which victim ideologies deserved precedence. In one such discussion, white feminists were criticized for making "testimonial-style" claims of oppression to which Chicana feminists felt they were not entitled. In another, arguments over the political implications of word capitalization got out of hand. In a paper he returned to a student, Rust had changed the capitalization of "indigenous" to lowercase as called for by the *Chicago Manual of Style*. The student felt this showed disrespect for her point of view. During the heated discussion that followed, Professor Rust leaned over and touched an agitated student's arm in a manner, Rust claims, that was meant to reassure and calm him down. It ignited a firestorm instead. The student, Kenjus Watson, jerked his arm away from Rust as if highly offended. Later, he and other "students of color," accompanied by reporters and photographers from UCLA's campus newspaper, made a surprise visit to Rust's classroom and confronted him with a "collective statement of Resistance by Graduate Students of Color." Then the college administration got involved. Dean

Marcelo Suárez-Orozco sent out an e-mail citing "a series of troubling racial climate incidents" on campus, "most recently associated with [Rust's class]."[15]

Administrative justice was swift. Professor Rust was forced to teach the remainder of his class with three other professors, signaling that he was no longer trusted to teach "students of color." When Rust tried to smooth things over with another student who had criticized him for not apologizing to Watson, he reached out and touched him in a gesture of reconciliation. Again it backfired. That student filed criminal charges against Rust, who was suspended for the remainder of the academic year. As if to punctuate the students' victory and seal the professor's humiliation, UCLA appointed Watson as a "student researcher" to the committee investigating the incident. Watson turned publicity from these events into a career, going on to codirect the Intergroup Dialogue Program at Occidental College in Los Angeles. As for the committee report, it recommended that UCLA create a new associate dean for equity and enhance the faculty's diversity training program.[16]

It was a total victory for the few students who had acted like bullies and the humiliating end of a career for a highly respected professor. It happened because the university could not appear to be unsympathetic to students who were, in the administration's worldview, merely following the university's official policies of diversity and multiculturalism.

Not even the most liberal of college administrators are immune to bullying. Smith College in Massachusetts is one of the most liberal schools in America and yet its president, Kathleen McCartney, found herself on the wrong end of a microaggression charge. In an e-mail in the wake of the 2014 Ferguson, Missouri, protests over a policeman's shooting of a black teenager, McCartney tried to show empathy with students who claimed to be suffering from emotional trauma. She was saddened that they had "lost faith in the quest for racial equality."[17] But at the end of her

e-mail, she made the mistake of using the phrase "all lives matter," which unbeknownst to her had been expropriated in protester code to mean "black lives don't matter." You would have
thought she had called for the reimposition of Jim Crow laws.
Protesters demanded she apologize for her remark.[18] In the classic recant of the shamed and the shunned, she did just that. She
thanked her critics for their "wisdom and wise counsel" and reas-
sured everyone that she was a "white ally" of "Black people."[19]

Such cowardice in the face of intimidation is not merely personal, it is systemic. It is built into the policies and the culture of
universities themselves. Take, for example, a recent case at Jesuit-
run Marquette University.[20] In a 2014 training presentation for
university employees, one projected screenshot noted that any
criticism of same-sex marriage, even if done privately, should be
reported to authorities as possible harassment. The presentation
also included a "liability avoidance tip" that stated that "[a]lthough
employees have free speech rights under the United States Constitution, in academic and other workplaces those rights are limited when they infringe upon another person's right to work in an
environment free of unlawful harassment." The training was part
of an "anti-harassment module" designed "in accordance with
federal law and university policy."

Never mind that Marquette is a Jesuit school that according to
its website still "support(s)" the "beliefs and values" of the Catholic Church, which officially opposes same-sex marriage. The university claimed to be merely enforcing new Labor Department
laws on discrimination. There is only one problem. Other universities that have to follow the same rules do not feel compelled
to behave in this manner. Lest we think this is an isolated event
at Marquette, consider this: in early 2015, the dean of its College
of Arts and Sciences started proceedings to rescind a professor's
tenure after he defended, on his own blog, a student who was told
by another teacher that any criticism of same-sex marriage would
not be "tolerated" in the classroom.[21]

America's universities have had a problematic relationship with free speech for a very long time. Speech codes were developed decades ago. They arose mainly as an outgrowth of the feminist movement, when feminist lawyers such as Catharine MacKinnon, Andrea Dworkin, and others began treating free speech as a barrier to gender equality. Free speech, they argued, allowed pornography to exist, which they insisted was a violation of a woman's civil rights.[22] A very important line had been crossed. Once free speech was interpreted as a threat to feminist and other multicultural values, it was only a short step to demanding speech codes and other attempts to stifle freedom of expression.

More imaginative ways to control speech have emerged in recent years. For example, consider the Inclusive Language Campaign at the University of Michigan at Ann Arbor.[23] Students are encouraged to sign a pledge to follow the campaign's guidelines by not using certain words and phrases that have been deemed offensive. Broadly worded, the guidelines could in practice result in some rather bizarre bans on speech. For example, in several mandatory sessions for freshmen, students reportedly were told that wishing someone "Merry Christmas" is a microaggression.[24] For students who did not comply with speech guidelines, punishment was swift. One student was fired from the campus paper for writing a satirical essay making fun of political correctness on campus. The head of student affairs was forced to attend sensitivity training on "white privilege" for saying that he was "going to die" if he heard about one more microaggression case on campus.[25] The movement to ban or control speech is limited neither to Ann Arbor or even to students and teachers. At the City University of New York, interim provost Louise Lennihan instructed all employees to stop using the salutations Mr. and Ms. The reason: they are not "gender inclusive."[26] At Johns Hopkins University, students tried to ban the Chick-fil-A restaurant from campus because of statements made by its owners that they considered a microaggression against the gay, bisexual, and transgender community.[27] And at the University of Missouri, a video captured a communications professor calling for "muscle" to eject a student journalist from a protest.[28]

As we saw at Berkeley, Smith College, Marquette University, and the University of Missouri, a significant part of the free speech problem lies with administrators. Entire bureaucracies have been established on campuses to monitor student behavior, presumably to improve their quality of life. George Mason University Professor Todd J. Zywicki relates how he crossed swords with "University Life" bureaucrats on campus. GMU is hardly a bastion of left-wing radicalism, and yet he ran into more trouble combating speech codes at GMU than at Dartmouth College, where he and others were successful in getting the codes overturned. The problem, as he saw it, was a new class of professional bureaucrats who were by their very nature hostile to free speech on campus:

> [T]he main stream of thought inside the University Life bureaucracy is decidedly hostile to free expression . . . [A]t one point one of the administrators told me that vagueness in a speech code is actually a positive virtue, because that way, students can be disciplined for disruptive conduct or speech that doesn't actually violate any rule.
>
> Such a principle turns ordinary standards of free expression and due process on its head. Whereas the First Amendment demands clear rules governing speech to ensure that protected speech is not chilled, the university actually sought to establish vague rules *precisely* to deter students from venturing near what otherwise would be protected speech, and reserving the right to punish them *ex post* if they didn't steer far enough away.[29]

Two things are happening here. One is that the war against free speech is now bureaucratized within the university system. It has its own army of professionals whose careers depend on finding ever new ways to slice and dice presumed offenses in order to justify the suppression of free speech. It may appear at first to be all about civility and good manners, but in reality it is about redefining and constricting the boundaries of thought and expression regarding social and political values. "University Life" bureaucrats are teaching the next generation of young Americans that the First Amendment is not a guarantee of constitutional rights; it is a potential weapon that can be wielded against one's enemies in the social justice wars.

Another trend is that progressives control the accreditation process for many colleges and universities. For example, 235 master's degree programs in the United States are accredited by the Council on Social Work Education (CSWE), which requires schools to "advocate for human rights and social and economic justice" as part of their curricula.[30] Colleges that refuse to toe the line could lose their accreditation. No wonder professors and administrators are intimidated and remain silent in the face of blatant discrimination against points of view that are not progressively liberal. Their very livelihoods depend on accreditation.

It can be astonishing how far some colleges will go to enforce ideological discipline. For example, at the City University of New York's Hunter College School of Social Work, Devorah Goldman was approached by a professor after class one day who quietly informed her, "I can't have you participate in class anymore."[31] The offense? Opinions she expressed in class were contrary to the school's guidelines—the same ones established by the CSWE. Emily Brooker, a Christian student at Missouri State University's School of Social Work (also accredited by CSWE), was asked in 2006 by her professor to sign a letter to the legislature in favor of adoption by homosexuals. When she refused she was interrogated for two and a half hours by the school's ethics committee and charged with a "Level Three Grievance," which is the most severe penalty.[32] Fearing the loss of her degree, Brooker eventually relented and signed a contract promising to "close the gap" between her religious views and the values of the social work professor.

There is no way to sugarcoat how bad this is for our society. It is thought control pure and simple. And it is systemic. It is not merely a lack of grace on the part of a few muddle-minded professors, but the corruption of our institutions of higher learning.

## SPILLOVER EFFECTS ON AMERICA'S EDUCATIONAL SYSTEM

Some Americans may take comfort in the fact that the illiberalism of the academy is not widespread—that it is limited to universities and colleges, and even then not to all of them. "It's just a bunch of eggheads," some may argue, "who have little influence over the rest of society."

This could not be more untrue. American universities and colleges have an enormous impact on the culture. It is not simply that they are shaping the minds of our young people, our future leaders. It is also that they are the avant-garde of the culture, providing in their intellectual laboratories the next new idea that will be taken up by political activists, lawyers, priests, preachers, entertainers, schoolteachers, and the public elementary and secondary education administrators of the future. The entire multicultural movement, which began in the halls of academe, is today practically the official doctrine of America's educational establishment. Far from being marginal or isolated, the political activism of the universities, including shaming rituals, is an influential part of America's mainstream culture.

Take, for example, an incident that occurred at a California school in February 2015. A group called the Queer Straight Alliance was invited to give a lecture on LGBT issues to fourteen- and fifteen-year-old freshman students at Acalanes High School in Lafayette.[33] The students were asked to stand in a circle and were grilled not only about their personal beliefs on homosexuality but also those of their parents. At one point the students were asked to step forward if they believed being gay was a choice and that their parents would accept it if they made that choice. According to the reports, those who refused to step forward were publicly ridiculed and humiliated. It was a public shaming ritual in which young students were pressured into making a public denunciation of their parents' value system. High school officials did not invent this game. Activists tutored in the hothouse ideas of identity theorists from Yale and Berkeley did.

Not only public school authorities but local and state officials use their positions to indoctrinate and discredit views with which they disagree. For example, even though Gordon College, a non-denominational Christian college in Wenham, Massachusetts, has a policy allowing any person of any sexual orientation to attend, teach there, or serve in its administration, as a Christian school it also has a "life and conduct" policy against sexual relations outside of marriage, including "homosexual practice."[34] This was too much for the local authorities. The city of Salem suspended a long-term contract with Gordon College that had allowed it to use the city-owned Town Hall. The nearby Lynn School Committee broke with long-term practice and started refusing to accept student teachers from Gordon College. Gordon's accreditor, the New England Association of Schools and Colleges, put it on probation, giving it a year to get rid of the offending policy. Without accreditation, of course, a college is doomed. Local authorities were threatening to shut the small college down for trying to stick, at least in part, to its Christian principles. The accrediting association eventually relented in May 2015, but only after conducting months of harassment.[35]

In their defense, school districts and public authorities have always had the authority to dictate the curriculum of public elementary and secondary schools. Control of the curriculum is no less of interest to liberals than to conservatives. It also is true that public school authorities in conservative districts are pushing back against what they believe is political correctness. In Tucson, Arizona, for example, the local authorities passed a resolution in

2012 that prohibits the state from teaching courses designed for a particular ethnic group.[36] Other conservative districts have put strictures on how human evolution should be taught.

The danger is not that authorities control school curricula, but that the federal government is attempting to control it for every school district in America. That is precisely the concern with Common Core, a federally prescribed program of education standards and tests rolled out under President Obama.[37] It purports to be all about educational standards, but it could just as easily be used to establish national criteria for the content of all school curricula.[38] What is excluded from textbooks can convey biases just as much as what is included. For example, a history textbook listed in the Common Core curricula highlights the destruction caused by World War II but is silent on why the United States entered the war. One of Common Core's designers, Dr. David Pook, admitted publicly that his belief in "white privilege" is the reason he helped write Common Core standards.[39] The problem is not only with Common Core. New standards established by the College Board for its Advanced Placement (AP) courses also are heavily biased in favor of a progressive interpretation of American history. For example, as one critic recently pointed out, "the 19th-century belief in manifest destiny is presented as a regrettable example of 'cultural superiority' rather than an attempt to expand and defend the realm of liberty."[40]

In both the AP program and Common Core examples, progressive liberals are trying to control what is taught not only to their own children but to everyone's children. They may complain that conservatives are trying to dictate content at the local level, but at least conservatives are not trying to impose particular ideas on the whole country. Conservatives want local control. Liberals want national control. Instead of allowing for the teaching of views that fairly represent all Americans, the College Board is, by pushing a one-sided agenda, excluding the views of millions of Americans. This is not merely a fight over who controls the education curriculum; it is ultimately a fight over ideas. Liberals are staking their claim for controlling the national curriculum on the basis of a single argument—that their ideas are right and correct, and as a result there is no room for a diversity of opinions.

Perhaps if there were a national consensus on what these ideas should be, it would not be an issue. A liberal society is perfectly within its rights to establish a national education curriculum if that is what most citizens in that society want to do. But there is no such consensus. In fact there are deep cultural divisions over the questions raised by Common Core. Trying to impose a national curriculum on local school districts under these conditions is not only contrary to America's tradition of local and state control over education, it is contrary to the spirit of pluralism that is at the heart of America's liberal democracy.

## KANGAROO COURTS AND THE
## CHARGE OF SEXUAL DISCRIMINATION

On June 23, 1972, President Nixon signed Title IX of the Education Amendments of 1972 into law. Title IX is a comprehensive federal law that prohibits discrimination on the basis of sex in any federally funded education program or activity. Originally intended to protect women against discrimination, in recent years it has been broadened to cover practically any issue associated with sex or gender. Since most universities receive some federal funding, it has been a powerful tool for progressive activists and the federal government to influence education at institutions of higher learning.

The Obama administration dramatically changed the procedures and guidelines for compliance with Title IX. It not only vigorously enforced Title IX rules, but also encouraged widening the scope of discrimination to include practically anything to do with sexual politics. The areas directly affected are investigations of sexual assault, sexual consensual-relations codes developed by universities, and even public utterances about these and other subjects related to sexual politics.

The new rules vary in implementation from one university to the next, but the tendency is to make it much easier to expel a student accused of rape, for example. New rules at Harvard University call for no hearing for the accused and thus no opportunity to question witnesses and mount a defense. A single Title IX compliance office, rather than an independent review committee, acts as investigator, prosecutor, fact-finder, and appellate reviewer; the pursuit of justice is wrapped up in one office. Some schools actually ban the accused from speaking with lawyers during the hearings, and in most cases the accused is not allowed under any circumstances to confront the accuser. Under the new federal requirements, university tribunals can find students guilty of rape or sexual assault under the lowest standard of proof. Instead of determining guilt beyond a reasonable doubt, as in a court of law, only a "preponderance of evidence"—that is, only 51 percent certainty—is required.

The result has been a rash of lawsuits filed by male students alleging false accusations. Most involve the application of the new Obama administration standards to cases that in the past would have been dismissed as incidents of consensual sex or as the misbegotten consequences of alcohol intoxication. Because of these new rules, convictions have been achieved in campus tribunals even when there are ever-changing accusations and testimonies. If alcohol was involved, it is used as a pretext to convict the accused, even though both the accused and the accuser may have been intoxicated. In some cases activist professors coached students to file rape charges even though the student was reluctant to do so. In others there is evidence that family members were involved in manufacturing rape accusations out of anger at discovering their child was having sex. Accused students were treated as if they were already found guilty and prohibited from visiting certain parts of campus for fear of making "retaliatory contact" with the alleged victims. Once a guilty verdict is rendered, even though an appeal process exists, the accused often leaves school and in many cases is unable to enroll at another college given his now blemished record as a sexual offender.

By changing the framework for adjudicating the charge of sexual assault on campus, two things were accomplished. First, by making it an issue of sexual discrimination rather than a violent crime, less stringent rules could be used in the investigation. Second, lesser offenses like unwanted touching could be called sexual assault, which would not have passed muster if it were treated as a crime of violence. In either instance, the point is driven home that rape is mainly about how men mistreat women in general—that it is, like "white privilege," a "systemic" problem—not about individual cases when men assault and abuse women.

The abuse of Title IX guidelines has increased in recent years, moving well beyond the rape charge. Students and activists harangue professors for holding contrary opinions. Professor Laura Kipnis at Northwestern University, for example, was investigated by a Title IX university "coordinator" after two students filed formal complaints against her.[41] They took issue with her public criticism of sexual consensual-relations codes, with one student calling her questions "terrifying." When she commented about one of the students on Twitter, she was accused of retaliation and creating a "hostile environment." As so often happens, the case began spiraling out of control once university administrators got involved. The university hired a law firm to investigate. Kipnis was interrogated for two and a half hours and forced to answer questions about what she meant by sentences in an essay and her tweets. She was told a report would be issued in sixty days and, in keeping with the new Title IX rules, only the standard of a "preponderance of evidence" would apply.

There is no better word to describe these practices than harassment. The campus tribunals may not be proper courts of law, but that does not mean they can act like kangaroo courts. They have no right to convict people on unsubstantiated, unproven, or tainted evidence. The accused should not be railroaded through a one-sided judicial process that favors the accuser over the accused. The accused have rights of due process that do not disappear simply because he happens to be a male or because she holds a politically incorrect opinion.

In the case of rape, no one should ever take an accusation lightly. It is undoubtedly true that many women are afraid of coming forward to report their experiences. As the unfolding case against Bill Cosby makes painfully evident, some men do prey on women for sexual favors in ways short of threatening force. Nevertheless, these facts should not be used as an excuse for short-circuiting due process in determining guilt. The presumed "narrative" of gender oppression should not be allowed to trump the rule of law, no matter how horrible the alleged crime may be. These are not only conservative principles. They are not only liberal principles. They are American principles. They are the principles that define a liberal democracy under the rule of law for everyone.

### THE HARASSMENT OF SCIENTIFIC DISSENTERS

The shunning tactics on American campuses mostly concern issues of race, gender, and sexual orientation. Occasionally foreign policy issues such as boycotting Israel enter the fray. Some academics and academic associations, for example, advocate cutting ties with any Israeli university or any U.S. company doing business with or in Israel.[42] For the most part, however, science and technical fields of study have been insulated from such political controversies. Most chemists, computer scientists, structural engineers, and astrophysicists go about their business without much thought of the political controversies of the day.

There is of course one notable exception: climate change research. Here the story is very different. While there are plenty of climate researchers and meteorologists who are not engaged in politicized research, there are unfortunately many others who are. The more activist scientists not only engage in direct political lobbying but have joined together to do the unthinkable in the scientific world—to ostracize their peers who dare to question their data, findings, and conclusions, and in some cases to try to drum them out of the discipline.

Take the case of Lennart Bengtsson.[43] A leading Swedish meteorologist working in the U.K. and approaching his eighties, Bengtsson was well respected in the international climate scientific community. But in April 2014 he joined the Global Warming Policy Foundation, a group that questions some of the climate change community's conclusions based on data. His main concern was that climate change predictions based on computer models were not validated by actual observations over time. "Since the end of the 20th century," he said, "the warming of the Earth has been much weaker than what climate models show."[44] He was not saying that global warming was not occurring. Rather he was raising a scientifically valid question about the difference between observational results and model simulations.

Within a matter of days he found himself in deep trouble. As happened to other scientists who questioned any aspect of the global-warming "consensus," Bengtsson was hounded by colleagues to the point that he felt forced to resign from the think tank. In his explanation of that decision, he complained:

> I have been put under such an enormous group pressure in recent days from all over the world that has become virtually unbearable to me. If this is going to continue I will be unable to conduct my normal work and will even start to worry about my health and safety. . . . Colleagues are withdrawing their support, other colleagues are withdrawing from joint authorship, etc. I see no limit and end to what will happen. It is a situation that reminds me about the time of McCarthy.[45]

Bengtsson's case is not isolated. There are many other in-stances involving not only intimidation over questions about data, but also data manipulation. The best-known involves the Climate Research Unit (CRU) of the University of East Anglia in the United Kingdom.[46] A hacker got access to over five thousand e-mails between CRU climate change scientists that showed dis-dain for scientists who questioned global-warming data. Climate change was referred to as a cause rather than as a subject of scien-tific inquiry. There was evidence that some scientists even tried to suppress data that pointed to a recent global cooling trend.[47] In one e-mail, former CRU director Tom Wigley, then of the University Corporation for Atmospheric Research in Colorado, complained that the editor of the journal *Climate Research*, cli-matologist Hans von Storch, published "crap science."[48] Wigley went so far as to say they "must get rid of von Storch" because he threatened the image of a united front of scientists concerned about climate change.[49]

And then there is Dr. Mitchell Taylor, a leading polar bear researcher and long-time member of the Polar Bear Specialist Group (PBSG). In 1996 the polar bear's listing in the *Red Data Book* of the World Conservation Union (WCU) was upgraded from "vulnerable" because its population was increasing. That did not sit well with the PBSG, which argued that polar bears were still endangered by climate change and thus should still be called vulnerable even if their numbers were growing. The group had concluded, on the basis of a presentation by one scientist which did not include supporting documentation, that global warming could reduce the bears' habitat and thus their population in the future. Taylor, however, decided to examine the climatology as-sumed in that presentation, and ultimately disagreed with its as-sertions. He contended that the data did not show that global warming posed a threat. But instead of examining his analysis of the data, the other scientists in the PBSG retaliated. The PBSG disinvited Taylor from its next meeting. Its outgoing chairman explained that he had been ousted because his views that run "counter to human-induced climate change are extremely unhelpful." Furthermore, lest there were any question about why he was being kicked out, Taylor was told that his ouster had nothing to do with his research on polar bears—"it was the position you've taken on global warming that brought opposition."[50]

It is clear that global warming is no longer exclusively a scientific issue. It is a political cause, and like all causes it has its hard-core believers. There are sensational cases such as the professor at the Rochester Institute of Technology who argued that climate change "deniers" should be punished for criminal negligence.[51] But extremist academics are not the problem. Mainstream scientists who do not speak up against such behavior by their colleagues are.

Political activism has so penetrated the science of climate change that one can barely tell the difference between a United Nations conference of scientists on global warming and a rally of political activists lobbying governments to adopt controls on carbon emissions. The bias arising from the alliance erodes even the peer-review process that is supposed to protect scientific research from charges of manipulation. The overriding goal of pushing the climate change political agenda is in full display in this excerpt from a peer-reviewed paper by two economists, Fuhai Hong and Xiaojian Zhao, in the *American Journal of Agricultural Economics,* published by Oxford University Press:

> It appears that news media and some pro-environmental organizations have the tendency to accentuate or even exaggerate the damage caused by climate change. This article provides a rationale for this tendency by using a modified International Environmental Agreement (IEA) model with asymmetric information. We find that the information manipulation has an instrumental value, as it *ex post* induces more countries to participate in an IEA.[52]

Thus as this peer-reviewed paper by respectable academics explains, accentuating or exaggerating the damage caused by climate change and manipulating relevant information has an actual "instrumental value"—in this case, inducing more countries to join a climate change agreement. This is a political agenda, not a scientific one. If this is what is meant by "settled" science, then climate change activists and advocates have an awfully shortsighted view of science.

I do not raise these examples to pass judgment regarding the reality of global warming: it appears to describe the recent temperature trend, though its current rate, causes, and future threat are in dispute. My point is rather that these efforts to shame and shun scientific colleagues violate the scientific spirit of open inquiry. Skepticism is a bedrock principle of science. Without it Copernicus and Galileo would never have challenged the established teachings on the planets. William Harvey and other scientists who explained blood circulation would not have done so had they not been skeptical of medieval notions about body humors inherited from the ancient Greeks. Scientists *should* argue and dispute one another's findings. But they should not be using their positions of power and prestige in their professions—not to mention their control of funding streams and journals—to silence other scientists and people who have legitimate questions about data and methodologies. If there is nothing to hide, they should not be afraid of bringing their findings into the light of scientific inquiry.

Sadly, too many climate scientists act more like advocates than scientists. They treat their conclusions as if they were doctrine rather than theory. They are not conspirators so much as groupthink careerists.[53] They do not lock themselves behind closed doors and intentionally draw up plans to mislead the public. They do rally the wagons to advance a policy agenda or, in some cases, to sustain political and financial support for their research. Climate "skeptics" may have a political agenda of their own, but their skepticism is not what is undermining the credibility of climate research with the public at large. It is the attempts to silence them, which most people rightly see as anti-scientific. If climate change skeptics are wrong, scientists should engage them and prove them so in an open and free debate.

If the abuse of science were limited to climate research, this might be alarming, but it would not constitute a crisis of confidence in science as a profession. Alas, climate change research is not the only area of science that experiences political bullying.

Consider the case of software engineer Curtis Yarvin. He was scheduled to deliver a presentation on a new computation framework at the Strange Loop programming conference in St. Louis, Missouri.[54] It was a purely technical talk. There was not even a hint of politics in the topic, which was to explore a new "universal computation platform." Yet when the conference organizer was told that Yarvin moonlighted as a self-professed "neoreactionary" blogger and some conference attendees did not like his views on unrelated topics, everything changed. Conference founder Alex Miller complained that a "large number of speakers and attendees" had contacted him "to say that they found Yarvin's writing objectionable." Even though he admitted to not having read Yarvin's blogs, Miller said, "[i]f Curtis was part of the program, his mere inclusion and/or presence would overshadow the content of his talk and become the focus."[55] Miller tried to make it appear that he was protecting the integrity of the scientific discussion by disinviting Yarvin, but it was the complainants who had politicized the discussion, not Yarvin. And it is they who wanted to censor his scientific work for political reasons.

Increasingly, scientists are lending their expertise and credibility to "studies" that are little more than thinly veiled political attacks. A study published by the journal *Psychological Science*, for example, "found" that people with "right-wing beliefs" have "poor abstract-reasoning skills."[56] As a result, they are supposedly more likely to have anti-homosexual prejudice and other authoritarian attitudes. Echoing the authoritarian personality theories of Erich Fromm, lead researcher Gordon Hodson concluded: "Socially conservative ideologies tend to offer structure and order. . . . Unfortunately, many of these features can contribute to prejudice."[57] For such "scientists," the evidence is in: conservatives are quite simply stupid.

This is junk science.[58] Anyone with an elementary knowledge of the scientific method knows that one cannot draw such broad conclusions from this narrow base of data. Social intelligence and political views are dramatically more complex than straight IQ tests can measure, and it is a ridiculous leap in logic to link right-wing ideologies to "poor abstract-reasoning skills." One could just as easily say the same thing about the conspiratorial views of left-wing populists such as Senator Elizabeth Warren. Are we to suppose they are stupid too? The "linking" of complex social attitudes to biologically based intelligence is a classic false comparison, and the attempt to explain prejudice as a lack of reasoning skills is absurd. Were Immanuel Kant and Thomas Jefferson, two extremely intelligent thinkers who held views that would be by today's standards considered racist, also stupid? Racial theorists such as Arthur de Gobineau were quite intelligent and possessed powerful reasoning skills, so much so that they used them to rationalize a reprehensible "scientific" ideology of racism. Where is the link to a low IQ there? You get the picture. The whole study published by *Psychological Science* is riddled with tendentious assumptions that should make a scientist blush, and yet there they are, presented as pure science.

It would be laughable if the subject were not so serious. There should be no room for such prejudice in science. Nor should scientists sit idly by while their colleagues are bullied for political gain. They should be horrified when one of their own, speaking on their behalf *as professional scientists*, abuses their prestige and position for political purposes. Science was politicized in the Soviet Union, Nazi Germany, and other totalitarian societies. We are not that far along yet, and thankfully most of our scientists are free of politicization. But all too many of them, especially in the social, psychological, and climate sciences, are not. They are succumbing to one of the oldest temptations known to science—letting prejudice affect the outcome of their work. It is tarnishing their profession and polluting our politics.

### NEIGHBORHOOD BULLIES, TWITTER TROLLS, AND OTHER INTOLERANT PEOPLE

Deborah Vollmer doesn't like mansions.[59] She really hates "McMansions" of the kind her neighbors, Linda and Arthur Schwartz, were building next door, so she tried to stop it. Starting in 2009, she sued the Schwartzes and the town of Chevy Chase, Maryland, five times, costing the city $50,000 and resulting in arrests, two misdemeanor charges, anger management classes, and a no-contact court order. It is not as if Vollmer were a pauper and had the proletariat's disdain for the rich. A retired lawyer who has been active in progressive causes, she is wealthy herself and like her neighbors lives in a million-dollar house. A child of the Sixties, Vollmer's backyard is rough-hewn and overgrown, while the Schwartz lawn is manicured. She drives a Prius; her neighbors have a Mercedes-Benz. In keeping with her old hippie values, Vollmer argues her aesthetic choices are about equality and not being "bullied" by rich people. "I just want equal control over the use and maintenance of a shared driveway," she says, although what she really wants is control over her neighbor's property. As in that old leftist adage, "think globally, act locally," Vollmer sees herself as acting out a grand progressive cause, and she seems to enjoy it. "If you can't take enjoyment out of these things," she tells a journalist, "you've got to at least find it interesting."[60]

Welcome to quarrelsome America. From neighborhood property wars to Twitter battles, the country is in a churlish mood. Tempers are set on a hair-trigger release. Arguments are like gladiator contests where only one side prevails and losers bleed to death in the dust. Whereas people used to shy away from appearing loathsome in public, today a hateful rant attracts millions of Twitter followers. People once thought neighborhood bullies were a pain in the neck. Today they are celebrated as working-class heroes. A protester can scream that the phrase "all lives matter" is a racial affront and get sympathetic coverage on CNN and MSNBC.[61] A presidential campaign can be waged on the premise that political enemies need to be demeaned and ridiculed and called names.

The cantankerous mood is part of our polarized political landscape. But it is not solely caused by politics. It is also caused by changes in our social values. As scholars from Robert Putnam to Charles Murray argue, the communal spirit in American society has been in decline for years.[62] There are many sociological reasons. Community-building institutions are weak. Suburban life can isolate people. The breakdown of the nuclear family has contributed to social ills. Economic disparities and the unequal distribution of social and economic capital have driven people apart. Even technology works against us. At the same time that social network sites like Twitter and Facebook bring us together, they also foster an insular anonymity that fuels the crabby temper of the country. The overall effect is to tolerate social malevolence as something other than what it really is: an indulgent narcissism masquerading as social concern.

Look, for example, at the phenomenon of Twitter trolls. They have no one political ideology: conservatives as well as liberals can be trolls. They stalk Twitter like predators, lying in wait for something with which to disagree and then angrily let loose a tirade of abusive language. They are sometimes part of organized efforts, even by foreign governments. The use of Facebook and other social media is often no better. Social media are stages upon which people play the political equivalent of computer war games. Hiding behind anonymity, they indulge in the habits of some computer gamers. They equate violence with winning, dehumanize their opponents as if they were no more than images on a computer screen, and become desensitized to the normal give-and-take of face-to-face interaction. All in all, it is a terribly antisocial way to debate anything, much less politics. And it is a social habit contributing greatly to the new intolerant mood of American politics.

Pew Research in 2014 estimated that 40 percent of online users have experienced bullying, harassment, and intimidation.[63] The numbers are highest for young people. Around 70 percent of users between the ages of 18 and 24 reported having been the target of harassment. Women and minorities report it the most, but frankly no one is immune. Some websites make a business of "outing" people and have been involved in online campaigns to defame and ruin careers.[64] According to British journalist Jon Ronson in *So You've Been Publicly Shamed* (2015), the mobbing of public figures is a commonplace feature of online life. The most notorious cases include public relations representative Justine Sacco, former Mozilla CEO Brendan Eich, and Nobel laureate biochemist Tim Hunt, all of whom had their careers ruined by online shaming campaigns.[65]

We may not understand all the reasons for the country's sour mood, but one thing is certain: intolerance is habit-forming. An angry teenager living in Alabama can do battle on Twitter with a grumpy old man in Vermont as if they were sitting across the table from one another. They are crossing generational lines, learning from each other the dark arts of online intolerance. When neighborhood bullies like Vollmer start wars over driveways, her neighbors have no choice but to respond in kind. What few communal values still exist are scorched in a fiery blaze of lawsuits and court orders. If a town council fines a baker for declining on religious grounds to bake a cake for a same-sex wedding, it should not be surprised when previously docile Christians in their town respond angrily. Much of the outcry against the jailing of Kentucky county clerk Kim Davis was a reaction to the overreach of the courts on gay marriage. Progressives who want to make the Charleston mass murder all about the traditions of the South should not be shocked to learn that Southerners who are not racist are offended and will fight back against such slurs, sometimes viciously, even raising the Confederate flag in defiance.

The spiraling effect keeps the hatred going and makes it worse. It was only when Donald Trump started saying outrageously insulting things about immigrants and his opponents that he shot to the top of the polls in the 2015-2016 GOP presidential primary contest. The whole system kicked into gear to reward mendacity as if it were authenticity, a kind of "speaking truth" to the power of political correctness. But it is nothing of the kind. It is quite simply rude and abusive behavior that coarsens American public life.

Americans are not a bad people. In fact most are decent and want only to live their lives in peace. But the problem is that the popular culture is working against them. It teaches every day that anything goes, so long as it is not *boring*. Intolerance and bullying may be titillating, if you have the mentality of a thirteen-year-old. But to an adult, calling people names and behaving like adolescents is boorish and antisocial. If we wish to be serious about fixing what ails our country, we need to think and act more like adults. Only then can we tell the difference between a charlatan and a statesman. Only then will the leader be separated from the fool.

# SEVEN

# The Death
# of the Liberal
# Intellectual

In 1783, a Berlin newspaper held an essay contest to answer the question, "What is Enlightenment?" Some of the greatest thinkers of the era responded. Immanuel Kant wrote that the Enlightenment was "man's emergence from his self-incurred immaturity," which he defined as "the inability to use one's own understanding without the guidance of another."[1] Philosopher Moses Mendelssohn provided an entry as well: enlightenment, he explained, is a process by which man is educated in the use of reason.[2]

The key word here is "process." Rationalism was viewed as a method of using human reason to educate oneself about the world. For it to work it had to be open-ended: you had to keep an open mind. There should be no attempt to stifle inquiry or establish another point of reference beyond reproach or outside the boundaries of criticism. All points of view should be heard. In the competition of ideas the truth would come out, provided the intellectual playing field was truly level. Trying to do otherwise would be the same "self-incurred immaturity" that was, in Kant's mind, the original sin of the old order. The commitment to free and open inquiry was the methodological cornerstone not only of the Enlightenment, at least in its moderate incarnation expressed here by Kant and Mendelssohn, but of the modern idea of "liberal" education from which it was derived.

It also is the core creed of the liberal intellectual. Ever since the *philosophes* first frequented the salons of Paris and David Hume and Adam Smith walked the halls of the University of Edinburgh, Western liberal intellectuals have seen themselves as free thinkers. It is no less true of American liberal intellectuals. From Thomas Jefferson to John Dewey, liberal thinkers were enemies of any idea that, in Jefferson's words, forms a "tyranny over the mind of man." Their bête noire was closed-mindedness, which Jefferson saw in the effort to establish a particular religious dogma, and which Dewey criticized as a characteristic of the turn-of-the-century American university. Both men were iconoclasts taking on the establishment, but their main intellectual complaint was not with the past per se or even frankly religious faith—after all both revered not only ancient philosophers but, in Jefferson's case, even the Bible. It was rather the fact that the old world had not been open to new ideas.

## THE DECLINE OF THE PUBLIC INTELLECTUAL

The free-thinking American intellectual was the iconoclast of the 20th century. Social critics such as Upton Sinclair, Sinclair Lewis, and H. L. Mencken established the profile of the public intellectual in the early part of the century. By the 1950s the American public intellectual was in full bloom. Mary McCarthy, Philip Rahv, C. Wright Mills, Dwight Macdonald, Lionel Trilling, Norman Podhoretz, Irving Kristol, Daniel Bell, Irving Howe, Edmund Wilson, Lewis Mumford, Malcolm Cowley, and other intellectuals were champions of free and open inquiry. Many of them operated outside of or at the edges of the academic world as independent intellectuals. Wilson made his living writing reviews for *The New Yorker, The New York Review of Books*, and other journals. Macdonald did much the same, starting, as Wilson did, as a magazine editor but ending up writing independently for *The*

*New Yorker* and *Esquire*. The outlets for intellectuals were not the academic tomes of the university press but such independent journals as *The New Republic, The New Leader, Partisan Review, Commentary, The Nation, Dissent*, and *politics*. Some, like Mills, were professors, but Bell, who began his career as a journalist, did not become a sociology professor at Columbia University until 1959.[3]

These were largely men and women of the left. Wilson was a bitter critic of U.S. Cold War policies, refusing at one point to pay taxes in protest. Macdonald, like many of his generation, had once been a communist but broke away and drifted toward an anti-Stalinist democratic style of socialism. One of the defining moments for this generation was the controversy over McCarthyism. It made them ardent defenders of free speech and freedom of expression and conscience. Seeing themselves as persecuted fighters for the truth, most were, despite their socialist leanings, civil libertarians in the negative sense—defenders of freedom of thought, whether from government control, suppression in the university, or censorship by the media. When the motion-picture producers, directors, and screenwriters of the "Hollywood Ten" were brought before the House Committee on Un-American Activities in 1947, they invoked their First Amendment right to free speech.[4] The belief in free speech was in fact so powerful in leftist circles in these years that it carried over into the birth of the Free Speech Movement at the University of California, Berkeley, in 1964, which was the beginning of the revolt of the New Left in the 1960s.

As outsiders, these public intellectuals knew that freedom of expression was in their self-interest. It was the necessary prerequisite for their vocation as writers of opinion. Since they were willing to compete in the open arena of ideas, they knew that they had to write in a persuasive manner. Their love of literature informed their intellectual sensibilities and made many of them excellent writers. Instead of articles laboriously inscribed in the turgid, impenetrable language of the specialized academic, they penned essays in delightfully accessible prose for a relatively large audience of educated people.

They were fiercely independent. Some writers, such as I. F. Stone, were accused of being Soviet spies; there were indeed professors and journalists who were spies or who at the very least came under the sway of Soviet influence.[5] But despite doubts about their loyalties during the McCarthy era, the New York intellectuals did not acquire their left-wing views at the behest of a Soviet paymaster. They developed them on their own as public intellectuals.

There was another important characteristic of the public intellectual of this time. They admired Western culture. They were men and women of letters who respected the West's achievements in art, literature, and philosophy. Often rooted in recent immigrant families, many of whom were Jewish, the New York intellectuals in particular saw themselves as cosmopolitan savants eager to bring the sophistication of European culture to America's shores. They were, at least in the early days, champions of the "two Ms"—Marxism and Modernism. Later, while retaining their socialist sympathies, most eventually broke with Marxism as a doctrinaire dogma.

Fast forward to postmodern leftist intellectuals of today. They could not be more different.[6] Whereas a Wilson or a Trilling admired Western culture, postmodernists such as Catharine MacKinnon, Richard Delgado, and Michael Walzer see it as confining, even oppressive. The Fifties intellectuals believed there was such a thing as universal justice, which they thought was the business of socialism; they would have been puzzled by the doctrinaire relativism of a Ronald Dworkin or any other postmodernist. Wilson and Trilling were more interested in art and literature than theory or doctrine, and they prided themselves on being free of cant and predictability. Even though some, like Mary McCarthy, could be fiercely rigid in their views, most cultivated the image of the free thinker willing to take an idea to wherever its logic took them.

The Fifties intellectuals approached knowledge and history with a sense of wonder, as something to be discovered by free and open inquiry and to be described with wit. By contrast, the postmodern intellectual treats knowledge like a scholastic, forever dissecting language in terms that only he or she understands. For the postmodern leftists, scholarship is not a craft in its own right, but a rigorous exercise in matching facts and information to preexisting theories. Whereas the Fifties liberals still operated well within the Enlightenment's tradition of universal humanism, the postmodernists—despite their professed egalitarianism—are the ultimate anti-humanists. They not only doubt there is such a thing as the universal human condition—they scoff at the very notion of universalism.

There is another crucial difference. Whereas liberal intellectuals sixty years ago were fiercely independent people, most intellectuals today are in some way or other creatures of the system. Some are members of the media who cheerlead or cover for officials and politicians they like. Others are part of a vast network of universities and research institutions funded either directly or in part by the federal government. Despite the immense amount of dollars involved, their work often escapes public scrutiny and evades rigorous congressional oversight. It can create anything but the kind of environment conducive to free and open thinking among scholars, because once the government gets involved, politics is often not far behind.

Those who are closest to the liberal public intellectuals of the 1950s today are the think-tankers, bloggers, opinion writers, and self-styled mavens of social media and the Internet. Liberal think tanks include the Brookings Institution, the Center for American Progress (CAP), and numerous other smaller research organizations, some of which may have only a handful of employees. Most of these are privately funded, although Brookings performs some government-funded research and CAP receives a small percentage of its funding from foreign governments. Equally influential are activist journalists like Matthew Yglesias of *Vox*, David Wald-man of the *Daily Kos*, and the shills of *Gawker* gossip. Many are young and some, like Facebook co-founder Christopher Hughes, are quite wealthy. Hughes in particular is making his mark by transforming the once venerable *New Republic* from a place of serious liberal thought into a glitzy platform for attention-deficit millennials.

They are close to the liberal public intellectuals of the 1950s, but not identical. Many are not really intellectuals at all, but rather pundits of popular culture. Forced to compete with Jon Stewart or Bill Maher on television and Kanye West and Kim Kardashian on Twitter, liberal opinion elites try to outdo one another in perfecting the adolescent snarky remark. They are masters of the frat-boy style of intellectual discourse—the separation of ideas into the equivalents of social cliques. Some ideas are "in" and others are "out" or, in Internet slang, "cringe-worthy." It is as if someone with the wrong idea shows up with a mullet haircut at a Manhattan hipster's party. There is scant knowledge of history and culture, unless it happens to fit a convenient political narra-tive. Unlike Mills or even McCarthy, who brandished their wits like daggers, the liberal bloggers of today are often petulant and given to childish name calling. They approach public debate not with a keen eye but with a sledgehammer, hoping to pound their opponents into submission with an "epic takedown."

The liberal blogger is the front man, but he is not alone. Be-hind him is an academic industry of far less colorful characters. They are the frowning multicultural professors of cultural stud-ies departments who see racism behind every innocent remark. They are the angry gender studies instructors who spin elabo-rate theories about the supposedly coded chauvinist language of white males. A tacit division of labor exists. These professors cre-ate the ideas, but it is up to the bloggers and journalists to explain, elaborate on, and popularize them in the fields of everyday life.

Like hummingbird hawk moths, bloggers and opinion elites drink nectar from the professors' Dianthus. They are symbiotically dependent. One cannot flourish without the other.

## THE QUASI-GOVERNMENT AND THE INTELLECTUALS' CONFLICT OF INTEREST

The most valuable intellectual currency of the scholar and the scientist is credibility. Even those who traffic in the theoretical relativism of deconstructionism claim their findings are grounded in scholarship. They may argue that there is no empirically objective truth, but they still act as if they arrived at their conclusions through—unsurprisingly—objective research. Even as the postmodern leftist spins theories about the unreliability of perceived reality or asserts that he knows for certain what cannot, by definition, ever be known, he still appeals to old-fashioned standards of scholarship and empirical research.

Objectivity also matters to scientists. They lack credibility without it. Willfully skewing data or evidence is still widely frowned upon in the broader scientific community and among the general public. Unlike in the social sciences, where it is nearly impossible to disprove a theory, theories in the hard sciences can be invalidated by experiments. There is a premium on objectivity that does not exist in the social sciences. At the same time, because science is highly technical, only the scientists themselves know for sure whether an experiment successfully upholds a theory or not. Their exclusive control of scientific knowledge makes their credibility all the more critically important. Most people are not knowledgeable enough to challenge a climate change scientist's analysis of a simple radiant heat transfer model. Nor do they have any independent source of data to discern on their own whether the oceans are in fact rising from global warming. They must, in short, take the climate scientists' word on it.

People's dependence on them is all the more reason for scientists to avoid conflicts of interest. One of the biggest temptations is to let funding sources get in the way of objectivity. The potential for just that is growing in what the Congressional Research Service (CRS), a nonpartisan research arm of Congress, calls the "quasi-government."[7] It is made up of agencies and entities that rely on billions of federal dollars to operate, often with little oversight, and that funding could be used to drive political agendas rather than objective research. According to the National Science Foundation (NSF) and the Association of American Universities (AAU), the federal government supports about 60 percent of the research performed at America's universities.[8] In fact, most of the funding that universities receive for research and development comes from the federal government. In fiscal year 2013, 645 universities were awarded federal research and development grants totaling nearly $40 billion.[9] Because of the 1980 Bayh-Dole Act, university-employed scientists and engineers are allowed to patent and retain title to inventions created by their government-funded research.[10] According to the AAU and the Association of University Technology Managers, 658 new products based on university-licensed discoveries were introduced in fiscal year 2009 alone, and there were 596 startups that year based on licenses from academic inventions.[11]

It is often assumed that most of this federal funding is for research related to national defense. That is incorrect. In 2012 the federal agencies investing the most in university research were the Department of Health and Human Services ($22 billion or about 50 percent of overall funding), followed by the NSF at $5.3 billion, the Department of Defense at $4.9 billion, and the Department of Energy at $2 billion.[12] The NSF is involved in a big way in funding environmental research. Though the largest share of the $3.9 billion it spent in 2012 on university scientific research went to the physical sciences, environmental sciences came in second ($792 million), beating out life sciences, computer sciences, and other scientific fields.[13]

The main funnels for federal research money—and the cogs in the wheels of the quasi-government—are the Federally Funded Research and Development Corporations, or FFRDCs.[14] These institutions are almost entirely funded by the federal government but not run directly by it. They are operated primarily by private entities and nongovernmental organizations on contract to the government. In 2014, forty of them were involved in research and development, and while some, like the RAND Corporation, are stand-alone operations, most are sponsored by nonprofit, university-affiliated, or private industry groups. Most university-affiliated FFRDCs are run either by universities or by a consortium of collaborating universities. Examples include the Ames Laboratory administered by Iowa State University, the Lawrence Berkeley National Laboratory run by the University of California, Berkeley, and the National Center for Atmospheric Research administered by the University Corporation for Atmospheric Research in Boulder, Colorado.

Three federal agencies—the Department of Energy (DOE), the Department of Defense (DOD), and the NSF—sponsor most of the research contracts. Between 2008 and 2012, the thirty FFRDCs sponsored by these three agencies received nearly $84 billion.[15] Most of the funding over that period went to the DOE to conduct long-range research on advanced technologies, including those that could be used for national defense; the DOE in fact spent 34 percent of its budget on FFRDC research. Next in line is DOD, which sponsored research on weapons systems and engineering. The NSF funded atmospheric and space research, among other things.

The conventional wisdom is that all such research is purely scientific and has nothing whatsoever to do with politics. If only it were so. In 2014 the case of MIT professor Jonathan Gruber made the news, exposing corruption in how government funding of research and consulting can serve partisan interests. Although there is no evidence that Gruber or any of his employers did anything illegal, between 2008 and 2014 he received at least $3.9 million from federal agencies and almost $2 million more from state governments for consulting work on Obamacare and Medicare. He received some of this money at a time when the issue of health care reform was being contested in Congress.[16] In other words, the federal government awarded taxpayer dollars to Gruber to help the administration devise and make the political case for implementing a policy that not only faced significant public and political opposition, but had not yet been decided by Congress. It was *not* about implementing policy, but about influencing the making or changing of laws, otherwise known as lobbying. All sorts of lobbying and conflict of interest laws exist to prevent this sort of thing from happening with regard to corporate interests, yet Gruber and others slip through the cracks, using government funding to influence the outcomes of pending legislation.

Gruber is of course not the only professor getting government money who works to influence changes in government policy. Some have much more influence than others. Penn State University Professor Michael E. Mann, for example, is the scientist who created the recently discredited "hockey stick" graph used by Al Gore and the United Nations Intergovernmental Panel on Climate Change (IPCC) to show rapid global warming.[17] According to his curriculum vitae on the Penn State website, for the years 2009 through 2018 he has received over $6.7 million in federal grants to study the effects of climate change on such matters as precipitation, inundation, droughts, water resources, malaria, and other diseases.[18] To put this figure in perspective, that is roughly equivalent to what the Department of Defense would spend on two Patriot PAC-3 missiles for our national missile defense systems.[19] Now consider that Mann is just one of thousands of federal research grantees.

The concern in Mann's case, though, is his political activism. He was involved in the so-called Climategate e-mail scandal that found some scientists associated with the Climate Research

Unit (CRU) at East Anglia University in the United Kingdom conspiring to suppress data that contradicted their theories. For example, in a private e-mail exchange that came to light after the CRU's computer system was hacked, Mann wrote that the data showing a temperature *decline* was "diluting the message" on climate warming.[20] To take care of the problem Mann was said, in another e-mail, to have altered the data, a maneuver the CRU director called a "trick."[21] In any other branch of science such a blatant attempt to control the portrayal of research results would be condemned out of hand. But unfortunately in the field of climate change science, too often the response is to circle the wagons and condemn critics as "deniers." Hiding behind the mantra of "settled" science, activists such as Mann often get a free ride inside the science community.

The problem is not merely the biases of certain scientists. It is a system that ignores a built-in conflict of interest. The quasi-government and universities conducting all this research, no matter what the subject may be, are part of a web of cozy professional relationships that are fueled by billions of federal dollars. It is a network of people who move in and out of government, sometimes even holding private and public posts at the same time.[22] As prominent scientific advisors, some could conceivably benefit from both ends of the federal funding trough at the same time, advising government how its research funds should be dispensed as well as receiving the benefits of some of that funding. The issue is not misappropriation of funds or outright fraud, but the legal and quite open conflict of interest involved in allowing many of the same people to wear too many of the same hats. Even if it is legal, it can give the appearance that today's intellectual class is more interested in job security and funding than in pursuing objective science and research.

Another example of the appearance of conflict of interest is Columbia University's Earth Institute. Founded in 1995, it is run by Jeffrey Sachs, who is also the director of the United Nations'

Sustainable Development Solutions Network. The Earth Institute, with an annual budget of around $130 million,[23] is focused on scientific research,[24] but that is not all it does. It openly acknowledges on its website and in news releases that it also advocates for federal policy changes related to climate change and the environment.[25] In case there is any doubt about this self-avowed advocacy role, Sachs was joined in 2012 by former NASA scientist James Hansen, who resigned his position at NASA expressly to get more involved in advocacy. His new job at the Earth Institute was to start up a "policy oriented" Program on Climate Science, Awareness and Solutions. Its task is to lobby for such policies as the disapproval of the Keystone XL pipeline.[26]

Privately funded think tanks across America conduct policy research all the time. There is absolutely nothing wrong with this kind of work. The private sector should be free to conduct any research it likes and to let the open competition of ideas decide its merits. The problem with the Earth Institute is that it is not really private. It receives most of its funding from the federal government, a fact its executive director acknowledged in 2014.[27] Between 2009 and 2010, the Earth Institute received 64 percent of its funding, or $71.2 million, from federal grants; by 2013 that amount had risen to 69 percent.[28]

There is another problem with the Earth Institute. Much of its work is not purely scientific. It takes scientific data, some of which are disputed, and quite openly uses them to buttress the case for making policy recommendations, including some that are politically controversial. There is a difference between pure scientific research and public policy analysis. How governments should respond to climate change is not merely a scientific question about its effects. It is also a political question involving choices and trade-offs that must be decided through the democratic process. The tactic of blurring the lines between the two under the flag of settled science is dishonest. Government-funded think tanks should stick to scientific analysis and leave the public policy recommendations based on that data to legislators and to privately funded think tanks that take no government funding (such as the Cato Institute or The Heritage Foundation, where I work).

Another example of the appearance of an overly cozy relationship involves Professor Steven Wofsy, the Abbott Lawrence Rotch Professor of Atmospheric and Environmental Science at Harvard University.[29] Between 2008 and 2014, Wofsy received some $2 million ($10 million since 2003) in U.S. government funding for research on the environment, greenhouse gases, and other issues related to global warming.[30] In 2012 he was awarded the Revelle Medal by the American Geophysical Union for contributing "in an outstanding manner to the understanding of Earth's climate systems."[31] In addition to his academic work, Wofsy regularly leads interdisciplinary teams doing research for NASA's Earth Science Division, including its climate change satellite project.[32] In 2005 and 2006 he served on the United Nations IPCC advisory group on climate change. These governmental and intergovernmental organizations are directly involved in climate change advocacy. NASA's Global Climate Change website reads like a commercial for the idea of climate change,[33] and IPCC reports regularly call for drastic measures to reduce greenhouse gas emissions.[34] Wofsy also is a member of the National Academy of Sciences and on the Scientific Advisory Board of a company that manufactures analyzers that measure greenhouse gases, which are specifically marketed to scientific researchers.[35] Wearing all these different hats, he stands at the influential nexus of the quasi-government between the private university and the federal government. Wofsy is a highly respected scientist, and there is no evidence he has ever engaged in any wrongdoing. But his receipt of government funding plus his involvement in so many government-affiliated organizations can and should raise questions about his objectivity as a policy advocate.

Any public policy question that touches on the sciences, or

any technical question for that matter, can be politicized. It is no less true for climate science than it is for a weapon system that some Congressman wants built in his district. But there are degrees of politicization. The RAND Corporation, for example, prides itself on the objectivity of its research work and, most of the time, especially in the defense area, it deserves the accolades. But even RAND can succumb to the myth of complete objectivity, especially when it concerns its work in the social sciences. If the Obama administration, for example, asks the RAND Corporation or any other FFRDC to study climate change or gays in the military, surely RAND's officials must know that there is a political purpose in mind. All the rigorous standards in the world can be maintained, and yet at some point subjective value systems, ones that cannot be quantified, come into play. Would RAND claim its analysis of gays in the military, which happened to conform to what the administration wanted as an outcome, is as completely objective as a study of the engine specifications for a fighter aircraft?

The quasi-government system is highly unfair to American taxpayers. Many may disagree with the *policy* recommendations of its studies, yet they have no say in the matter. This is true even in the contentious case of climate change. Regardless of what Americans may or may not believe about global warming, they have every right to disagree with the *policy* recommendations that activist scientists make. It is wrong to demonize all objections to climate change policies as the result of ignorance or conspiracies. There is sufficient evidence of bad behavior and conflict of interest to raise legitimate questions not only about the intentions of some of the scientists involved, but also about the objectivity of some government-funded research. Climate change is ultimately a political issue. Even if it were completely true that global warming is occurring as some claim, non-scientist citizens have a right to weigh in on the question of what to do about it, of whether, for example, draconian measures to stop it are more costly than adapting to it.

There is a place for federally funded research. Work in the physical and life sciences and on national defense, engineering, and advanced scientific discovery are of vital interest to the United States. But funding for research in the social sciences should be curtailed, and support for research on environmental and climate sciences should be watched closely for bias and politicization. Even research in the hard sciences should be scrutinized for conflicts of interest and abuse. If there is even a hint of political advocacy or conflicts of interest on the part of the scientists receiving federal grants, it should be stopped. At stake is not only the credibility of the research, but also the fairness and openness of the democratic system.

### THE RULE OF THE MANDARINS

Chapman University Fellow Joel Kotkin calls opinion elites today the clerisy of the administrative state. Academics, he says, supply the ideas and the intellectual legitimacy for a "new class" of "ultra-wealthy" people who align themselves with "the instruments of state power."[36] Kotkin is on to something. Most intellectuals today, far from being the scrappy outsiders of the 1950s, are the quintessential insiders. They attend White House parties, get invited to all the best conferences, and control and benefit from billions of dollars of government research funding. They bring to mind Chinese mandarins, the bureaucrat scholars who once advised the emperor and gave his rule intellectual cover and moral legitimacy.[37] Occupying positions of power, which means never having to say you're sorry, many of today's intellectuals revel in dissembling and cultivating the air of the eminent official who knows better than everyone else.

Like mandarins, far too many academics operate at the nexus between intellectual inquiry and government interest. They endeavor to create an official ideology for the state—in the case of progressive liberals, the welfare state. They hold a monopoly over the course of research and the content of ideas, as the mandarins once did in establishing the imperial examination system. And many draw their prestige and influence from their access to government and its dependents, from which many also make a very good living.

The problem is not that intellectuals and scientists have well-paid jobs at universities. American industry and government have been dependent on academic research for over 150 years. Rather, the problem is twofold: 1) a monopoly of one point of view; and 2) a lack of self-awareness on the part of some of the more activist professors about the relationship of the intellectual to power. As Richard Hofstadter said in his landmark study *Anti-Intellectualism in American Life* (1966):

> It would be tragic if all intellectuals aimed to serve power; but it would be equally tragic if all intellectuals who become associated with power were driven to believe they no longer had any connection with the intellectual community: their conclusion would almost inevitably be that their responsibilities are to power alone.[38]

Hofstadter is correct. Independence is indispensable to the intellectual, and once it is lost, it is very difficult to regain. And yet it is or nearly is already gone. The federally subsidized scientists or the six-figure salaried chairs of gender studies academic programs are hardly the Greenwich Village beatniks of the Fifties. They live in nice suburban neighborhoods, not some dark hovel off Washington Square. Instead of sacrificing for their cause, they are rewarded handsomely for it. The well-endowed chairs of ethnic studies departments may be many things; they may even be alienated from the traditional culture of most Americans. But oppressed minorities they are not.

The problem is that intellectuals have forgotten their calling.

They are supposed to "speak truth to power." And yet today they *are* part of the power. Much of the problem stems from universities turning their backs on open inquiry and a well-rounded education. We should remember that the ideal of the liberal arts college was originally a progressive idea. In the 1890s, largely under the influence of Progressive leader and Governor of Wisconsin Robert La Follette, the University of Wisconsin developed what was called the "Wisconsin Idea," namely, the idea of the university as a place to explore knowledge impartially. As Hofstadter described it:

> The role of the university, it must be emphasized, was to be wholly nonpartisan; it would be impartial between the political parties and, in a larger sense, it was expected to serve "the people" as a whole, not a particular class interest. It would not offer propaganda or ideologies, but information, statistics, advice, skill, and training. By the same token, it was hoped that the prestige of the university would grow with its usefulness.[39]

Most of America's elite universities today do not come close to meeting this ideal. They are monotonously uniform in their ideologies. They are places where shaming rituals are conducted against ideological enemies. And they increasingly are dependent on official recognition and funding. Whatever this is, it is not the "nonpartisan" institution free of "propaganda" that Hofstadter and other progressives dreamed of. It is more like the reactionary and insular class of intellectuals that once helped propel the Chinese empire into decline.

### THE ILLIBERAL INTELLECTUAL

The liberal intellectual in America has traveled a long way from the creed established by Kant, Mendelssohn, and other founders of the Enlightenment. Kant's abhorrence of "self-incurred immaturity" was at the time aimed at the Church. But today it is not Christianity that threatens to enslave the mind of mankind; it is a secular ideology that purports to impose a new authoritarian order on society. The "other" that Kant feared would tyrannize the mind is today not religion, but an illiberal ideology devised by America's intellectuals and funded by, entrenched in, and enforced by an increasingly illiberal administrative state.

It all comes down to the open mind. Edmund Wilson and others like him believed that in the competition of ideas, the truth would prevail. They were, in this respect, classic liberals even as they wanted to be socialists. Since many of the old liberal intellectuals were men and women of the left, they could not have imagined the current situation, in which today's intellectuals actually become rich in the capitalist society they profess to hate. The beggar-thy-neighbor mentality of the downtrodden remains strong in the mindset of many American intellectuals, supposedly giving them "street cred." But that image cannot be squared with the reality of the multiple award-winning professor who chairs an Ivy League university department and rakes in millions of dollars of federal grant money.

Liberal intellectuals come by their illiberalism honestly. They have a choice. They can maintain their independence, at which point we have some obligation to listen to them. Or they can cash it all in and become shills for the administrative state. Too many have chosen the latter option, which means they have forfeited their right to be taken seriously as intellectuals. We should not be surprised that the ideology they adopt is one that openly makes the case against human freedom. Who needs freedom when you have power, prestige, and money? What is freedom if it can be bought and sold by a government contract or exchanged for a comfortable post at a university? Now that so many intellectuals are in positions of power, they want to close the gates behind them.

Liberal intellectuals have given up their birthright. As Norman Podhoretz explains:

The basic truth is that the fundamental values on which this country was founded as expressed in the Declaration of Independence, in the Constitution, in the writing in *The Federalist Papers*, used to be called liberal. And it is wanton and reckless to tamper with them, as many people now called liberals are always eager to do.[40]

Not only are these intellectuals *not* liberals, they are not true intellectuals either. They have become the Establishment they once loathed. The intellectual today is dead, at least on the left side of the political spectrum. They have "come a long way, baby," all right, in the words of the popular ad from the 1960s. They have ended up closing their minds to the wonders of knowledge, the cultivation of which had once been their most sacred mission.

# EIGHT

# The Troubled Legacy of the Radical Enlightenment

The dangers of illiberal liberalism are very real. They threaten our civil liberties, the rule of law, and our constitutional form of self-government. It may be that the perils of liberal intolerance are caused in some cases by the character flaws of individuals. But that is a wholly unsatisfactory explanation for why so many otherwise good and open-hearted people behave in such atrocious ways toward their fellow Americans. There must be something else going on. There has to be something enticing liberals to surrender their heritage to one of the oldest intellectual temptations known to mankind—the irrationalism of the closed mind—something other than personal animosity or mendaciousness of character.

There is something else indeed, and it is called ideology.[1] It is a certain kind of ideology, though, with a very specific and very long history. I have spent a great deal of time tracing the intellectual historical roots of modern liberalism for a reason: the very same ideas used today to excuse and justify the illiberalism of the American left have been around for a very long time. Put simply, there is a common historical thread between the hard illiberalism of the far left of the past and the soft illiberalism of the postmodern left today. To know what that thread is we must understand its origins. The Western Enlightenment has given us the liberal tradition, but it is not monolithic. We must ask: what element of the Enlightenment is behind progressive liberalism's slide toward authoritarian thinking?

## WHAT KIND OF ENLIGHTENMENT?

There are essentially two Enlightenments. Think of them as jet streams flowing through the broader atmosphere of the Enlightenment. One is the *moderate Enlightenment* exemplified by Francis Bacon, John Locke, Montesquieu, Adam Smith, and even François-Marie Arouet (Voltaire).[2] These men celebrated the rights of man and believed in a universal secular philosophy separate from religion, but they stopped short of egalitarian democracy and atheism. They were radicals by the standards of their day, but they were reluctant to overthrow the old social and political order. The other is the *radical Enlightenment* of Baruch Spinoza, Pierre Bayle, Denis Diderot, and Jean-Jacques Rousseau. They were the first to indulge in the dreams of radical egalitarianism as harbingers of a new populist kind of democracy. They also challenged religious thinking nearly to the point of atheism.

Each of these two Enlightenment traditions started from a common concern. They were both interested in the nature of man, religion, and the political order. But they ended up going in very different historical directions. Whereas the moderate Enlightenment jet stream flowed largely into the classical liberalism of the British and the Americans, the more radical ideas of Diderot and Rousseau poured into the more radical traditions of the Germans, Russians, and French—namely, socialism, communism, and modern and postmodern ideas of egalitarianism. One gave rise to the classic liberal revolution of the Americans; the other to the first experiment in modern totalitarianism, the Reign of Terror of the French Revolution.

*The Radical Enlightenment Tradition.* The radical tradition starts with Dutch philosopher Baruch Spinoza. The son of a Portuguese Jew who fled from religious persecution to Rotterdam, Spinoza reflects the cosmopolitan liberalism of the Netherlands in the 17th century. He challenged French philosopher and mathematician René Descartes's idea of mind–body dualism, insisting that there is only a "one substance monism."[3] In other words, there was no dualism between body and mind, but a material continuum he broadly described as "nature." Nature was a material machine that operated all on its own. Metaphysics was not the study of the great beyond and how it relates to the physical world, but of the material world itself.

This is a historically momentous idea. Nature, as understood through human reason, had replaced God as the source not only of all human knowledge but of morality and ideas about the proper political order. For Spinoza and other materialists who would follow him, the material world of nature was all there was. And it was indivisible. Spinoza actually believed Nature was God and God was Nature, which is a kind of pantheism. From this all-powerful nature mankind derived its capacity to reason and to understand the world. The study of ethics became all about discovering the inherent good that resides in nature, including the virtuousness that supposedly exists in human nature. The goal of politics was to create a new order in which these ethics could be realized. Men were indeed now like gods. They could set their own destiny. They had the power to know and to understand the world sufficiently to make it perfect.

This view of how mankind relates to nature is the key to what historian Jonathan Israel calls the radical Enlightenment.[4] It was picked up by French *philosophes* Pierre Bayle and Denis Diderot and then conveyed to Jean-Jacques Rousseau, who developed it into a full-blown philosophy. Historians often cite the anti-clerical religious views of Bayle and Diderot as evidence of their radicalism. It is true that they were fierce critics of Christianity. But as far as the history of liberalism is concerned, it is their view of the good and all-encompassing power of nature that is most important. It distinguishes them from more moderate Enlightenment figures such as Thomas Hobbes and John Locke, who believed in natural rights but held a far dimmer view of the utopian potential of mankind.

The contrast becomes clear when comparing the views of moderate and radical Enlightenment figures. Take for example perhaps the most conservative figure in the Enlightenment, Thomas Hobbes. He famously had a grim view of the state of nature. Life was "solitary, poore, nasty, brutish, and short."[5] Hobbes shared Bacon's and even Spinoza's mechanistic view of things, and he even believed in a social contract and popular sovereignty. But the purpose of that contract was to end the "war of all against all" and to establish an absolute state that could bring the peace. His view was hardly a vote of confidence in the natural goodness of man, and it showed that the ideas of nature at the time could be decidedly pessimistic.

This is not at all how Diderot and other radicals saw the possibilities of mankind. Drawing on the influences of Niccolò Machiavelli, Spinoza, and Bayle, Diderot thought Hobbes was way too pessimistic. The original state of nature was not a place where violence and inequality were rampant, but a kind of Eden in which mankind's natural goodness was revealed. Since man was inherently good, so too were his natural rights. Rather than suppress them with an absolutist monarchy, they needed to be carried over from nature into civil government where they could be made manifest. There should be a continuum between the rights of nature and the obligation of civil government to guarantee those rights. For the radicals the implication was obvious: it meant a republican form of government. But it also implied that the purpose of government was not merely negative—to protect people from other people trying to deprive them of their rights—but positive, insofar as the state was expected to create a new social order in which all sorts of rights were to be realized.

At play in this debate are two totally different conceptions of popular sovereignty. For Hobbes, the royalist sympathizer in the middle of the bloody English Civil War, the liberty of nature was to be feared. Democracy was distrusted because it meant too much liberty. By contrast Diderot and Rousseau (and Spinoza before them) had no such fears. Trusting human nature rather than fearing it, they imagined a government of the people to be totally benign. They could not fathom a true republican government abusing the rights of the people because, if constructed properly, it would automatically reflect the natural goodness of man as he had once existed in the state of nature.

What is emerging in the minds of the radicals of this period is the nascent idea of modern democracy. It decidedly is not the democracy of ancient Athens, with its respect for hierarchy. And it is not the limited notion of popular sovereignty found in Hobbes or even John Locke. Rather it is the notion of government embodying the ultimate common good. Spinoza had taught that once tyranny had been eliminated man would naturally be cooperative. Diderot, Rousseau, and other radicals agreed but took it one step further. They argued that the new state should provide not only security and liberty but also equality. The public good—or the "general will" as Diderot and Rousseau called it—was not merely the sum of all individual wills, but something bigger, a supersession of them all, precisely because the general will represented an equal collection of all individual wills combined.

This vision of a new society run by a state dedicated to the common good rested squarely on a radically new understanding of equality. There were many thinkers in 17th-century Europe who like Spinoza believed in social equality. François Poullain de La Barre, a French Catholic priest who converted to Protestantism, published a treatise anonymously in 1673 calling for the equality of the sexes.[6] Adriaan Koerbagh, a Dutch scholar writing in the middle of the 17th century, also spoke of the need for social equality. Others such as the Italian free thinker Alberto Radicati—and even, much later, Rousseau himself—developed their own interpretations of human equality. They all owed a debt to

Spinoza's "monist" view of nature in assuming that all men were part of one substance, which assumed as well that all men (and for some, women) must be truly and completely equal.

*The Moderate Enlightenment Tradition.* The moderates of the Enlightenment took a different view of equality. It was not only Hobbes who believed that inequality was inevitable in human society. David Hume, the Scottish philosopher, thought the same. "[I]deas of *perfect* equality," he said, "would be extremely *pernicious* to human society" because "men's differing degrees of art, care, and industry will . . . break that equality."[7] Locke, too, accepted the need for social hierarchy. Even someone as supposedly radical as Voltaire was skeptical. Being a cultural elitist, he looked down his nose at the ignorant poor, whom he believed lacked a proper education to appreciate the blessings of liberty. Some moderates wanted to have it both ways—to have the moral authority of claiming equality in nature but not to delve more deeply into what this meant for actual civil society. John Locke thought this way. Like the radicals he believed that natural rights were equal and should be carried over into civil government. But unlike the radicals he drew very different conclusions about what these rights were. When he said that "all men by nature are equal," he meant it to be true only with respect to certain rights—namely, the right of free conscience and property. Once the civil government was established to protect these rights, all sorts of social differences were not only tolerated, but in the case of property, actually welcomed. Equality meant the freedom and opportunity to pursue one's individual interests and desires within the confines of the law. It did not mean equality of outcomes, since in Locke's mind trying to achieve absolute social equality would inevitably end up in tyranny.

Jonathan Israel believes that along with differing interpretations of nature (especially human nature), interpreting equality was a central difference between the moderate and radical Enlightenments. He says:

The tension between the moderate mainstream and Radical Enlightenment was certainly a schism between Deism and atheism, belief in supernatural agency and materialism, and over whether the *philosophes'* fight was solely against intolerance, superstition, and censorship, or also against existing structures of authority. But, at a deeper level, it was perhaps especially a struggle about whom and how far "to enlighten" and ultimately . . . a contest between hierarchy and equality.[8]

These different streams of ideas burst into the political arena at the end of the 18th century. They became hotly contested property in two events that changed the world forever—the American and French revolutions.

### TALES OF TWO REVOLUTIONS

The American and French revolutions are like identically named plays using very different scripts. The revolutionaries in Paris and Philadelphia used many of the same words to justify their actions, but they meant different things. John Adams no less than Maximilien de Robespierre was a fierce lover of liberty. But Adams was horrified by the Terror. Thomas Jefferson was famously a Francophone and flirted with the Terror, but even he in the end was forced to admit its errors. George Washington believed as did Louis Antoine Saint-Just that virtue was a republican value upon which the safety of liberty depended. But Washington's idea of virtue was that of an English gentleman, not a firebrand revolutionary calling for the blood of traitors.

One reason for these differences is that the American and French revolutionaries drew differently on the two Enlightenments, the moderate and the radical. The Americans tended to look to the Anglo-British moderates like Locke, whereas the French drew on the radicals like Diderot and Rousseau. The American Revolution was the moderate Enlightenment in action, while the French Revolution embodied the radical Enlightenment. The differences partially explain why American liberalism and radicalism were so different from European liberalism and radicalism. It helps also to clarify why the postmodern left today, as an heir to the radical Enlightenment, is so out of step with the original American conception of liberalism.

Let's start with how the Americans and French viewed the state of nature. To do so will help illuminate why America's revolution was socially modest while France's was not. It turns out that the differences account not only for how equality, rights, and republican government were viewed, but also for the dramatically different uses and abuses of violence in the two respective revolutions.

We know that Jefferson's interpretation of the state of nature was heavily influenced by John Locke. Inspired by his *Two Treatises of Government* (1689),[9] Jefferson and most of the Founders believed governments should be instituted to protect natural rights. As many have noted, Jefferson's use of "Life, Liberty and the pursuit of Happiness" in the Declaration of Independence is an obvious revision of Locke's views.[10] The natural rights Jefferson entrusts to civil government are vague and significantly limited in number. They are defined in such a way that they could be interpreted negatively or positively; the "pursuit of happiness" could mean almost anything. While most Americans instinctively adhered to Locke's negative view—that governments were instituted to protect specified rights from tyrannical governments—there was enough vagueness in Jefferson's rendering for even radicals such as Thomas Paine to embrace the cause of the American Revolution.

One will search in vain for Rousseau's romanticized myth of the golden age of nature—and hence his equally romanticized conception of human rights—in the Declaration of Independence. After a brief reference to the "Laws of Nature" in the first paragraph, Jefferson turns to the real business of making the practical case for independence from Britain. Despite the hortatory appeal to the rights of mankind, the Declaration's main complaint was arbitrary government and a lack of proper representation in legislatures. The "long train of abuses and usurpations" did not include grievances about social or economic inequality, but listed laws not passed and legislatures wrongly suspended. This is what one would expect from a people steeped in the English common law and still sincerely committed not only to social order but to religion.

For the French, it was completely different. Professor Dan Edelstein argues in *The Terror of Natural Right: Republicanism, the Cult of Nature, and the French Revolution* (2009) that myths about the golden age of nature were common in the French Revolution.[11] They were used by radicals to justify nothing less than mass murder. The Jacobins who followed Robespierre in establishing the Reign of Terror shared what Edelstein calls a philosophy of "natural republicanism"; they believed that individuals who transgressed the laws of nature must be executed without judicial formalities. Anyone who stood against the republic stood against the people who were, by right of their natural goodness, above reproach. An enemy of the people became an enemy of the human race and thus guilty of treason.

It was not only a propensity to mass violence but to authoritarian government that distinguished the French from the Americans. The difference, in a nutshell, is that the Americans distrusted state power while the French glorified it. At the outset of the French Revolution, the French quite consciously rejected the American idea of checks and balances, choosing a unicameral legislature instead.[12] They made their courts weak and subservient either to the legislature or the executive, unlike the Americans, who gave the judiciary independent powers. By the time the Jacobin dictatorship was established, all power had been put into the hands of a few members of executive committees. This set the precedent for Napoleon Bonaparte's imperial dictatorship, all in the name of saving a revolution that had been originally republican.

If the Americans and French did not see eye to eye on the state of nature, rights, and government, they were positively at odds over the principle of equality. For the Americans, it was largely a matter of equality before the law. When Jefferson wrote in the Declaration, "We hold these truths to be self-evident, that all men are created equal, that they are endowed by their Creator with certain unalienable Rights, that among these are Life, Liberty and the pursuit of Happiness," he meant that human beings were equal in their possession of political rights. He did not mean that all people were equal in talent, merit, wealth, or social status. They were equal as human beings in their right to pursue their interests and their dreams without interference from the government or other people.

In Federalist No. 10, James Madison made it clear that he had no use for the French idea of equality either. He wrote, "Theoretic politicians, who have patronized this species of government, have erroneously supposed that by reducing mankind to a perfect equality in their political rights, they would at the same time be perfectly equalized and assimilated in their possessions, their opinions, and their passions."[13] For Madison, who was heavily influenced by Hume, there was no single or general will in mankind. There was rather only a society of individuals with diverse interests and opinions whose natural freedoms needed to be preserved by government.

Since the French Revolution unfolded in phases, it would not be accurate to say there was a single concept of equality that captured all its variations. It is true that the constitutional monarchical views of the Marquis de Lafayette were not the same as the radical egalitarianism of Saint-Just and François-Noël Babeuf. Nevertheless, for the French republicans, who included in their ranks more people than the radical Jacobins, the demands of overthrowing the social order behind the political order of the *ancien régime*, with its estates of clergy and noblemen, were a concern from the start. It is this social interest that drove that revolution in an egalitarian direction.

As the French Revolution progressed, egalitarianism became more radical. It first surfaced in the rule of the Jacobins but continued afterwards. When the French Directory tried in February 1796 to revoke the bread and meat subsidies established by the Jacobins a few years earlier, Babeuf and other radicals conspired to overthrow the government and create a communist-like government. Babeuf's "Conspiracy of Equals" failed, but his legacy endured in socialist revolutions to come. Equality would henceforth mean in radical circles the complete social and economic equality of all people and classes.

It is understandable that the French and the Americans would have different understandings of political morality. One was a late feudal society of aristocrats and priests while the other was a society of relatively free Englishmen—property owners, small farmers, merchants, craftsmen, lawyers, and doctors. In Marxist terms, the Americans had already had the equivalent of a "bourgeois" revolution by overthrowing the feudal order. Moreover, unlike the French revolutionaries who were anti-clerical in their views, the Americans embraced religion as a positive force in civil society and as a prerequisite for freedom. In *Democracy in America* (1835, 1840), French historian Alexis de Tocqueville wrote:

> On my arrival in the United States the religious aspect of the country was the first thing that struck my attention; and the longer I stayed there, the more I perceived the great political consequences resulting from this new state of things. In France I had almost always seen the spirit of religion and the spirit of freedom marching in opposite directions. But in America I found they were intimately united and that they reigned in common over the same country.[14]

And:

> Religion in America . . . must be regarded as the first of
> their political institutions; for if it does not impart a taste
> for freedom, it facilitates the use of it. . . . I am certain
> that they hold it to be indispensable to the maintenance
> of republican institutions. This opinion is not peculiar to
> a class of citizens or to a party, but it belongs to the whole
> nation and to every rank of society.[15]

The French Revolution gave history its first instance of modern leftist illiberalism—an embrace of tyranny in the name of the people. All the symptoms were there: the use of coercion against the individual in the name of the public good; a fierce closed-mindedness and the suppression of dissent; the appeal to romanticized, utopian myths to justify ruthless acts in the "name of the people"; and a complete rejection of the moderate Enlightenment's respect for narrowly defined (largely negatively defined) individual rights and the rule of law. Over 40,000 people were executed in less than a year during the Terror, some 17,000 by the guillotine. Tyrants had existed for millennia before the French Revolution, but what made the new dictators in Paris different, and historically dangerous, was that they committed their illiberal acts in the name of liberalism itself.

## JEFFERSON'S RADICALISM AND
## THE MODERATE ENLIGHTENMENT

Thomas Jefferson's ambivalence toward the French Revolution is legendary. He started out as a passionate enthusiast. Indulging in his feelings for the "martyrs to the cause," he wrote to William Short in 1793 that rather than see that Revolution fail, he "would have seen half the earth desolated."[16] But as the news of the king's execution and the Terror reached him, his ardor cooled. Late in life he tried to put the French Revolution in perspective, condemning both Robespierre and Napoleon equally for betraying it, and he was clearly shaken by the bloodshed it had unleashed on the world. But even then he could not quite break its hold on his dreams. In a letter to John Adams in 1823, a mere three years before his death, Jefferson admitted that he still believed the "object" of "representative government" was worth "rivers of blood."[17] It was simply the price that had to be paid to attain its "glorious achievements to man, which will add to the joys even of heaven."

Jefferson's ambivalence toward the French Revolution matters. As a key founder of the American republic, he bridges the moderate and radical Enlightenments. He tried to have it both ways. At times he was a fire-breathing radical. At others, as a U.S. minister to France for example, he was a cool voice counseling constitutional monarchy for France. Given his later views about desolating "half the earth" for the republican cause, he might have been expected to take a radical position. But in practice he did not. Instead, as American minister he advised the French revolutionaries to "secure what the [French] government was now ready to yield"—namely, freedom of the press, freedom of conscience, habeas corpus, and a representative legislature, because "with the exercise of these powers they would obtain in [the] future whatever might be further necessary to improve and preserve their constitution."[18] Jefferson was a pragmatist when he had to be. His rhetoric was sometimes bloodthirsty, but as a government official—as minister to France, governor of Virginia, secretary of state, and as president—he never indulged himself in bloody purges or violence.

Why does this matter? When push came to shove, even the most radical of America's Founders (not including Thomas Paine, who was not strictly a founder) ended up siding with the moderate Enlightenment. Jefferson could not escape the fact that he was born an English gentleman and was not an angry French lawyer who hated priests as much as he despised kings and aristocrats. As both a thinker and a statesman, Jefferson acted as if there were no great differences between the dreams of the radicals and the worries of the moderates. That he was wrong made no difference to him. To his ultimate credit, despite his theoretical flights of fancy, Jefferson remained a classical liberal statesman. He remained true to his Locke and Montesquieu, and though he loved the French, he only dabbled with them like an old man flirts with a pretty young girl. He was free to indulge in his fantasies for France because he knew in America he would never act on them.

### THE HEAVENLY CITY OF PHILOSOPHERS AND THEIR CRITICS

In 1932, a bespectacled Cornell University professor published a book that shook the intellectual world's view of the Enlightenment. His name was Carl L. Becker, and the book was *The Heavenly City of the Eighteenth-Century Philosophers*. Becker was a New Deal progressive who had become disillusioned with the rosy optimism of the Enlightenment. Its promise of never-ending progress was not based on reason but on a kind of blind faith—or, as the author of the preface to a recent reprint edition, Johnson Kent Wright, put it, "a secular version of the same chimerical hopes for which the philosophes had ridiculed Christianity."[19] The Enlightenment, Becker said, had "demolished the Heavenly City of St. Augustine only to rebuild it with more up-to-date materials."[20] It was not modern at all, but essentially old medieval wine poured into new bottles.

Historians today dismiss Becker's interpretation as outdated, but he was right about one thing. The philosophers of the 18th century had always evoked opposition from monarchs, aristocrats, and priests. But as the Enlightenment project became associated with the French Revolution and the Napoleonic Empire, even liberals and moderate conservatives were repelled. Edmund Burke is the most famous of the conservative critics of that revolution and the Enlightenment in the Anglo-American world, but John Adams, James Madison, and Alexander Hamilton also shared some of Burke's concerns. They all felt the trauma of the French Revolution as the Enlightenment gone mad. On the European continent French conservatives like Joseph de Maistre were disgusted by the excesses of the French Revolution, which he also blamed on the Enlightenment. In Germany the negative reaction to Napoleon manifested itself in the Romantic Rebellion against the "Age of Reason" and the rise of chauvinistic nationalism.

Serious intellectual questioning of the Enlightenment started in the most unlikely of places—in the remote Baltic Sea coastal city of Königsberg, which at the time was part of Prussia. The philosopher was Immanuel Kant, who more than anyone at the time revolutionized the way we think about the Enlightenment's ideas. Under the influence of the Scottish philosopher and historian David Hume, whom he said had awoken him from his "dogmatic slumber,"[21] Kant turned against the Enlightenment's supreme rationalists, Gottfried Wilhelm Leibniz and Christian Wolff. At the same time he fell under the spell of Rousseau and his highly positive, romanticized view of the natural rights of man. Eventually Rousseau's optimism made Kant wary of Hume's skepticism and changed his mind about empiricism. It was a momentous turn. By rejecting Hume in the name of Rousseau, Kant opened the way for modern idealism, which established absolute freedom as the new project of human consciousness.

Kant faced a philosophical dilemma: On the one hand he did not believe that truth and morality could be known by merely observing the world, as Hume did. On the other hand he thought that it was possible to know the absolute truth, particularly the moral law, as Rousseau believed. So how did Kant resolve the dilemma? By proposing a compromise, what he called a "synthetic" solution: we do know certain truths about our world (including what is right and wrong), but it is not because our observations of nature tell us so; it is because we are following an *innate truth*, provided by nature, that is etched into our knowledge and into our very consciousness.

From these metaphysical speculations Kant gained the confidence to make strong assertions about the nature of human freedom. He believed not only that freedom was possible, but that actualizing freedom was the primary obligation of states. Kant was skeptical of whether Plato's perfect state could exist, but in the end he accepted that we must believe and act as if it does.[22] A universal and permanently peaceful life requires that freedom be adopted as the ultimate and absolute goal of the state. Freedom is an a priori ideal to be achieved through the state's organization of people's lives, an idea that would be later taken up and expanded by German philosopher Georg Wilhelm Friedrich Hegel.

The difference with Locke and Jefferson is that whereas they both assumed that rights were sacrosanct because they were natural—"self-evident," as Jefferson put it—Kant believed that they were absolute because they were etched into mankind's moral being. It is a subtle but important difference, essentially reflecting the contrasts between English natural law and Rousseau's myth of omnipotent nature. What is more, whereas Locke and Jefferson believed that freedom (liberty) was attained only when the government protected those rights from the "tyranny" of the state (or the majority), Kant suggests something quite different—that freedom is an "absolute ideal" that can only be achieved through the laws established by the state itself. Kant does not say it outright, but he is hinting (showing the influence of Rousseau) that a properly constituted republican state cannot possibly be tyrannical because it is by definition the embodiment of freedom. It was a subtle philosophical difference based on how Anglo-Americans and Germans conceived freedom. Hegel would later take the idea of positive freedom to even greater heights, essentially arguing that the state was its historical embodiment.

Kant and Hegel's idea that freedom can be realized only through the state drove a stake even deeper into the split legacies of the moderate and radical Enlightenments. Anglo-American liberalism remained committed to concerns about too much state power, while the continent of Europe moved increasingly in the direction of accepting Kant and Hegel's notions of positive freedom granted by the state. Communists and socialists took this proposition to its logical (if extreme) conclusion, conceiving the all-powerful state as the necessary agent to create a revolutionary new order. On the right side of the political spectrum, nationalists saw the state as the highest embodiment of the *Volk*. Even European liberals and American progressives began to move away from classical liberalism's fear of state tyranny. The story of European socialism is largely one of envisioning state power as the deliverer of radical egalitarian visions, first made possible by Spinoza, Rousseau, and Kant, and modernized by Hegel and Marx.

Kant is a bridge from the radical Enlightenment to the modern world. The project that started under Bayle and Rousseau ended up through Kant giving Western liberals something that Locke, Hobbes, and Montesquieu would not have expected or approved: the notion that freedom is an absolute that can be realized through the positive action of the state. In this respect every modern ideological movement that claims the mantle of egalitarianism, whether socialism, progressivism, or the postmodern left of today, owes a debt of gratitude to Kant and his critique of the Enlightenment. It was he who first channeled Rousseau's romantic liberalism into a positive project of the modern state, making possible all the left's subsequent utopian dreams of abolishing the human condition of inequality.

◆  ◆  ◆

Rousseau and Kant are the intellectual founders of the modern radical left. That is to say, they are the intellectual forefathers not only of Karl Marx but Michel Foucault and Jacques Derrida. But that is not all they are. The history of ideas never unfolds in a straight line, and nowhere is this truer than in how Kant and Rousseau influenced Western thought. It is correct that they inspired the critical thinking that gave rise to Hegel, Marx, and the leftist tradition. But Rousseau and Kant also spurred the thinking of some conservatives who hated the Enlightenment. It is a bit of a strange twist in history, but in addition to their progeny on the left, they are also great intellectual grandfathers of the European right tradition.

To understand how this happened we must begin with the Romantic movement in the mid-18th century. In 1774 the German poet Johann Wolfgang von Goethe wrote *The Sufferings of Young Werther*, a novel that was part of the German Sturm und Drang period of literature. Goethe was deeply inspired by Rousseau's sentimental writings, and other romantic writers all over Europe followed suit by celebrating the passions of the new "natural man." William Wordsworth, Samuel Taylor Coleridge, John Keats, Lord Byron, and Percy Bysshe Shelley wrote stories, poems, and articles exploring the dark worlds of myths and emotion, taking the old Enlightenment idea of the natural virtue into an entirely new direction. They opened the door to a radically new idea—that human emotion and passions took precedence over human reason. Nature was now not about rational discourse but about discovering the inner authenticity of the natural man.

Most historians see the Romantics as part of the Counter-Enlightenment—a broad political and intellectual movement that rejected the tenets of the Enlightenment. But it would be more accurate to describe them as fomenting a revolt inside the Enlightenment tradition itself. Their original inspiration was indeed Rousseau, who we should remember as a major Enlightenment figure in his own right. Later in the early 19th century Rousseau's legacy, as processed by both the Romantics and Kant, took a sharp right turn. It was picked up by German idealists like Johann Gottlieb Fichte, Friedrich Schelling, and Johann Gottfried Herder who had studied Kant closely, but who also drove Rousseau's sentimentalism to new extremes. Under the influence of Kant and the Romantics, they turned their backs on rationalism—thus inventing the modern notion of irrationalism—and on the other traditions of the moderate Enlightenment, including empiricism and skepticism, or the British spirit of liberalism. As cultural nationalists, Fichte and Herder laid the theoretical groundwork for both radical nationalism in the 20th century and the cultural tribalism of identity politics in the 21st.

Thus did the German idealist tradition, first (and rather innocently) created by Kant, morph into a new kind of illiberalism. It was a revolt not from "behind" but from the "front" of history, a revolt inside modernity itself. Politically it evolved into an attack on liberalism from the *right*. Over the centuries that followed this new movement produced such brilliant and highly influential illiberal philosophers as Arthur Schopenhauer, Friedrich Nietzsche, Martin Heidegger, and yes, even Foucault and Derrida who, strictly speaking, saw themselves as men of the left.

The primary intellectual enemies of right-wing illiberalism were classical liberalism and the moderate Enlightenment, particularly of the British sort. Proponents included radical nationalists and *völkish* racists in 19th-century Central and Eastern Europe who believed in the historical myths first invoked by the Romantics. They tended to be authoritarian and anti-democratic in their politics and occupied European nationalist parties and even the government of Imperial Germany. They despised socialists and liberals alike, seeing them as two peas in a modernist pod and mutual enemies of hierarchical order despite their ideological differences. In America, the radical right was not shaped by the experiences of the Europeans, but by indigenous developments related mainly to slavery, racism, and immigration.

We should not be confused by the dissimilar ideological claims of the far left and far right. The left may argue for universal equality while the far right champions hierarchy and particularism. In their extremes they are equally illiberal. Communism and National Socialism became totalitarian because they shared modern man's hubris of believing he could build a perfect society. They had very different views of what that society should be, and they certainly had different ideas of the nature of mankind. Because of their unbridled ambitions, they were willing to pursue their plans regardless of the high cost in blood and treasure.

Modern illiberalism is thus a child of the radical Enlightenment. It can be either liberalism gone astray (the far left) or liberalism rejected (the far right). The two share a deep and abiding contempt for the ideas of the moderate Enlightenment. On the far right, an irrational idealism allied itself with reactionary social and political forces to make war not only on socialism but rationalism and liberalism. On the far left it was pushing the promise of radical egalitarianism to its revolutionary limit. Either way, illiberal variations represent a betrayal of the original promise of the Enlightenment—namely, the freedom of mankind. They may be children of the Enlightenment, but only in the tragic sense of the son slaying the father.

The turn toward tragedy began very early. It happened the moment the radical *philosophes* began thinking of freedom as something absolute and of society as perfectible. Without knowing it, they had reduced mankind to a mere instrument in a grand social cause (whether communism or fascism), which meant that people's lives and freedoms were only as safe as the whims of the general will (and the state) would allow. That thinking—that hubris—is the original sin of the radical Enlightenment. It set up an intellectual trap for modern liberalism. What began long ago as a dream of natural perfection has today been reduced to a hideous nightmare of nihilism and degradation.

### THE TROUBLED LEGACY OF THE RADICAL ENLIGHTENMENT

Progressive liberals today see themselves as heirs to the radical Enlightenment. They proudly trace the recent advances in gay and women's rights to the ideas of Spinoza, Bayle, Diderot, Rousseau, and other radical figures. They seem to forget that this same tradition also gave us the Terror, the Gulag, and Mao Tse-tung's Cultural Revolution. This totalitarian legacy is ignored because it is

assumed to have nothing whatsoever to do with the noble sentiments of progressive liberalism. Unfortunately this is not true. As
I have argued, there is a broad continuum of ideas flowing from
the radical Enlightenment up to today's radical identity theorists,
and that historical road also runs right through the French Terror
and the Russian and other communist revolutions. To pretend
otherwise is to whitewash history.

"Utopia" is often used to describe the dreams of the far left, but
the word is misleading. It conjures up images of innocents frolick-
ing around in communes, or young people casually experiment-
ing with alternative lifestyles. It ignores a reality that is far more
complicated and frankly more sinister. The intellectual problem
is not trying to imagine a better world. Rather it is presuming
that human reason is capable of perfection. Historian Jacques Barzun believes the intellectual problem is sentimentalism,[23] and he
blames Rousseau. Enamored as he was by the potential of human
sentiment, Rousseau lifted human reason up from the mulchy
soils of empiricism and skepticism and transformed it into an
all-powerful force for utopian change. Human beings were perfectible because they were inherently good, but they were good
because they possessed a perfect kind of reason. That is the seed
of modern utopianism. If humans are perfectly equal, not in some
theoretical spiritual way but in their very real capacity to build a
perfect society, then there are virtually no limits to what can and
should be done to force equality on humankind.

This way of thinking accounts not only for the hubris of violence that has possessed countless revolutionary movements in
Western history. It also explains the paradox of a political movement seemingly based on human reason veering off into wild passions of vengeance and mass hysteria. It is witnessed not only
in the orgies of violence of Stalin's Purges and Mao's Cultural
Revolution but more recently in the hybrid revolutionary movement of Islamist Jihadism that fuses the nihilism of anarchism with
the messianic goals of a religious revolution. Islamist extremism

may be rooted in medieval notions of religion, but its expression and politicization are thoroughly postmodern—in glorifying the boundless nihilism of the postmodern age. Nihilism is also surfacing in the dark reaches of the postmodern identity movements with their totalitarian ambitions to revolutionize the mores governing sexual and gender relations.

It turns out, then, that the legacy of the radical Enlightenment is not all sweetness and light. It has a malevolent side. We are, frankly, witnessing a takeover of progressive liberalism by the same illiberal spirit that has moved all the authoritarian leftists of the past. It is no accident that the very same radical notions that inspired Saint-Just, Marx, and Foucault are today animating the minds of professor Catharine MacKinnon and other radical multicultural theorists. They come from the same source—from radicals who centuries ago imagined that human beings could be totally and utterly equal in all measures and in all things, regardless of how much it destroyed freedom and crushed the human soul.

# NINE

# The Closing
# of the
# Liberal Mind

Ask millennials, even relatively conservative ones, why they support same-sex marriage and the likely answer will be that they do not want to be seen as judgmental. Note the phrase "seen as." What matters is that everyone sees themselves as fitting into a clique, a class, a team, or some group cohort. The main concern is the group dynamics of managing the appearance of compassion—of being seen as getting along within the group or team. When millennials speak of equality, what they mean is openly accepting anyone and everyone on their own terms. It is about caring and being open-minded. In fact, open hearts and open minds are seen as pretty much the same thing. One leads to the other. Just be nice to everyone and avoid judgmental criticism and all will be well.

## THE PARADOX OF THE OPEN HEART

An open heart can indeed be a virtue. It can contribute to all sorts of good things—love, compassion, kindness, and a society that cares for those who cannot care for themselves. But are open hearts really the same thing as open minds? After all, my heart tells me to love my wife and children, yet if someone unfairly criticizes or threatens them, my mind will not be terribly open to what that person has to say. Love in this case rightly inspires a loyalty that quite intentionally rejects negative ideas about my loved ones. By the same token, I may have compassion for a street person who begs for money, yet I may think twice if I believe my charity will be used for drugs or alcohol. In that case, it is not my heart alone that makes this judgment, but my knowledge of a street person's entire situation. It likely may not be hunger motivating his begging but a serious, life-threatening addiction.

The point is this: It is not the sentiment alone that determines whether an act is charitable or venal—right or wrong—but the moral context in which the sentiment is acted upon. Seeing the whole picture requires a rational assessment by the human mind of all the factors involved. In other words, virtue is a balance of reason and sentiment—an open heart informed by the reasoning abilities of the open and inquiring mind.

We are familiar with the problem of good intentions gone awry, but what causes it? C. S. Lewis once drew a distinction between "being in love" and the actual state of love. The former is a fleeting feeling, the latter a permanent state maintained by will and rational decision. In other words, the state of love is an affair not only of the heart but of the mind. It needs rational defenses against temptations and selfishness that can threaten it. The same is true for compassion. It, too, needs a rational basis to withstand the most obvious things that threaten it, like selfishness and hatred, and also the more subtle confusions of life that can transform even good intentions into evil ones. It turns out, then, that despite the claims of moral relativists, all intentions are not utterly moral-less—most of them cannot be deemed good or evil without a rational assessment of their consequences. The difference between good and evil is not between good and bad feelings, but between good and evil consequences—and between good and evil actions decided by the mind and the heart working in tandem.

Human passions, emotions, and sentiments require rational guidance. Completely unmoored from reason, they can, despite the best of intentions, be transformed into evil. It is not a matter of one "good" sentiment against a "bad" one, but the moral reasoning that sorts out the difference and decides which direction to take. At their most basic instinctive levels, human emotions are not all that different; they arouse passions and feelings that are deeply rooted in the unconscious and even irrational part of the human mind. Psychologists describe human emotions as arising not only out of the archaic history of the brain but from the instinct of survival. It is no accident that emotions and feelings such as wrath, fright, passion, love, hate, joy, and sadness are so-called "mammalian inventions" of the brain originating in the limbic system. They arise from parts of the brain that evolutionists say developed in the intermediate stage of human existence. The more rational faculties of the neopallium part of the brain came later and involve the process of reasoning and judgment. All this is to say that we need both emotions and reason to be human; of the two, it is our greater ability to reason that makes us distinctly different from other mammals.

The mistake so often made today, especially by young people, is to confuse compassionate feelings for virtue. It is the belief that certain kinds of feelings are always good regardless of their purpose. But consider, for example, love. In marriage love is obviously a good thing; it is not good in adultery, where it involves betrayal and deceit. What matters is not where one starts but where one ends up. One can believe that even the hardest of totalitarians like Stalin and Lenin began their journeys into darkness with an open heart; Stalin was once a seminarian and Lenin's radicalization began after the execution of his beloved brother, Alexander Ilyich Ulyanov. A misguided and heightened sense of wanting to correct an injustice can spill over into vengeance, which is one of the surest ways to slip into a closed, dictatorial state of mind. Again, the moral context is everything. In the heart of an American soldier fighting for a noble cause, mental fortitude is heroic. In the mind of a Waffen-SS soldier overseeing a firing squad, it is pure evil.

History has shown us what happens when passion—and its ideological offspring irrationalism—reigns supreme. The Nazi regime was an orgy of human passions directed against enemies, all in the name of a perverted kind of "racial" justice. The same was true for the Italian fascists who tapped into the irrational philosophies of vitalism. The genius of the classic Anglo-American liberal tradition (and its source, the moderate Enlightenment) had been to treat the dark passions like the plague. It sought a balance between passion and reason. There was always a fear, going back to Hobbes and certainly prevalent in Madison's thinking, that the dark side of human nature had to be contained. Later liberals like John Stuart Mill moved away from this caution, but in doing so they, like so many other radicals at the time, were succumbing to the lure of sentimentalism that had been prevalent all along in the radical Enlightenment.

The human heart is indeed a paradox. Guided by moral reasoning it can be sublime. Left to its own devices it can lead mankind into unimaginable darkness. The essence of moral reasoning is to draw distinctions. Although we may think that "having a heart" always means well, we should think again. Sometimes it does not. Sometimes it is an ill will pretending to be good. At other times it is an innocent but misguided delusion about what is good. Either way, "going with your gut" or "having a passion for justice" is not good enough.

### THE AUTHORITARIAN MIND OF IDENTITY MILITANTS

The rapidity with which acceptance of same-sex marriage and transgender rights is spreading has been remarkable. Values that existed at the margins of society only a few years ago are now front and center. Today it is not uncommon to have city ordinances establishing transgender-friendly public bathrooms. The sexual rights movement in America has been around a very long time. It was first launched in the 1920s and exploded in the 1960s, but it is now heading for the stratosphere. It is about many things—women's rights and sexual freedom primarily—but it has always been about more than seeking tolerance for different attitudes and lifestyles. Its larger goal has been to change the moral fabric of modern society.

The makers of this sexual revolution have been quite candid about it. For example, a statement called "Beyond Marriage," signed by an influential group in the same-sex marriage movement, says their goal is not merely to gain tolerance for gays to marry but to change the institution of marriage beyond recognition. As Jonathan Last of *The Weekly Standard* explains:

> [The Beyond Marriage letter argues] that same-sex marriage is merely the first step on the path to redefining the family itself. Ultimately, they want legal protection for a host of other relationships, including, as they delicately put it, "Queer couples who decide to jointly create and raise a child with another queer person or couple, in two households" and "committed, loving households in which there is more than one conjugal partner." This group is not a collection of cranks: It includes professors from Georgetown, Harvard, Emory, Columbia, and Yale. The Beyond Marriage project has at least as much elite support today as the entire same-sex marriage movement had in 1990.[1]

Only a few years ago people would have scoffed at such ideas, but then again over a decade ago they did not suspect that gay marriage would be socially acceptable either. Already new sexual lifestyles are gaining respectability among the media and academic elites. For example, in 2015 Cambridge University Press published Ronald C. Den Otter's book *In Defense of Plural Marriage*, which attempts to offer a detailed study of why the constitutional case for plural marriage (polygamy) is stronger than the case against it.[2] Rutgers-Camden law professor and Harvard graduate Margo Kaplan has written opinion pieces to say that our understanding of pedophilia is all wrong; apparently it is a mental disorder, not a crime, because not all pedophiles are child molesters.[3] In 2014, *New York* magazine, which is hardly a tabloid, ran a story about a man who was dating his horse.[4] In 2015, it published an interview with a young woman titled "What It's Like to Date Your Dad."[5] Even that old mainstream standby, *The Atlantic*, is pushing the envelope. It printed an article in 2014 by Olga Khazan arguing that "some studies suggest" polyamorous people "handle certain relationship challenges better than monogamous people do."[6] In June 2015 *The Washington Post* ran a front-page article arguing that gay couples make better parents than families composed of married men and women.[7]

Before we dismiss these stories as extreme, remember this: *The Washington Post* is the most influential newspaper in our nation's capital. Cambridge University Press is not Beau to Beau Books or some other explicitly gay-friendly publishing house. It is a reputable academic press.[8] *The Atlantic* and *New York* are not the *National Enquirer* or *Queer'd Magazine*; they are mainstream magazines. Now that the cat is out of the bag, the only limitation on acceptable sexual and marriage relationships appears to be a lack of imagination, and there seem to be precious few limitations on that. A man in Florida, for example, came up with the idea of marrying his porn-laden computer: "If gays have the right to marry their object of sexual desire," he said, "even if they lack corresponding sexual parts, then I should have the right to marry my preferred sexual object."[9]

The issue is not whether any of these practices will become commonplace. They will not, if for no other reason than that most people do not want to marry their dog, dad, or computer. It is rather why such stories are attracting such widespread attention in the press. It is true that the tabloid character of weird sex will always sell magazines, but that is not why serious magazines, newspapers, and publishing houses are covering them with an air of respectability. It is because doing so widens the range of what is considered normal. If the "orange" of marriage plurality is now the new "black,"[10] then it will not be long before same-sex marriage will look positively Victorian.[11] The argument is always the same: no one anywhere or under any circumstance has the slightest right to criticize a person's private sexual choices. You simply have no right to hold a negative view, much less express it. That is really what the same-sex marriage movement is about. It is not even about equality or tolerance, but about a new legal and moral order in which only one view of sexuality and marriage must prevail.

While gay rights advocates sometimes let slip their true intentions, the more publicly involved groups are less forthcoming. Knowing full well that declaring war explicitly on the family would not be popular, they first launched the same-sex marriage campaign as if it were all about respecting family values rather than destroying them. Activists argued that all they wanted was equal recognition for the same long-lasting, monogamous relationships that characterized marriages between men and women. Some went so far as to goad social conservatives into accepting that same-sex marriage was really only about fidelity and the right for gay couples to be officially recognized for their love and devotion. Put aside for a moment that studies have found same-sex unions are not as monogamous as traditionally married ones.[12] The real problem is deception. Today many LGBT activists are dropping the pro-family façade and openly declaring war on the family as a social unit. In a fit of candor, the Beyond Marriage letter makes it clear that the group's ambitions are not to sanctify fidelity or glorify monogamy, but to destroy the traditional family and blaze a path for other sexual and gender relationships to replace it.

This penchant for dishonesty is evident also in the way militants treat religious liberty. The more militant activists are quite candid. They believe that religion, particularly Christianity, is the enemy and must be discredited across the board. Savvy activists are more careful. They downplay the threat and argue that religious conservatives are just paranoid. But look at how rapidly things have changed in the past several years. Only a few years ago, even Hillary Clinton and Barack Obama dismissed the possibility of gay marriage. Now bakers, florists, and photographers are fined for refusing to participate in same-sex marriages. Adoption and foster care services of Catholic charities already have shut down in Illinois, Massachusetts, and the District of Columbia. In recent Supreme Court deliberations, U.S. Solicitor General Donald Verrilli refused to rule out that religious universities could lose their tax-exempt status if they opposed same-sex marriage.[13]

Now that the Supreme Court says that same-sex marriage is a constitutional right, the door has been thrown wide open for more aggressive demands. Indeed now, because same-sex marriage is the law of the land, officials such as Kentucky clerk Kim Davis can be jailed for refusing to enforce it. In Ohio judges are being told they cannot decline to marry same-sex couples because of their personal beliefs.[14] Once a moral issue such as gay marriage becomes enforceable by law, there is no dodging it. Even conservative constitutionalists and other staunch supporters of law and order have to get in line, becoming enforcers of a moral position with which they disagree.

◆ ◆ ◆

It would be useful to deconstruct the mindset of sexual militants. It is a swirl of claims and counterclaims that sometimes make it nearly impossible to understand what they really want. What makes them so intolerant? Why are they prone to authoritarian thinking? And why do they appear to be filled with an unquenchable rage at their enemies? There are a number of contributing factors.

*Construction of Alternative Realities.* Let's start with social psychology. The aim of the sexual militant is not just to create a totally new subjective reality in their own minds (the first act of identity politics). Nor is it to ask for mere tolerance of their views or behavior. Rather, it is to force everyone else to accept their views and behavior as *normal*. In other words, it is to control the entire public "narrative" of social morality. The topic may be gay rights, but it might as well be radical women's or racial rights. There is a common thread running through all radical identity politics. It involves first deconstructing the old morality and then constructing a new one to replace it.

Take, for example, a college student offended by comedian Jerry Seinfeld's complaint that he would not perform on college campuses anymore because students are so easily offended. In an anonymous open letter published by the *Huffington Post,* a student responded to Seinfeld's statement by claiming "sexist humor and racist humor can no longer exist in comedy because these concepts are based on archaic ideals. . . ."[15] Note the phrase "no longer exist," which implies that the only reality tolerated is the one the student allows. As far as the new rules on humor are concerned, it must "construct" (according to the student) a "valuable dialogue about white male privilege." That construct must be created only by the student, who sets the boundaries of the so-called "dialogue" that in reality is a monologue. In an obvious bid to retain some campus street "cred" and perhaps emboldened by his or her anonymity, the student ends the letter in a profanity-laced appeal stating it is not about *not* offending people. It is, rather, about offending "the right—people."[16] Could the point be any clearer? All the high-minded talk about not giving offense is a sham. The whole point is precisely to offend people who have "archaic ideals" like Jerry Seinfeld (of all people).

The claim of the social construct is a lot stronger than merely holding an opinion. We all have opinions. But those who believe in social construct theory argue that they do not have mere opinions; they are relating scientific and objective facts. They cite studies with questionable methodologies and patently nonsensical conclusions, but such studies are not the ace up their sleeves;

it is the argument of epistemic relativism that they wield like a shield, deflecting every counterthrust of an argument. Occupying the privileged status of victim, they and they only get to decide whether an offense has been made or not. Only they get to determine whether a joke is funny or not. Only they get to say for sure whether Bruce Jenner is a man or not. The only thing that matters is the supremacy of the construct, which decides everything and which only they get to assemble.

The fascination with social constructs explains the obsession sexual, racial, and other identity militants have with symbolism. Symbols must be elevated to the point where nothing in particular about any individual case is interesting, least of all hard facts. To their minds, symbols are actual social facts with near totemic powers. They provide their own context, which has been manufactured heuristically in countless academic studies and repeated ad nauseam by tendentious media stories. Since meaning is already provided by the symbol—and the construct preceding it—all that is left to do is grind historical and social axes on the basis of the symbol itself. No historical context is necessary. No distinctions are allowed. After the Charleston, South Carolina, massacre, you would have thought it was actually the Confederate flag itself, rather than Dylann Roof, that had murdered those innocent people in Emanuel AME Church. That is because the main interest was not to understand or punish the man who actually committed the crime, but to validate the narrative that most Southerners are racist.

It would be tempting to call such narrative-mongering a lie, but that would imply that those who advance such ideas actually believe them to be untrue. They do not. To identity militants, nothing could be truer than their own concept of identity. Bruce Jenner is a woman if he says he is. A white woman working for the NAACP, Rachel Dolezal, is a black woman if she says she is. A Southern man is a racist if singer-songwriter Neil Young says he is. The pure subjectivity involved in all these arguments—

in defining political reality only according to the dictates of a preconceived social construct—is what makes them so politically successful in debates. People are shadowboxing over symbols, not reality, which means that facts, social context, and distinctions get lost inside the alternative reality created by the construct.

*The Authoritarian Personality.* Sadly and even ironically, given the youthful nature of the protagonists, we are witnessing in many of these militants a postmodern version of the authoritarian personality.

Erich Fromm, Theodor Adorno, and other sociologists developed the authoritarian personality as a psychosocial type in the late 1940s to describe the Nazis and other right-wing authoritarians.[17] Characteristics include: personal insecurities leading to rigid stereotyping and adherence to social norms (called authoritarian submission); the projection of one's harsh passions onto inferior groups (projection); fierce denunciations of those who violate conventional values (authoritarian aggression); a tendency to believe in mystic determination (superstition); and a very cynical view of power relations that becomes an "us-versus-them" mentality.

Most of these sociologists were Marxists. But shorn of its socialist baggage—specifically the presumption that psychological insecurities only arise when men are psychologically traumatized by capitalism—the theory need not apply only to right-wing authoritarians. Stalin or Mao Tse-tung could just as easily fit the personality type if you strip away the tendentious ideological narrative assumed by Adorno and others. Stalin persecuted Jews, stereotyped races and Kulaks, and was as authoritarian and paranoid as dictators come. He created a new communist order that was hierarchical along Communist Party lines and that attracted paranoid authoritarian personality types like Lavrentiy Beria and Vyacheslav Molotov to be his henchmen.

LGBT and other radical identity militants are not communists, but they do share with the hard left an affinity for the authoritarian personality. They viciously stereotype people who disagree with them. They project their own paranoia and conspiracy theories onto their enemies. They harshly condemn people who disagree with the conventional wisdom of the gay agenda (authoritarian aggression). They demand absolute submission from people in their own ranks (authoritarian submission). They cynically and deceptively play power politics with peoples' fears and emotions. And they create fabulist theories of racial consciousness and white privilege that are as irrational as any old Nazi's fantasies. The one big difference—and it is a crucial one that separates these militants from totalitarianism—is an unwillingness to advocate physical violence. Most do not advocate violent revolution. But then again they do not have to. They are winning without it.

*The Tyranny of Passions and Pride.* Identity militants are deeply attached to the power of human sentiment. It is no accident that gay activists speak of pride; it captures the emotion of supremacy that is crucial to the solidarity of the movement. It is not reason that makes a cause or a person authentic, but the level of passion he or she brings to the cause. It is "breaking away" and "becoming free" so "I can be like everyone else." For gay activists, "love" alone is what defines marriage, not that it produces and provides a stable environment for children. It is an odd mixture of selfish egoism and sentimentalism made to look like a cause of equality. And it is a perfect strategy for a popular culture steeped in the politics of authenticity.

In intellectual terms, it means that human sentiment (with the irrational faculties associated with it) is the sole arbiter of morality and justice. In more down-to-earth language, it means "I go with my gut" or "whatever feels right for me." Essentially human passions are erected as the final court of appeal in deciding a moral issue. We may analyze the facts and talk about the logic of ethics, but at the end of the day what matters most is how we feel.

For example, gay activists argue that love is the only thing that matters in marriage. Not children. Not the traditional family's role throughout history. Only love alone between two consenting adults. Note the ethical case for same-sex marriage is not made in terms of freedom—namely, that two consenting adults should be able to do whatever they please. Observe as well that it is not even a case of what is best for society. Nor is it even what will make the people involved better persons. It is rather quite simply that "the heart wants what it wants," the sentiment revealed starkly in the Human Rights Campaign's Twitter campaign, *#lovecantwait*. It is the passion of love elevated to be the *summum bonum* of human ethics and human rights. It is a case made solely on the basis of asking people to empathize with gay people's feelings of wanting to be seen as married. From that right all other claims are made, including the legal demands for equal benefits associated with marriage. After all, Supreme Court Justice Anthony Kennedy argued that gay marriages should be afforded equal protection under the law not because gays are a class in need of special protection, but because lacking that protection offends the way gay people feel about themselves—namely, their dignity.[18]

Creating new constitutional rights based exclusively on people's self-awareness (their identities) opens up endless problems. What about the dignity of a white supremacist who claims his "pride" is offended by the presence of black people at public events? We can rightly dismiss his argument as absurd, but not because he has no right to self-esteem, which is the logic of identity politics. Rather, it is because he is a hateful bigot. What he thinks about himself has nothing to do with whether we should accord him respect. His is a position of professed pride, and it is no accident that Christians count that particular emotion as a cardinal sin; it destroys the grace that opens up the way to all other virtues. One does not have to be a Christian to see the problem with allowing conceit or vanity to be the arbiter of constitutional rights. They are ultimately selfish and hopelessly subjective. In the final analysis, dignity defined in this way is morally and socially formless. It can be anything, depending on the subjective views of its beholders. It can be pride in honorable behavior or the arrogance of driving your enemies into the dust. Surely we can do better than this in deciding the validity of constitutional rights.

There is a way to respect the humanity—or Justice Kennedy's "dignity" if you will—of same-sex marriage aspirants without succumbing to the illiberal implications of identity politics. Justice Clarence Thomas pointed the way in his dissent to *Obergefell v. Hodges*. He said that dignity is not a matter of individual pride, but a natural right existing objectively and shared by everyone equally. It cannot be bestowed or taken away by governments or the law. Applying that principle, the case can be made that gay people, like all people, are to be treated with respect not because of their sexual practices or preferences, but because they are human beings deserving of equal protection under the law. In this respect, the equal humanity argument of gay rights activists—that they deserve the same respect as straight people—is half right; they should not be singled out by the law for persecution or discrimination, even if they do things of which the majority disapproves. Nevertheless, there is no compelling state interest, nor is there a natural right, that requires the state to recognize a gay person's special identity claims. They are, after all, cultural declarations of independence, a demand that their "differences" be recognized as equal. Those differences should indeed be tolerated; but there is nothing in them, short of a passed statutory law to the contrary, that demands that they be accepted as a fundamental right.

*The Mob Mentality*. Identity militants are experts at exploiting human passions. Shouting down errant public speakers is a weapon of choice in academic venues. Street demonstrators work themselves up into a frothing mob as they denounce one enemy after another. Their manifestos are laden with a black–white worldview more appropriate for Mao's *Little Red Book* than an American democratic movement. The more extreme the argument and the more implausible the comparisons the better, because it polarizes the debate and mobilizes people to act against enemies. An ugly tactic with a long sordid history in politics, it has a name: the mob mentality.

Ever since social psychologists Gabriel Tarde and Gustave Le Bon wrote about the psychology of crowds in the 19th century, social scientists have debated it. Le Bon took a dim view of crowds, seeing them as manifestations of dark primeval forces in the human mind. In the 20th century his theories were vindicated by the vicious primitivism of the Nazis' Nuremburg rallies and by the genocidal movements of fascism and communism. In recent years social scientists and psychologists have taken a more favorable view of crowd mentalities. They speak of crowd wisdom and group intelligence as often being superior to the decisions of individuals.[19]

The crowd mentality of identity militants is definitely of the Le Bon variety. It is true both in terms of group dynamics and in the way they view human nature. The average organizer of a campus protest or street demonstration is not reaching out to the public in order to find a practical solution to a problem, as a group intelligence theorist might do. He is tapping into one group's base emotions in order to mobilize them against other people. It is more like a tribe gearing up for war than a committee inquiry. This is precisely how Le Bon and others like him understood the dark motives of crowds. What matters is not the logic of the argument, but the authenticity of the passion used to convey it. Ultimately, it is about power. The militants' behavior in groups and their propaganda methods are of the same species as 20th-century totalitarians, and they have absolutely nothing in common with the practical, business-oriented group dynamics favored today by some social psychologists.

*Postmodern Authoritarianism.* Identity militants are not fascists or communists. Strictly speaking they are not even socialists; they do not care all that much about controlling the means of production. But they are authoritarians, and uniquely so—with a postmodern twist. As with all authoritarian movements, they employ deception as a means to shape public opinion. They appeal to the darker passions of people—to their fears and social prejudices—in order to mobilize support. They present a public face of tolerance, compassion, and humanitarianism, but it masks a deep-seated hatred of certain classes of people. They intentionally sow confusion about their intentions and goals in order to minimize opposition. And they seek to pass laws to punish their enemies and to restrict freedom of speech and expression, and thereby constrict the political space in which ideas can be debated, all done of course in the name of demanding respect for their dignity.

A conclusion is unmistakable: The extremism of the identity militants is not a case of mistaken zeal. It is not a good heart going too far. It is not even good intentions getting out of hand. It is the direct consequence of a closed mind addled by ideological prejudices. The offense is both of the heart and the mind. It is the mind closed to objective tests of reality and other points of view. And it is a heart hardened by the same hubris that drives dictators to abuse power in the name of a good cause.

I am speaking here of the militants—the true believers—not the millions of Americans who casually support the various causes of identity politics. Nor am I even thinking of moderate gay rights supporters like Andrew Sullivan and Jonathan Rauch, who are horrified by the dark illiberalism of the militant sexual rights activists. Nevertheless, even moderates have been infected with the paranoid mentality of the militants. Rauch, for example, lumps most opponents of gay marriage together as "homophobes."[20] He apparently finds it impossible to distinguish between a gay-bashing redneck who abhors homosexuality and a thoughtful Christian like Professor Robert George of Princeton University who explains that the best of human reason counsels against same-sex marriage.[21] The inability to make such distinctions is a telltale sign of the ideologue and of the authoritarian mindset. Even moderate supporters of the gay rights agenda are finding themselves pulled over to the dark side.

## THE ABOLITION OF HUMANITY

British philosopher Roger Scruton once made this observation about contemporary liberalism:

> Every conflict is seen in terms of power: who enjoys it and who suffers it—"who? whom?" in Lenin's summary. But the deep conflicts concern not power but knowledge. Which institutions, which procedures, and which customs preserve and enhance the store of social knowledge?[22]

One can argue that political ideologies all care about political power. Conservatives and liberals alike want to gain power to enact their agendas. But there is a difference between wanting power to preserve and enhance knowledge and wanting it in order to create and control knowledge. Although progressives may be loath to admit it, conservatives can draw on a vast body of knowledge to justify their careful approach to historical change. Knowledge is not something they claim they invented, but something they inherited. Progressives on the other hand, being forever in the business of reinventing knowledge, have no real need for knowledge except as an expedient political tool with which to gain and hold on to power. That is why, as Scruton suggests, progressive liberalism is ultimately all about the power to control knowledge, and not what is really true and right since, as any good postmodernist will tell you, searching for a single truth is a fool's errand.

All liberals, even classic ones, are to some extent guilty of wanting to invent knowledge rather than discover it. Liberal philosophers from Rousseau to John Stuart Mill were keenly interested in, and almost obsessed with, revolutionizing the way we view knowledge. But whereas the liberal always believed that he was discovering knowledge in nature and would then spread this new light around the world in order to emancipate mankind, today's postmodern leftists have an entirely different mindset. They see themselves in the business of actually inventing knowledge from the slippery material of human perception. It is not even called knowledge anymore, but a "construct" or some other subjective invention of the mind.

There is something profoundly troubling going on here. The old left, including the hard left of communism, made war on the accumulated wisdom of the ages. It hated customs and traditions. It sought to revolutionize and change social conditions in order to liberate the inner communist that supposedly dwelled in us all. But even Marx felt the need to keep his feet on the ground. He detested Hegel and the German idealists because he believed their endless theoretical debates would stand in the way of making the communist revolution. Not so the postmodern leftists. They have turned their endless theoretical debates into a form of agitation-propaganda. They believe they have discovered a whole new way of making revolution—a revolution that starts first with the human mind and then proceeds to overturn society itself. The philosophers who created this worldview were not Marx but Arthur Schopenhauer, Friedrich Nietzsche, Albert Roussel, and Martin Heidegger, the forefathers of postmodernism.

In the hands of today's leftists, the postmodernist component has been reduced to a crude project: to make war on society by making war on knowledge itself. That in essence is what "deconstructionism" means. It is breathtakingly radical in its ambitions, even though it eschews (for the most part) the physically violent revolutionary methods of the past. But we should not underestimate the violence that it is doing to language, philosophy, meaning, and knowledge, which after all is the stuff of civilizations. Postmodern leftists are quite consciously navigating without a historical compass, or any moral instruments for that matter. Nothing that came before is useful except as material to revise the past in order to suit the future. Not even reason is said to exist. The urge to start anew makes Locke's *tabula rasa*[23] look like it was written on with disappearing ink: nothing is for certain except for the ever-changing verities of the perceptual moment.

It may very well be that, as historian Jacques Barzun suggests, Western civilization is imploding.[24] The very things that
once made it great—its openness to change and embrace of independence and liberation—today may be bringing it down. The
once noble cause of emancipation that freed men and women
from the chains of slavery is now enlisted in the cause of providing state subsidies for sex-change operations. The hope to invent
oneself anew that once inspired the Protestant Reformation and
the American Revolution is today reduced to primitive beliefs in
secular eschatological causes, from eliminating all fossil fuels to
basing all human relations, including marriage, solely on fleeting
emotions of sexual attraction. The impatient fondness for change
that enabled the West to reinvent itself while other civilizations
languished seems to be stuck in an endless loop of trivial causes,
spinning wildly out of boredom or simply because it is too hard to
deal with a world that refuses to conform to the fantastical perfection imagined by a five-year-old.

The challenge may go even deeper than Barzun imagines. It
may be that many of the basic precepts of the postmodern left are
actually hostile to the very idea of an advanced civilization. For
example, how do you organize the complex arrangements of a
society and state, not to mention all the attending support systems
of bureaucracies, armies, and belief systems, if you truly believe
that no objective, and reliable, theory of knowledge exists? How
do you expect a civilization to thrive, much less survive, if the
traditional family and its role in rearing children are completely
cast aside? How can you expect to erect a reliable rule of law if all
laws are nothing but social fictions, lacking any foundation other
than the whims of a passing fancy? Just as the Supreme Court
cited the Fourteenth Amendment in finding a right to abortion
in the "penumbra" (a space of partial illumination at the edge of
a shadow!) of the right to privacy, it found the right to gay marriage in that same amendment in *Obergefell v. Hodges*; it apparently
was lurking there all the time as a constitutional right to identity

undiscovered by over two centuries of constitutional review. Can it be said any longer that the Supreme Court has *not* gone "full postmodern"?

All across America, in our hospitals and the science departments of universities, knowledge qua knowledge still exists. It has not been suspended. The natural order is actually respected for what it is—a reality that must be acknowledged, discovered, and understood. Moreover, even though many law schools indulge in all sorts of multicultural legal theories, American jurisprudence in practice carries on remarkably *as if* natural law still exists.

And yet the postmodern left spins cultural, legal, and moral narratives as if it is all a joke. For a while, gay and gender activists seemed to believe that a person was born with a sexual orientation and identity. That is no longer the case. It is now a full-blown choice—identity à la Bruce Jenner and Rachel Dolezal. Identity theorists will occasionally cite a study showing the natural inclination for some deviant sexual practice or trying to show that homosexuality is common in other cultures, but their main line of argument is a moral one of rights—that people get to choose their identities, full stop. It is as if they had issued a decree that "the natural order is hereby suspended" and anyone who does not agree is hereby pronounced unnatural. It is the new abnormal sold as normal. It is not merely an attempt to control nature or to use it for the benefit of mankind. It is the desire to abolish it.

This understanding of knowledge is unsustainable. The only way it will survive is if we escape into cultural schizophrenia. We apply one set of rules in some areas (scientific research, medicine, and engineering) while reserving a special set of rarified rules for the rest of our lives (our culture, morality, and politics). For this to work requires a very determined kind of compartmentalization. The walls around the two different worldviews will have to be built ever higher. This is where the power politics Scruton warned of come into play. The only way to force an artificial order on civilization is with brute force. The only way to make something unnatural appear to be natural is to force everyone to think alike. If you are making war on both nature and reality, you will need to do more than break a few eggs and make an omelet. You will have to start slaughtering the chickens.

Getting back to Scruton's suggestion, if society is utterly indifferent to knowledge—not caring about knowing what is true and right—then the only option left is to prefabricate knowledge as if it were a modular house. You build it cheaply knowing full well it is not meant to last. It is intended only to serve some transient purpose such as getting gay marriage legalized or banning guns. All knowledge is expedient and politicized. It must be assembled and packaged for a certain cause. This is true even in some areas of science, such as in climate change research, where the political objective of getting the government involved in controlling $CO_2$ emissions actually drives the research. If knowledge has no objective basis but is merely a tool to be manipulated to suit political agendas, then what is the point of even speaking of it as knowledge—as *understanding* and as the accumulated wisdom of the ages? If knowledge is purely utilitarian, then we might as well skip all the theorizing and get down to what is really important—gaining political power in order to invent and control what people think.

There is no mistaking the implication. Trying to abolish knowledge is taking direct aim at our humanity. By trying to break the human being into separate identities—by focusing on what makes us different and then pretending that we are all equal in our differences—we are not serving the cause of universal equality, but erasing our common humanity. In order to justify the plethora of self-generated identities, the very notion of the human being must be eradicated. It must be sliced and diced only according to what each identity establishes as its own local truth. If we are only who we *think* we are, then we can just as easily imagine we—or more likely *others*—are nothing at all. If we believe, as identity theorists do, that the individual human being as we commonly understand him or her is a social fiction, then it is not a tragedy if some people are sacrificed for the sake of others. Without a respect for *all* human beings, regardless of their place in the identity pecking order, it is fairly easy, even necessary, to separate people into winners and losers in a game of power. The next step is obvious and even inevitable: a prison for the losers.

### THE REAL ESCAPE FROM FREEDOM

In 1941 German-born psychologist-sociologist Erich Fromm predicted the kind of freedom we are experiencing today in America. In *Escape From Freedom*, he described freedom in the age of mass politics as a quest for personal authenticity.[25] It was an internal affair, the psychology of trying to be "true" to oneself. The person involved in this quest sees himself on a journey of self-discovery. Overcoming obstacles requires courage and determination. "There is only one meaning of life: the act of living it," Fromm said.[26] In other words, the only way we can get in touch with others is first to get in touch with ourselves. It is "all about me." Thus was born the modern culture's fixation on the inner life of authenticity as the true and only source of human freedom.

Fromm was a socialist channeling all the fashionable ideas of the time—Freudianism and those of the neo-Marxist Frankfurt School of dialectics. But he was tapping into something larger. He sensed that, in the new age of mass politics, social psychology was the new frontier. Dissecting the inner world of the "masses" was the way to predict where they wanted to go. He understood that in an age of mass communications large groups of people would define their freedoms by how they felt emotionally. Fromm had Nazism in mind, but he was also fascinated by advertising campaigns in the West and how they could move public opinion with carefully calculated messages.

Another German-born philosopher of the neo-Marxist Frankfurt School, Herbert Marcuse, had a different take on the politics of passions.[27] He believed they were a window into a whole new concept of freedom and justice. The new revolution against capitalism did not involve a communist seizure of the means of production, but a capture of the culture. It was not workers' alienated labor that would be liberated, but everyone's passions, including their sexuality. Revolution and politics were about liberating Eros, the god of love, from the oppression of capitalist morality. Marcuse's ideas were among the early siren songs of the sexual revolution that swept the West in the 1960s. Today they are as ubiquitous as the *#lovecantwait* campaign of gay marriage activists.

Behind the romantic façade of humanitarian love lurks a demanding lover determined to have its way. As Polish philosopher Leszek Kolakowski once remarked, Marcuse's notion of revolutionary passion "depends on replacing the tyranny of logic by a police tyranny. . . . The Marcusian union of Eros and Logos can only be realized in the form of a totalitarian state, established and governed by force; the freedom he advocates is non-freedom."[28] That is indeed the logical extreme, and although things need not end up that way, it must be admitted that any political order that strives to press political power into the service of human passions is playing with fire. There are no natural or logical limits on politics if passions are to be their guide. Once logic (Logos) is made the servant of passions (Eros), then all human reason, including the practical reason that runs the everyday world, is subordinated to whatever human emotions demand.

How can the complex interests of human beings be weighed and compromised in a political order that promises unlimited freedom of the passions? How can a person who supposedly has the complete freedom to define his or her own identity possibly be expected to care if that freedom interferes with someone else's rights? Can we really expect the gay rights activist to respect the religious passions of a born-again Christian who thinks those who live the gay lifestyle are likely to burn in hell? By the same token, how can we expect a Christian to restrain himself if all he is doing is expressing his own feelings about his religious convictions? And, to push the argument to an extreme, why should a white supremacist's identity not be as valuable as a black's if he should find himself a minority living in a black majority country? By the logic of identity politics it cannot, unless of course we suspend logic in favor of something else—namely, the theory of white privilege.

Trying to define human identity solely on the basis of passion is a dead end. A gay or transgender person's identity as a human being is greater than what they do in their bedrooms or even what they may think about their sexuality. They have families and friends who need to be nurtured and protected outside the confines of their sexual and gender identities. They surely have ambitions to be scientists, lawyers, politicians, and even presidents that involve the concerns and issues of all human beings, regardless of what they think about sex and gender. At some point reducing everything in their identity to those two characteristics becomes restraining and restrictive, not to mention off-putting and boring. The unremitting vigilance needed to sustain their cause in society can only lead to hatred and heartache. Coercing others to accept their cause will deprive them of sympathy and in some cases make them look like bullies. It is not really freedom at all, but a psychological prison of one's own making. It is the very definition of Kolakowski's "non-freedom."

As it turns out, Fromm's "escape from freedom" has come full circle. The foray into psychologizing about inner freedom has become a new kind of psychological enslavement. People are imprisoned by identities of their own making. They cannot endure objective freedom because it will expose the fragile unreality of the world they have created for themselves. In the postmodern leftists' desire to escape the mundane freedoms of the real world—and biological nature—they have created an imaginary world that can only be imposed by establishing an illiberal political order. The only way to empower Eros is to fine pastors and to restrict people from speaking out against the new freedoms

Eros demands. Everything that conflicts with the new Eros—even traffic signals and bathrooms—must be made to conform. Kolakowski was right: the union of Eros and Logos requires the actual use of force and coercion, because in normal life, as well as in the public life of a liberal democracy, people do not want other people telling them how to feel, love, believe, or live.

## A NO-LIMITS GOVERNMENT

So much of the illiberalism of progressivism today stems from a single attitude: a boundless confidence in the power of government to wipe out all vestiges of inequality and unfairness in life. We have gone through periods in our history when people were highly skeptical of liberal government action, but today is not one of those times. Today we live in a moment when many people are skeptical of the skeptics of government. Because so many of the country's cultural and communications institutions are in the hands of progressive liberals, the old gospel of small-government conservativism does not ring as true as it once did.

Many Americans may not embrace small-government philosophy. But that does not mean they have a lot of confidence in government itself. Polls show most Americans have little faith in government, even as they continue to ask it to do many things for them.[29] That Americans want more for less is typically a schizophrenic attitude. They want more government services efficiently provided, but they do not necessarily want to pay more for them. Most Americans do not want the government interfering with their daily lives, but many also are all too happy to see someone they dislike being told what to do. Americans may hate an overbearing and incompetent government in theory, but they seem to like it well enough in practice. There is always some government benefit upon which they think they depend and which they wish to save from some fiscal axe–wielding conservative.

These contradictions help explain why otherwise liberal-minded Americans are willing to tolerate an overbearing government doing illiberal things. It is not only a lack of interest in the finer points of constitutional government or even the result of a complete befuddlement over the implications of identity politics; it is also a matter of confusion over what government is supposed to be and do. For most Americans, government is at best a distant annoyance to which they do not give much thought beyond the next election. But for liberal activists it is quite different. Government is literally identified with the populace, or as a liberal once said to me privately, "How can you distrust government? The government is us!" It is as if government is, to refer back to Rousseau, a physical incarnation of the "general will." It is an idea with a very long historical pedigree, but it is alive and well today not only in the liberal mind, but thanks to the megaphones of the popular media and academia, the American mind in general.

The question is, what is the destiny of a nation that thinks this way? The dangers are plain enough to see. Without some check on social entitlement spending, at some point a reckoning of the nation's massive debt will have to occur. The roller-coaster ride of a zero-interest-rate economy is bound to come to an end—possibly even crash. When it does the artificial nature of our current prosperity will become painfully obvious as the true value of goods and services (including those provided by governments) are reflected in much higher prices. If we think that the Europeans spend mindlessly and get away with it, we need only to be reminded of the crushing fiscal crises in Greece, Spain, Italy, and Portugal. It is true that the private American economy remains quite strong and still attracts foreigners willing to invest and hold our debt. But that cannot last forever. We cannot endlessly abuse "the goose that lays the golden eggs." At some point we are going to have to come to terms with our spending habits, but that day will never come so long as we believe that there are really no limits on what the government can do.

We sometimes forget how much our civil stability as a nation depends on a strong economy. Without the promise of ever-rising prosperity all the social divisions that have been stoked by the postmodern left will get far worse. People will head to their respective corners, the rich behind their gated communities and the poor and minorities into the streets. Each side will justify its radicalism by pointing to the extremism of the other. One crisis after another will cause people to throw caution to the wind, and the institutions necessary to sustain a flourishing liberal democracy[30]—the rule of law, constitutional checks and balances, civil society organizations, freedom of expression, and a pluralistic political system—will fray even further. A radical populism will become the order of the day. Everyone calls for "new" leadership, but it is never forthcoming because people insist on electing politicians who only tell them what they want to hear: that justice and equality require even more spending and more debt, and that it is okay to persecute certain people with unpopular opinions. They are far too willing to settle for the simplistic answers of populist demagoguery.

I can scarcely imagine a popular culture less able to deal with such crises than the one we now have. It is steeped in the myths of the postmodern left, which are perfectly disabling. The mystifying confusion of metanarratives and identity symbolisms hangs over the culture like a thick fog over a swamp. You cannot make anything out for sure. Everything you have been taught is suspect. But at the same time anything and everything is at least plausibly true. Maybe it is okay after all for a guy to marry his porn-laden computer? Who's to say what is right or wrong anyway? Who cares about all those stuffy rules about the separation of government powers, or the First Amendment rights of free speech and religious expression? They are just rules, and we all know from the likes of Steve Jobs and Donald Trump that we get to make up our own rules as we go along. This is a culture ripe for mass delusion, because as any summer superhero blockbuster will show, there are millions of dollars to be made by pretending reality does not exist. As Supreme Court Justice Antonin Scalia famously said after the court's ruling on the Affordable Care Act, "words no longer have meaning. . . ."[31]

If we ever hope to solve our problems, we must at least return to a semblance of reality-based thought. All the fantastical thinking about unlimited federal budgets and using police powers to enforce identity mandates would have to disappear. So, too, will simplistic government solutions for the most pressing problems of our lives, such as illegal immigration. Whether that will happen any time soon is questionable. Delusion can be a lot more palatable than hard reality. Entertainment is more enjoyable than policy white papers. What is not contestable is that we cannot continue on our current course without destroying the American system as we know it. Unless we find it within ourselves to rediscover the age-old American wisdom about the limits of government, including a deep and abiding respect for the Bill of Rights, we will surely lose a lot more than our wisdom. We will lose our ability to govern ourselves.

## THE DANGERS OF THE CLOSED MIND

One of the most important achievements of the Enlightenment was the commitment to the open mind. It is a principle on which practically all the *philosophes* and thinkers agreed. Voltaire no less than Hobbes believed in open inquiry, and all the great liberal thinkers of the 19th century from Humboldt to Mill were champions of freedom of expression and speech. It was a founding principle of the American republic as well, enshrined in the First Amendment. Liberal thinkers and statesmen understood clearly what Allan Bloom said in *The Closing of the American Mind* (1987): "Freedom of the mind requires not only, or not even especially, the absence of legal constraints but the presence of alternative thoughts. The most successful tyranny is not the one that uses force to assure uniformity but the one that removes the awareness of other possibilities."[32]

Unfortunately, the open mind is dying. It is under fire from the very same people who claim to embody the spirit of the Enlightenment—namely, progressive liberals. It is not only the most egregious of abuses such as hate speech ideology or campus controls on free speech that shock. There is the much larger problem of groupthink. Liberal intellectuals these days simply cannot be bothered by critical analysis outside their own frames of reference. They are profoundly uncurious about anything that does not fit their predetermined narratives of reality and politics. It is as if they are latter-day scholar-monks who receive their wisdom from a transcendent source and feel no need whatsoever to question its premises or assumptions. Knowledge, like human progress, must be created and managed by state policy, bureaucratized and forced on all people equally despite the infinite differences that exist between individual human beings. It is a sad state of affairs, especially for intellectuals who are expected to know better.

History is replete with the casualties of the closed mind. We all know what happens when totalitarian and authoritarian regimes get people acclimated to the routines of thought control. But as Bloom recognized, for America the danger is much more subtle. Despite all the hate speech rules and speech code campaigns, the real threat is not legal but cultural. We as a people may be slipping into a complacency about one of our most cherished government principles without even knowing it. The culprits oppressing us are the very ones we expect to be the guardians of the open mind—namely, the progressive liberals themselves, who never tire of telling us how committed they are to dissent and civil rights. People have a hard time imagining that liberal iconoclasts like Jon Stewart and Bill Maher are threats to open inquiry and freedom of expression. And yet every day they set a tone of ridicule that is every bit as dismissive and controlling—not to mention in sync with a broader *official* culture—as any directive from a government propaganda ministry. People think that the ACLU must be out there championing free speech, and yet the only speech it seems to care about is that which advances its agenda.

It all comes down to controlling what people believe. The postmodern left is using subterfuge to transform *all* of America's culture. To do that requires upending America's values. And to do that necessitates redefining what things mean. As a result, all distinctions are lost, indeed they are considered to be singularly uninteresting. The broad brush is now the analytical tool of choice, covering one's own cause in a shiny glaze while painting one's cultural enemies in a very flat Midnight Black. All the care liberal intellectuals once took to deconstruct the culture—the parsing of language, the rigorous analysis of subtexts, a skepticism about everything—disappears the moment their own theories are the object of scrutiny. Who needs critical analysis when you are in charge? Far better to steamroll the opposition with the actual control of institutions and money.

What does it mean to stop thinking? It means intellectual atrophy. Curiosity shrivels up. Ideas become slogans. Debate degenerates into a war of ideas. Clichés mount and political conversations devolve into wild shouting matches or boring repetitions of politically correct bromides. The worst is that the very class we expect to uphold the values of the open mind—our academics and intellectuals—become like mandarins codifying, recording, and propagating the party line and in constant search for grants and academic and government sinecures. After Bloom wrote his book on the American university, furious academics such as Lawrence W. Levine mobilized to denounce him.[33] It was a pitiful thing to watch. Completely missing the point, Levine argued that radical multiculturalism was merely reflecting the "diversity" of America, not causing it, as if that were the problem. Bloom was not worried about ethnic diversity; he was, after all, the son of Jewish social workers. Rather, he was horrified by the inability of intellectuals to think openly and clearly about problems. Everything was getting precooked by ideology which, to his mind, had been the trademark of all authoritarians, including fascists.

Civilizations can survive with closed minds, at least for a time.

Rome lasted for centuries after its rulers succumbed to the tyrannies of the empire. But liberal democracies cannot long endure a political culture that refuses to entertain alternatives. Certainly the American republic cannot bear it. The problem is not only the attempts to chip away at the legal protections of freedom of expression, which are bound to increase. More important is the normalization of a political and intellectual culture of mediocrity and dishonesty. Everything becomes aimed at getting and keeping political power. Even academic agendas are set to serve this purpose. All the principles of liberty and freedom that made the country great are mocked and dismissed as silly fictions. All in all, it is impossible to know what is up and what is down, because cultural confusion is actually a weapon in the arsenal of cultural war.

It is true that there are still vast swaths of American life where the open mind is king. American businesses still value innovation and experimentation. And even in some corners of academia (the hard sciences, engineering, and technology for example), a fierce dedication to open inquiry still persists. But that is not true in the study of the humanities. Nor is it the prevailing mindset in progressive political circles. There the clock has stopped. History is over. The truth has been revealed and we need not concern ourselves further with anything except finding the data and methodologies to prove our points and to implement our plans. The exploration of ideas is the work of officially sanctioned intellectuals, activists, and bureaucrats who represent the interests of the state and its quasi-government industries.

Most people go about their day with little notice of politics. To many it is just white noise. And who can blame them? What passes for political and intellectual discourse in this country is designed by communications specialists and political consultants with specific agendas in mind. To this extent everyone involved in politics, not just liberals, is to blame for the sad state of political affairs. Nevertheless, progressive liberals bear special responsibility. As the savviest of political activists (as anyone who worked on

Obama's campaigns will tell you), they are not only fully committed to the corrupt practices of the political class, but often are also
its most passionate innovators. They are masters of the cultural
fog, spreading a faux compassion across the political landscape as
if it were a comfort blanket. They are, in this respect, not merely
deconstructionists, but "deceptionists." Just as Barack Obama
once claimed to be against same-sex marriage, progressives today
hide their radical intentions from the American public. It is white
noise all right—a din of obfuscation intended, like a fan whirring
in the night, to lull Americans to sleep.

No one better captures the spirit of the Enlightenment than
Thomas Jefferson. He really and truly believed in the open mind.
As he once said, "I have sworn upon the altar of god eternal hos-
tility against every form of tyranny over the mind of man."[34] Are
America's progressives listening?

CONCLUSION

# The Way Forward

American liberalism is in dire straits. The question is, can anything be done about it? Admittedly, the prospects do not look good. Progressive militants are on a roll and show no signs of backing down from their increasingly strident positions. A leading grant-maker for "gender rights" organizations, for example, told business leaders in 2015 that he wants to shut down the political fight for religious-freedom exemptions in three years.[1] Many courts seem to be moving in an illiberal direction, and their decisions could help freeze in law the postmodern left's cultural agenda for generations to come. Demographic trends also seem to favor the progressives. Ethnic and racial minorities who otherwise would have no use for the radical identity politics of white progressives seem to be unable to break the Democratic Party's spell over them. Republicans appear to be at sea as well, fighting among themselves and unsure of which direction to take.

The roots of cultural liberalism in America today go very deep. Part of the problem lies with classical liberalism itself. The notion of the autonomous individual freely choosing his or her destiny, which is a fundamental principle of classical liberalism, does contain at least the seeds of gender and sexual identity choice. It is true that this is not the way John Locke, Thomas Jefferson, or even John Stuart Mill interpreted liberty, but the similarities are close enough for gay activists (and some libertarians) to argue, often convincingly and in public, that all they want is the same freedom everyone else has. Even capitalism can work in their favor. The autonomy capitalism affords to the individual can just as easily be applied to choice of gender and sexuality. After all, if you have unfettered choices in the commodities you buy, why not the same in the choice of sexual orientation and identity? This is not really a fair analysis—rational people can distinguish between buying an iPhone and choosing a different gender than nature gave them. But suffice it to say that the mantra of choice, with which everyone is supposedly enamored, is a feature of our free market system that feeds the expectation of unlimited freedom.

True enough. Nevertheless, another outcome is possible. In the culture wars the pendulum always swings back and forth. The excesses of the Sixties and Seventies gave rise to the conservative era of Ronald Reagan. Conservatives maintained their dominance for a while, but their successes were met with strong resistance from the cultural left. Today the pendulum has swung back in the left's direction. Progressives are in the ascendency and conservatives are on the defensive. Times always change. For every action there is a counterreaction. The postmodern left is on top politically now, but who knows which way the country will turn next?

It is highly likely that progressive liberals will overplay their hand. Heady with their victories over gay and contraceptive rights, they are trying to ostracize and bully people with whom they disagree. This does not bode well for their cause. Americans do not like bullies. They are turned off by scolding of any persuasion, left or right; and they do not like powerful elites pushing other people around. Nor do they like hypocrites. The image of activists shouting down speakers in the name of tolerance or hurling insults at someone over the simple statement "all lives matter" does not go over very well with average Americans. Many will see that it is not puritanical conservatives who are forcing "their kind of morality" on others, but instead it is the progressive liberals. As it becomes increasingly clear that left-leaning liberals are the dominant ruling elite—the Establishment protected even by their court jesters in the world of comedy—conservatives will be seen as the new cultural insurgents.

There are already signs of unrest inside the liberal camp. Moderate Democrats such as Senator Joe Manchin of West Virginia[2] and reporter Juan Williams bemoan the illiberal tactics of others in their party. Occasionally commentators on liberal news and blog sites recoil from the beast they helped create. For example, when an American dentist was hounded by an online campaign for killing an African lion, the reliably liberal *Vox* World site ran a story lamenting that "Internet mob justice is out of control."[3] Moderates such as Andrew Sullivan who support gay rights are clearly discomfited by militants who want to criminalize opposition to gay marriage.[4] Conor Friedersdorf, a libertarian-minded staff writer for *The Atlantic* who once was hired by Sullivan, put it this way:

> The owners of Memories Pizza [the O'Connor family] are, I think, mistaken in what their Christian faith demands of them. And I believe their position on gay marriage to be wrongheaded. But I also believe that the position *I'll gladly serve any gay customers but I feel my faith compels me to refrain from catering a gay wedding* is less hateful or intolerant than *let's go burn that family's business to the ground.*[5]

This is what real tolerance looks like. It is not the fake kind that fines people while striking the self-righteous pose of the open-minded liberal.

A backlash against progressive illiberalism may be building. The transgender-backed Houston "bathroom" referendum was defeated in a landslide in the November 2015 elections, as was a ballot proposal in Ohio to legalize marijuana. The pendulum, it seems, may be starting to swing back in the other direction.

It is entirely possible that a diverse coalition could emerge to challenge the illiberalism of the postmodern left. It could include many moderate liberals who are aghast at the authoritarianism of the militants and horrified by the rank oppression of free speech

occurring on college campuses, such as *Washington Post* columnist Catherine Rampell.[6] It could also include libertarians who
are sympathetic to gay rights and other cultural liberal causes but
alarmed by the abuse of government power done in their name.
Obviously, social conservatives and religious people would need
to be part of this coalition, but it may require them to shed their
aversion to working with people who do not share their views
one hundred percent. It is remarkable what can happen when
people actually talk to one another. They may find in some instances they have more in common than not.

If there is to be any chance for such a coalition to emerge,
there has to be the realization that radical illiberalism of any sort—
far left or far right—is a mortal danger to both liberalism and
conservatism. It threatens the moderate progressive who still believes in the American system no less than it does the conservative who believes that system is under attack. It may be a stretch
to expect progressives and conservatives to forge a united front
against radical illiberalism, but at the very least they should agree,
tacitly if not openly, that certain things are beyond the pale. The
bloody-minded authoritarianism raging in radical circles on campus, in the entertainment industry, and in the blogosphere and
social networking worlds should be shunned by everyone. By
the same token, bigotry of any sort, whether expressed by a racist
or an anti-Christian gay rights activist, should be labeled as such.
The criminalization of speech and even of things we do in our
day-to-day lives must be stopped. The silly intolerance-in-the-
name-of-tolerance campaigns should be dismissed as the height of
hypocrisy. Any abuse of executive authority, which is a politically
double-edged sword if there ever was one, should be repudiated.
Overt efforts by the courts or the president as the chief executive
to bypass the legislative process should be seen as direct assaults
not only on our constitutional order, but on our republican democracy.

For a coalition against illiberalism to work, some distinctions are in order. It would be helpful if liberals stopped buying into the radicals' meme that conservatives are all illiberal extremists. The KKK, racists, and fascists are illiberal and extremist. Conservatives are not. Moreover, it would be helpful to understand the difference between a real American conservative and an illiberal authoritarian posing as one. The American conservative tradition has classical liberalism as one of its pillars. That is why it supports limited government and freedom of speech and religion. It is quite different from the European right, which reviled classic liberalism almost as much as it did socialism. Trying to pretend that all conservatives are closet authoritarians (or worse, racists) merely because they believe in traditional and longstanding morality or the rule of law should be unacceptable.

By the same token, conservatives should draw some distinctions as well. First, they should police their own, drawing clear distinctions between real conservatism and its counterfeit, illiberal populism. Second, they may dislike the progressive liberalism of the New Deal, the Great Society, and the neo-liberalism of Bill Clinton's "New Democrat." They may believe that progressive liberalism has severely damaged the country. But they should not conclude that all moderate Democrats have always been and still are all socialists and the same as the postmodern left. These days it is getting harder to tell the difference, but conservatives should not demonize the entire progressive tradition without distinction. Most American progressives prior to the rise of the postmodern left were not by and large illiberal. They were statist and culturally liberal; and, yes, some were by today's standards no less illiberal than others living in their historical moment.[7] But they did not by and large swallow the noxious authoritarianism of the radical left. Postmodern leftists are inspired, not by Alexander Hamilton, Herbert Croly, or John Dewey, but by Karl Marx, Jacques Derrida, and Che Guevara. Realizing this simple historical fact could help prevent misunderstandings. At the very least it may help avoid the overuse of broad-brush condemnations of which both liberals and conservatives are guilty.

What is at stake is nothing less than the constitutional order that has preserved American freedom for nearly 240 years. Liberals and conservatives alike have an interest in conserving it. They do not have to agree on everything to know that it is wrong to shun dissent and shut down debates, or that is injurious to abuse executive power for short-term gain. They can vigorously dispute gay marriage without wanting to see our democracy undermined by judicial fiat, or our religious freedoms trampled by petty administrative fines, or worse. They can care about the environment without throwing people in jail or fining them for picking up an eagle feather or using it in a decoration.[8] And above all, they can vigorously disagree over political philosophy without closing their minds to alternative ways of solving problems. It does no one any good when people stop thinking. And yet for all its intellectual gyrations and pretensions, that is precisely what the postmodern left is doing. There is closed-mindedness on the right, too, but these days it is caused mainly by panic over losing the American system and by the fact that the successes of the postmodern left leave conservatives little choice but to rally the wagons around their causes.

For most of our history the constitutional order worked remarkably well. It was open and flexible. One side never got quite enough power to shut out the other completely. There was no end of history, and except for the showdown that was the Civil War, no one expected one party or ideology to prevail completely over the other. There were "eras of good feelings" and periods in which one side dominated over the rest, but things always changed. There were rules and precedents that everyone respected because they were to everyone's mutual benefit. It was this order that made America a great nation. And yet it is precisely this same order that the postmodern left, particularly President

Obama and his supporters, want to "transform." By this, they do not mean merely to tinker with it, but to change it root and branch. They are after nothing short of purging what remains of the classical liberal dream in our constitutional order.

Call this order whatever you like. To me it is a conservative-liberal order. By this I mean a constitutional order that is largely (although not exclusively) classically liberal superimposed over a unique kind of civil society—one that encompasses a raging competition on the one hand between a moral and religious conservatism (think Edmund Burke and William F. Buckley, Jr.), and on the other an impatient, progressive desire for radical change (think Thomas Paine, Gore Vidal, and the counterculture). The battles over values rage on, and there will always be bids by one side to gain power to demonstrate the "rightness" of its views over the other's. But the constitutional order should keep one side from gaining complete predominance over the other. The purpose of the constitutional order is to preserve freedom and to keep society in equilibrium. If that constitutional order ever were to completely break down, the battles over values would no longer be mere debates, but fights to the death. This happened in the Civil War, after all, when the political system could not settle the nation's visceral differences over slavery.

This is an order worth saving. But it will require restoration work. We will need to give people more authority over their lives, enabling them once again to make decisions on their own without the government telling them what to do. Americans will need more freedom, not less. At the same time we must recognize the absolute necessity of a moral order in sustaining liberty. Freedom is not license, and anyone who thinks otherwise might as well get it over with and choose between anarchy and dictatorship. Liberals and conservatives may never agree on the scope and reach of government, but at the very least they should recognize that there are limits to what government can and should do. If not, then there is no hope for reviving the fiscal health of the country. Nor will our democracy long survive if the powers of the legislatures are taken over by overweening courts, an imperialistic presidency, and the insular authorities of the regulatory-administrative state. Our precious freedoms of speech, religion, expression, and association will not endure either. Treating the First Amendment as an inconvenience, or worse as a fiction, will inevitably lead to new legal and administrative authorities for the government to control the direction and boundaries of political and religious thought and expression. That is truly the road to an illiberal regime, one democratic in name only.

Above all, liberalism needs to regain its respect for the open mind. There is no other way to put it: the closing of the liberal mind is an American tragedy. America needs a viable liberal philosophy. Not only is liberalism part of the country's historical DNA, it is vitally important to have a political movement that pushes the culture and the system to adapt to changing circumstances. We need an open competition of ideas. We need people to remind us that everyone should be included in the American dream. But we also need a liberalism that does not pretend that history ends the moment progressivism gains power. To make true progress, liberals need to be open as well to real change. They need to entertain all possibilities, including the possibility that sometimes they can be wrong.

This is not to say that some conservatives do not also have closed minds. They do. But liberals are the ones who are supposed to fight to the death for the open mind. After all, it is not conservatives but liberals and socialists who proudly wear the mantle of the Enlightenment. They are supposed to be the ones representing the philosophy of "light." They claim this as their birthright, and yet they are selling it out. It is not only a betrayal of their cause. It is a potential calamity for the nation.

## ACKNOWLEDGMENTS

Writing a book about ideas is like flying in a glider. You constantly search for air currents to sustain the flight, knowing full well at some point gravity will take over. People want to know if ideas are "real," if they actually make a difference. I believe they are and do, but it is no easy task to explain how or even why. In the end the history of ideas involves a complex interaction between people's thoughts and deeds that often remains as elusive as an evening breeze. I hope I captured some of that complexity, but I know, as Kant once said about human reason, there are limits to our ability to reach a complete understanding of what actually happens in history.

I would like to thank the Heritage Foundation, particularly its president, Jim DeMint, for the opportunity to write this book. He encouraged me every step of the way and I benefited enormously from his insights and guidance as I worked my way through the manuscript. I would also like to thank Matthew Streit, Vice President for Strategic Communications at Heritage, and David Fouse of the Pinkston Group for their personal efforts to bring this book to publication.

As always, no writing project I undertake would ever get off the ground if it were not for Janice Smith, my senior editor and researcher. Her hours upon hours of research, editing, and fact checking were indispensable. She was always there reminding me never, ever to take the word of a single source as gospel. I greatly appreciate her editing skills, suggestions, and due diligence, but mostly I cherish her deep dedication to standards of excellence. Quite simply, I could not have done the book without her.

I also thank my Heritage Foundation interns, Elizabeth Sparks, Patrick Kearney, and Curtis Walter, who provided valuable research assistance. Research for this book was challenging because of the wide-ranging nature of the subject. Moreover, since the topic is controversial, it was crucial to provide more examples with sourcing than would normally be the case. This presented quite a challenge, and I am very much grateful for their due diligence. Much appreciation goes out as well to Heritage program manager Kathy Gudgel, who like a master magician made lost drafts reappear and always kept me on schedule for all of my commitments.

Some of the subjects I covered can be quite specialized. To review chapters that touched on them, I sought out the wisdom of a number of experts. I am very much indebted to former Attorney General Ed Meese and Heritage's Group Vice President for Research, David Addington, who reviewed the chapters on law and the Constitution. Heritage colleagues in the Institute for Economic Freedom and Opportunity—David Kreutzer, Senior Research Fellow for Energy Economics and Climate Change, and Nicholas Loris, Herbert and Joyce Morgan Fellow in the Thomas A. Roe Institute for Economic Policy Studies—were an immense help in shaping the sections dealing with the politicization of science; and Ryan Anderson, William E. Simon Senior Research Fellow in American Principles and Public Policy at Heritage, helped guide me through the thorny thicket of the gay marriage issue.

I am grateful as well for the support of the fine people at Encounter Books, particularly Roger Kimball, its president and publisher; Heather Ohle, Director of Production; Katherine Wong, Production Manager; Sam Schneider, Director of Marketing; Lauren Miklos, Director of Publicity; and their copyeditor, Rebecca Tolen.

As thankful as I am to all these people, I stand on the legacy of many liberty-minded liberals who helped the world discover the values and principles that have made America great—people like John Locke, Thomas Jefferson, and James Madison. Their ideas continue to feed my own.

# NOTES

## INTRODUCTION

1 Joe Burris, "Student Suspended for Pop-Tart Gun, Josh Welch, Files Appeal with Maryland County School System," *Baltimore Sun*, March 3, 2013; see also Alexandra Petri, "Pop-Tart 'Gun' Suspension: Seriously, Folks?," *Washington Post*, March 5, 2013.

2 Petula Dvorak, "Free-Range Kids and Our Parenting Police State," *Washington Post*, April 13, 2015.

3 The differences between the moderate Enlightenment and the radical Enlightenment are discussed later in this volume.

4 See, for example, Sharyl Attkisson, *Stonewalled: My Fight for Truth Against the Forces of Obstruction, Intimidation, and Harassment in Obama's Washington* (New York: Harper, 2014). See also Kirsten Powers, *The Silencing: How the Left Is Killing Free Speech* (Washington, DC: Regnery Publishing, 2015).

## CHAPTER ONE

1 S. V. Dáte, "O'Malley, Sanders Shouted Down at Netroots by 'Black Lives Matter' Protest," *National Journal,* July 18, 2015.

2 Edmund Fawcett, *Liberalism: The Life of an Idea* (Princeton, NJ: Princeton University Press, 2014), pp. 10–11. Kindle edition.

3 Stephen Holmes, *The Anatomy of Antiliberalism* (Cambridge, MA: Harvard University Press, 1996), p. 4.

4 See Fawcett, *Liberalism*, pp. 34–35; and Biancamaria Fontana, ed., *Constant: Political Writings* (Cambridge: Cambridge University Press, 1988), p. 177.

5 See, e.g., Steven Lukes, *Individualism* (Colchester: European Consortium for Political Research Press, 1973).

6 Holmes, *The Anatomy of Antiliberalism*, p. 4. Emphasis added.

7 François Guizot, *History of the Origins of Representative Government in Europe*, trans. Andrew R. Scoble (London: Henry G. Bohn, 1861), p. 264.

8 Fawcett, *Liberalism*, pp. 118–19.

9 Thomas Jefferson, "Thomas Jefferson to James Madison, 6 Sept. 1789," in *The Papers of Thomas Jefferson*, vol. 32, ed. Barbara B. Oberg (Princeton, NJ: Princeton University Press, 2005); see also Philip B. Kurland and Ralph Lerner, "Popular Basis of Political Authority," in *The Founders' Constitution*, ed. Philip B. Kurland and Ralph Lerner, vol. 1, chap. 2, document 23 (Chicago: University of Chicago Press, 1985).

10 For an analysis of these ideas, see Fawcett, *Liberalism*, pp. 120–21.

11 Ibid., p. 120.

12 Ibid., p. 127.

13 Louis Hartz, *The Liberal Tradition in America: An Interpretation of American Political Thought Since the Revolution* (Orlando, FL: Harcourt, Inc., 1991). First published by Harcourt, Brace & World (New York), 1955.

14 Richard Allen Epstein, *The Classical Liberal Constitution: The Uncertain Quest for Limited Government* (Cambridge, MA: Harvard University Press, 2014).

15 Clinton Rossiter, ed., *The Federalist Papers* (New York: New American Library, 1961).

16 Madison, for example, wrote in Federalist No. 49 that "[t]he passions ought to be controlled and regulated by the government." Ibid., p. 317.

17 Ibid., p. 322.

18 Ibid., p. 324.

19 Ibid., pp. 324–25.

20 John C. Calhoun, "A Positive Good," *Speech in the U.S. Senate* (1837), http://www.stolaf.edu/people/fitz/COURSES/calhoun.html.

21 In order to secure Southern votes for the Constitution, the framers agreed to a provision that gave the states twenty years to eliminate the slave trade. Madison argued at the Constitutional Convention that even those twenty years were "dishonorable." In Federalist No. 42, he wrote that it would be a "great gain" that a "period of twenty years may terminate for ever within these States," a practice he called "unnatural" and "the barbarism of modern policy." Matthew Spalding, ed., *The Heritage Guide to the Constitution*, 2nd ed. (Washington, DC: Regnery Publishing, 2014), p. 196; see also Rossiter, *The Federalist Papers*, p. 266.

22 See, e.g., M. Stanton Evans, *The Theme Is Freedom: Religion, Politics, and the American Tradition* (Washington, DC: Regnery Publishing, 1996).

23 Wilson, who argued for his administration's policy of segregation in federal departments, once said: "Segregation is not humiliating, but a

benefit, and ought to be so regarded by you gentlemen." William Loren Katz, *Eyewitness: The Negro in American History* (New York: Pitman Publishing Corp., 1967), pp. 389–90. Croly wrote, "The Southern slave owners . . . were right, moreover, in believing the negroes were a race possessed of moral and intellectual qualities inferior to those of the white men." Herbert David Croly, *The Promise of American Life* (Los Angeles: Library of Alexandria, 2012), ch. 4, section II, paragraph 2. Kindle edition.

24 "Birth control itself, often denounced as a violation of natural law, is nothing more or less than the facilitation of the process of weeding out the unfit, of preventing the birth of defectives or of those who will become defectives." Margaret Sanger, *Woman and the New Race* (New York: Brentano, 1920), chap. 18, republished by Bartleby at http://www.bartleby.com/1013/18.html.

25 Melvin I. Urofsky and Paul Finkelman, "Abrams v. United States (1919)," in *Documents of American Constitutional and Legal History*, 3rd ed. (New York: Oxford University Press, 2008), pp. 666–67.

26 George Novack, "American Intellectuals and the Crisis," *New International*, February 1936, pp. 23–27, and June 1936, pp. 83–86.

27 Marisa Schultz, "Obama Says N-Word in Racism Discussion," *New York Post*, June 22, 2015.

28 Allen J. Matusow, *The Unraveling of America: A History of Liberalism in the 1960s* (Athens, GA: University of Georgia Press, 2009), p. 310.

29 Ibid., p. 312.

30 Ibid., p. 313.

31 See, e.g., Gerald Sorin, *Irving Howe: A Life of Passionate Dissent* (New York: New York University Press, 2005), p. 218.

32 Brian Doherty, *Radicals for Capitalism: A Freewheeling History of the Modern American Libertarian Movement* (New York: PublicAffairs, 2009), location 480. Kindle edition.

33 Ibid., location 484.

34 Ibid., location 878–1511; see also Steve J. Shone, *American Anarchism* (Chicago: Haymarket Books, 2014).

35 Doherty, *Radicals for Capitalism*, locations 1310, 4348, 4753.

36 Albert Jay Nock, *The Myth of a Guilty Nation* (Auburn, AL: Ludwig von Mises Institute, 2011); see also Doherty, *Radicals for Capitalism*, locations 1158, 1195, 1201.

37 Leslie J. Vaughan, *Randolph Bourne and the Politics of Cultural Radicalism* (Lawrence, KS: University Press of Kansas, 1997), p. 1.

38  He formed the Bastiat Circle with fellow libertarians George Reisman, Robert Hessen, Ralph Raico, and others. See Doherty, *Radicals for Capitalism,* locations 747, 4628.

39  Ibid., locations 2734–2753, 2850, 4703–720.

40  Ibid., locations 6444–501.

41  Ibid., location 6501.

42  Ibid., location 7189.

43  Ibid., location 5423.

44  John Rawls, *A Theory of Justice* (Oxford: Clarendon Press, 1971).

45  The White House, Office of the Press Secretary, "Remarks by the President at Presentation of the National Medal of the Arts and the National Humanities Medal," September 29, 1999, http://clinton3.nara .gov/WH/New/html/19990929.html.

46  Alan Ryan, *The Making of Modern Liberalism* (Princeton, NJ: Princeton University Press, 2012), p. 510. Kindle edition; see also Rawls, *A Theory of Justice*, pp. 244ff.

47  Ryan, *The Making of Modern Liberalism,* p. 512.

48  Ibid., p. 513.

## CHAPTER TWO

1  For additional information on the origins of postmodernism, see Quentin Skinner, ed., *The Return of Grand Theory in the Human Sciences* (New York: Cambridge University Press, 1985); and Stanley Fish, *Doing What Comes Naturally: Change, Rhetoric, and the Practice of Theory in Literary and Legal Studies* (Durham, NC: Duke University Press, 1989).

2  Alan Sokal and Jean Bricmont, *Fashionable Nonsense: Postmodern Intellectuals' Abuse of Science* (New York: Picador USA, 1998), location 124. Kindle edition.

3  Ibid., "Epilogue," location 2747.

4  For example, Jason Read of the University of Southern Maine writes in a book review of Simon Choat's *Marx Through Post-Structuralism: Lyotard, Derrida, Foucault, Deleuze* that "Foucault's texts are overtly critical of Marx, relegating him to the nineteenth century." Jason Read, review of *Marx Through Post-Structuralism: Lyotard, Derrida, Foucault, Deleuze* by Simon Choat, *Notre Dame Philosophical Reviews: An Electronic Journal,* November 5, 2010, http://ndpr.nd.edu/news/24534-marx-through-post -structuralism-lyotard-derrida-foucault-deleuze/. See also Mark G. E. Kelly, "Foucault Against Marxism: Althusser Beyond Althusser," in *(Mis)readings of Marx in Continental Philosophy,* ed. Jernej Habjan and

Jessica Whyte (Basingstoke, UK: Palgrave Macmillan, 2014). According to Kelly, Foucault sees "Marxism as a tendency that closed down Marx's critical opening [in the history of thought] in favour of 'a reign of terror'" and "Foucault's dictum that Marx, qua coherent, unitary thought, 'does not exist,'" p. 93.

5 See Lois Tyson, *Critical Theory Today: A User-Friendly Guide* (New York: Routledge, 2006); Keith Windschuttle, *The Killing of History: How Literary Critics and Social Theorists Are Murdering Our Past* (New York: Encounter Books, 2000); John M. Ellis, *Literature Lost: Social Agendas and the Corruption of the Humanities* (New Haven, CT: Yale University Press, 1997); Daniel A. Farber and Suzanna Sherry, *Beyond All Reason: The Radical Assault on Truth in American Law* (New York: Oxford University Press, 1997); and James Lindgren, "Measuring Diversity: Law Faculties in 1997 and 2013," *Northwestern Law & Econ Research Paper* No. 15-07, March 20, 2015, http://dx.doi.org/10.2139/ssrn.2581675.

6 Sandhya Somashekhar, "How Autistic Adults Banded Together to Start a Movement," *Washington Post*, July 20, 2015.

7 Tyson, *Critical Theory Today*, pp. 378–80.

8 Latin term denoting Catholic Church teachings that have been definitively decided on as a matter of faith by the Magisterium in an infallible manner.

9 Jean-François Lyotard, *The Postmodern Condition: A Report on Knowledge* (Paris: Minuit, 1979). For more on grand narratives and postmodernists, see Rainer Friedrich, "The Enlightenment Gone Mad (I): The Dismal Discourse of Postmodernism's Grand Narratives," *Arion, a Journal of Humanities and the Classics*, vol. 19, no. 3 (2012), pp. 31–78.

10 Jacques Derrida, *Of Spirit: Heidegger and the Question*, trans. Geoffrey Bennington and Rachel Bowlby (Chicago: University of Chicago Press, 1989). See also Friedrich, "The Enlightenment Gone Mad"; and Leonard Lawlor, "Jacques Derrida," in *The Stanford Encyclopedia of Philosophy*, ed. Edward N. Zalta (Stanford, CA: Metaphysics Research Lab, Spring 2014), http://plato.stanford.edu/archives/spr2014/entries/derrida/.

11 See, e.g., William D. Gairdner, *The Book of Absolutes: A Critique of Relativism and a Defence of Universals* (Montreal: McGill-Queen's University Press, 2008), pp. 250–56.

12 A microaggression is an assertion that some remark, even if innocently made, is actually an insult intentionally made. See Chapter Six for more on this topic.

13 Michel Foucault, *The Order of Things: An Archaeology of the Human Sciences*

(New York: Pantheon Books, 1970); and *The Archaeology of Knowledge and the Discourse on Language*, trans. A. M. Sheridan Smith (New York: Pantheon Books, 1972).

14 Max Ehrenfreund, "The FBI Director Just Quoted from Avenue Q's 'Everyone's a Little Bit Racist.' That's Huge," *Washington Post*, February 12, 2015.

15 *Huffington Post,* "Jon Stewart LIVE on Fox News, Tells Host 'You're Insane' (VIDEO)," updated August 19, 2011, http://www.huffington post.com/2011/06/19/jon-stewart-fox-news-sunday-video_n_879964 .html.

16 Will Dana, "A Note to Our Readers," *Rolling Stone*, December 5, 2014, p. 1, http://www.rollingstone.com/culture/news/a-note-to-our-readers -20141205; and T. Rees Shapiro, "Charlottesville Police Find No Evidence in U-Va. Sexual Assault Case," *Washington Post*, March 23, 2015.

17 Asked what is the difference between a Democrat like Hillary Clinton and a socialist like Bernie Sanders, Wasserman Schultz replied, "The more important question is what is the difference between being a Democrat and being a Republican." See "Chris Matthews vs. Debbie Wasserman Schultz: 'What's the Difference Between a Democrat and a Socialist?,' " *RealClearPolitics* video, July 30, 2015, http://www .realclearpolitics.com/video/2015/07/30/chris_matthews_to_debbie _wasserman_schultz_whats_the_difference_between_a_democrat_and _a_socialist.html.

18 For more on this topic, see Kim R. Holmes, *Rebound: Getting America Back to Great* (Lanham, MD: Rowman & Littlefield, 2013), pp. 84–94.

19 For more on how Marx, Nietzsche, Heidegger, and others influenced these philosophers, see Stephen R. C. Hicks, *Explaining Postmodernism: Skepticism and Socialism From Rousseau to Foucault* (Tempe, AZ: Scholargy Publishing, 2004), pp. 21–22, http://www.stephenhicks.org/wp -content/uploads/2009/10/hicks-ep-full.pdf.

20 David G. Savage and Timothy M. Phelps, "Supreme Court Ruling: 'Equal Dignity in the Eyes of the Law,' " *Seattle Times*, June 26, 2015.

21 John Stuart Mill, *On Liberty*, ed. Alburey Castell (Northbrook, IL: AHM Publishing Corporation, 1947), p. 19.

22 Ibid.

23 See Leo Strauss, "Relativism," in *Relativism and the Study of Man*, ed. Helmut Schoeck and James W. Wiggins (Princeton, NJ: Van Nostrand, 1961), pp. 135–57.

24 See Leo Strauss and Joseph Cropsey, *The History of Political Philosophy* (Chicago: University of Chicago Press, 2012), p. 889.

25 Leo Strauss, "Political Philosophy and the Crisis of Our Time," in *The Post-Behavioral Era,* ed. George Graham and George Carey (New York: David McKay, 1972), pp. 222–23.

26 Leo Strauss, *On Tyranny* (New York: Free Press, 1991), pp. 22–23.

27 Farber and Sherry, *Beyond All Reason*, p. 17.

28 Ibid., p. 23.

29 See Joe Cohn, "Colleges Are Not the Place to Try Rape Cases," *Washington Post*, January 16, 2015, p. A21.

30 Farber and Sherry, *Beyond All Reason,* p. 43.

31 American Civil Liberties Union, "ACLU Sues Ferguson-Florissant School District, Charging Electoral System Undermines African-American Vote," press release, December 18, 2014, https://www.aclu.org/racial-justice-voting-rights/missouri-naacp-v-ferguson-florissant-school-district.

32 On racial contract quotas at the Department of Defense, which were struck down by an appeals court, see Washington Legal Foundation, "Appeals Court Ruling Against Racial Quotas in Pentagon Contracts Apparently Will Stand; Administration Reportedly Won't Appeal to Supreme Court," press release, February 11, 2009, http://www.pacificlegal.org/page.aspx?pid=3959.

33 Joseph Curl, "Obama Set to Force Affordable Housing into Affluent Communities," *Washington Times,* June 11, 2015.

34 S. V. Dáte, "O'Malley, Sanders Shouted Down at Netroots by 'Black Lives Matter' Protest," *National Journal,* July 18, 2015.

35 Farber and Sherry, *Beyond All Reason,* pp. 4–5.

36 Ibid., p. 11.

## CHAPTER THREE

1 Fareed Zakaria, "The Rise of Illiberal Democracy," *Foreign Affairs,* November/December 1997.

2 Richard Hofstadter, "The Paranoid Style in American Politics," *Harper's Magazine*, November 1964.

3 Richard J. Ellis, *The Dark Side of the Left: Illiberal Egalitarianism in America* (Lawrence, KS: University Press of Kansas, 1998), p. 11.

4 Fritz Richard Stern, *The Failure of Illiberalism: Essays on the Political Culture of Modern Germany* (New York: Columbia University Press, 1992), p. xxix.

5 Ibid.

6 See, e.g., Henry A. Rhodes, "Nativist and Racist Movements in the U.S. and Their Aftermath," in *Racism and Nativism in American Political Culture,* Yale-New Haven Teachers' Institute Curriculum Unit 94.04.05, vol. 4, chap. 5 (1994), http://www.yale.edu/ynhti/curriculum/units /1994/4/94.04.05.x.html.

7 Ellis, *The Dark Side of the Left,* p. 20.

8 Ibid., p. 31, n. 56, citing William Lloyd Garrison, ed., *Liberator,* vol. 33, no. 11 (March 13, 1863), p. 4.

9 Ibid., p. 67.

10 Robert Nozick, *Anarchy, State, and Utopia* (New York: Basic Books, 2013). Kindle edition.

11 Randolph Silliman Bourne, *The Radical Will: Selected Writings, 1911–1918,* ed. Olaf Hansen (Berkeley, CA: University of California Press, 1992), p. 354; and Ellis, *The Dark Side of the Left,* p. 93.

12 For example, in a 2015 address to the U.S. Conference of Mayors, Clinton said, "For a lot of well-meaning, open-minded white people, the sight of a young black man in a hoodie still evokes a twinge of fear. And . . . too rarely do [news reports about poverty and crime and discrimination] prompt us to question our own assumptions and privilege." Steve Benen, "Clinton: 'Our Problem Is Not All Kooks and Klansmen,'" MSNBC News, June 22, 2015, http://www.msnbc .com/rachel-maddow-show/clinton-our-problem-not-all-kooks-and -klansman#break.

13 See, e.g., Elinor Burkett, "What Makes a Woman?," *New York Times,* June 6, 2015.

14 Yana Wang, "Feminist Germaine Greer Still Pummelled for 'Misogynistic Views Toward Transwomen,'" *Washington Post,* November 2, 2015.

15 Blake Neff, "Missou Protesters Now Segregating Their Members by Race," *Daily Caller,* November 11, 2015, http://dailycaller.com /2015/11/11/mizzou-protesters-now-segregating-their-members-by -race/.

16 Herbert David Croly, *The Promise of American Life* (Los Angeles: Library of Alexandria, 2012).

17 John Dewey, *Democracy and Education: An Introduction to the Philosophy of Education* (New York: The Macmillan Company, 1916), p. 5.

18 Indeed, as Croly wrote, "The destruction or the weakening of nationalities for the ostensible benefit of an international socialism would in truth gravely imperil the bond upon which actual human association is

based. The peoples who have inherited any share in Christian civilization are effectively united chiefly by national habits, traditions, and purposes; and perhaps the most effective way of bringing about an irretrievable division of purpose among them would be the adoption by the class of wage earners of the programme of international socialism. It is not too much to say that no permanent good can, under existing conditions, come to the individual and society except through the preservation and the development of the existing system of nationalized states." Croly, *Promise of American Life*, p. 211.

19  See Leslie J. Vaughan, *Randolph Bourne and the Politics of Cultural Radicalism* (Lawrence, KS: University Press of Kansas, 1997).

20  Croly, for example, criticized Marx's "false" predictions in *Progressive Democracy* (New York: Macmillan Company, 1915), p. 178. On his admiration of Hamilton, see Croly, *Promise of American Life*, pp. 29, 44–45.

21  Edmund Fawcett, *Liberalism: The Life of an Idea* (Princeton, NJ: Princeton University Press, 2014), pp. 118–19. Kindle edition.

22  See, e.g., ibid., p. 120; and Steven Lukes, *Individualism* (Colchester: European Consortium for Political Research Press, 1973), p. 105.

23  Fawcett, *Liberalism*; see also Alan Ryan, *The Making of Modern Liberalism* (Princeton, NJ: Princeton University Press, 2012), p. 512. Kindle edition.

24  See, e.g., Do-Hyeong Myeong, "Eisgruber, BJL Come to Compromise After Two Days of Protests," *Daily Princetonian,* November 19, 2015, http://dailyprincetonian.com/news/2015/11/eisgruber-bjl-come-to -compromise-after-two-days-of-protests/?wpmm=1&wpisrc=nl_daily 202; and Eric Owens, "Movement to Rename Schools Honoring Confederate Leader Widens to Reach Progressive Woodrow Wilson," *Daily Caller,* July 4, 2015, http://dailycaller.com/2015/07/04/move ment-to-rename-schools-honoring-confederate-leaders-finally-widens -to-reach-progressive-woodrow-wilson/.

25  Tony Lee, "White House Defends Ignoring Ferguson Police Officers While Giving Al Sharpton Seat at Table," *Breitbart News,* December 2, 2014, http://www.breitbart.com/big-government/2014/12/02/white -house-defends-not-inviting-ferguson-police-officers-while-giving-al -sharpton-seat-at-table/.

26  Dana Milbank, "'Liberal:' So Hot Right Now," *Washington Post*, June 21, 2015, p. A17.

27  See David A. Reidy, "John Rawls," *IVR Encyclopedia,* March 10, 2008, pp. 30–31, http://ssrn.com/abstract=1069953; David Gauthier, *Morals*

*By Agreement* (Oxford: Oxford University Press, 1986); and Ann Cudd, "Contractarianism," in *The Stanford Encyclopedia of Philosophy,* ed. Edward N. Zalta (Stanford, CA: Metaphysics Research Lab, Winter 2013), http://plato.stanford.edu/entries/contractarianism/.

28  Reidy, "John Rawls," p. 31; see also Ronald Dworkin, *Taking Rights Seriously* (Cambridge, MA: Harvard University Press, 1977), p. 156; and Cudd, "Contractarianism" in Zalta, *Stanford Encyclopedia of Philosophy.* For more on Dworkin's theory of justice, see, e.g., Dragica Vujadinovic, "Ronald Dworkin–Theory of Justice," *European Scientific Journal,* 8, no. 2 (February 2012).

29  Reidy, "John Rawls," p. 32; see also Michael Walzer, *Spheres of Justice: A Defense of Pluralism and Equality* (New York: Basic Books, 1983), p. 79; and Daniel Bell, "Communitarianism," in Zalta, *The Stanford Encyclopedia of Philosophy,* Fall 2013, http://plato.stanford.edu/entries /communitarianism/.

30  Reidy, "John Rawls"; see also Susan M. Okin, *Justice, Gender, and the Family* (New York: Basic Books, 1989), p. 89; and Martha C. Nussbaum, "The Future of Feminist Liberalism," *Proceedings and Addresses of the American Philosophical Association* (November 2000), p. 60, http://www .jstor.org/stable/3219683.

31  Reidy, "John Rawls"; see also, e.g., Richard Arneson, "Rawls, Responsibility, and Distributive Justice," Faculty Paper, University of California, San Diego, April 1997, accessed August 18, 2015, http:// philosophyfaculty.ucsd.edu/faculty/rarneson/rawlsresponsibilityand distributivejustice.pdf; Will Kymlicka, *Contemporary Political Philosophy: An Introduction* (Oxford: Clarendon Press, 1990); Tan Kok-Chor, *Toleration, Diversity, and Global Justice* (University Park, PA: Pennsylvania State University Press, 2000); and Amartya Sen, *The Idea of Justice* (Cambridge, MA: Belknap Press, 2009).

32  Reidy, "John Rawls"; see also Will Kymlicka, *Multicultural Citizenship: A Liberal Theory of Minority Rights* (Oxford: Oxford University Press, 1995), pp. 5, 128. Kymlicka writes, e.g., "when Rawls emphasizes the 'fact of pluralism'—particularly religious pluralism—he equates the political community with a single 'complete culture,' and with a single 'people' who belong to the same 'society and culture' . . . There is no discussion by contemporary liberal theorists of the differences between nation-states and polyethnic or multination states, or of the arguments for modifying liberal principles in countries which are a 'federation of peoples.' This shows, I think, that it is a mistake to subsume the issue of minority rights."

33 See, e.g., Richard Rorty, *Philosophy and the Mirror of Nature* (Princeton, NJ: Princeton University Press, 1979) and *Contingency, Irony, and Solidarity* (Cambridge: Cambridge University Press, 1989).

34 Fawcett, *Liberalism,* p. 333.

35 Ibid., p. 120.

36 Ibid.

37 Ibid., p. 122. See also Lukes, *Individualism.*

38 Fawcett, *Liberalism,* p. 122. See also Immanuel Kant, *Groundwork of the Metaphysics of Morals* (Radford, VA: Wilder Publications, 2008), p. 46.

39 Fawcett, *Liberalism,* p. 280.

40 See, e.g., Arthur A. Ekirch, Jr., *The Decline of American Liberalism* (Oakland, CA: Independent Institute, 2009).

## CHAPTER FOUR

1 Amos N. Guiora, *Tolerating Intolerance: The Price of Protecting Extremism* (New York: Oxford University Press, 2014).

2 Martha C. Nussbaum, *The New Religious Intolerance: Overcoming the Politics of Fear in an Anxious Age* (Cambridge, MA: Belknap Press, 2013). See also Carl W. Ernst, ed., *Islamophobia in America: The Anatomy of Intolerance* (New York: Palgrave Macmillan Press, 2013).

3 D. A. Carson, *The Intolerance of Tolerance* (Grand Rapids, MI: Wm. B. Eerdmans Publishing Company, 2013), pp. 40, 42.

4 Rosalie907, "It's Treason," *Daily Kos* (blog), October 15, 2013, http://www.dailykos.com/story/2013/10/16/1247681/-It-s-treason#.

5 Tony Lee, "Reid: 'Radical' 'Tea Party Anarchists' Holding Gov't 'Hostage,'" *Breitbart.com*, September 23, 2013, http://www.breitbart.com/big-government/2013/09/23/reid-radical-tea-party-anarchists-holding-gov-t-hostage/; Office of U.S. Senator Harry Reid, "Reid Remarks Prior to a Vote to Avert a Government Shutdown," press release, September 27, 2013, http://www.reid.senate.gov/press_releases/reid-remarks-prior-to-a-vote-to-avert-a-government-shutdown.

6 Dan Farber, "Obama Explains His Remark about Punishing His 'Enemies,'" CBS News, November 1, 2010, http://www.cbsnews.com/news/obama-explains-his-remark-about-punishing-enemies/.

7 Kristi Keck, "GOP: Power Players or 'Hostage Takers'?" CNN, December 9, 2010, http://www.cnn.com/2010/POLITICS/12/09/republican.strategy.taxes/.

8 Alexander Mooney, "Rep. Grayson Calls Cheney a Vampire," CNN, October 24, 2009, http://politicalticker.blogs.cnn.com/2009/10/24/rep-grayson-calls-cheney-a-vampire/.

9 Brian Montopoli, "Alan Grayson 'Die Quickly' Comment Prompts Uproar," CBS News, September 30, 2009, http://www.cbsnews.com /news/alan-grayson-die-quickly-comment-prompts-uproar/.

10 John Nolte, "Rainbow of Hate: Catholic Priest Reports Being Spit On at Gay Marriage Parade," Breitbart.com, June 29, 2015, http://www .breitbart.com/big-government/2015/06/29/rainbow-of-hate-catholic -priest-reports-being-spit-on-at-gay-marriage-parade/.

11 Frances Kai-Hwa Wang, "George Takei Apologizes for Calling Clarence Thomas 'Clown in Blackface,'" NBC News, July 7, 2015, http://www .nbcnews.com/news/asian-america/george-takei-apologizes-calling -thomas-clown-blackface-n387886.

12 Amanda Mikelberg, "Jerry Seinfeld Says Political Correctness Is Hurting Comedy," CBS News, June 8, 2015, http://www.cbsnews.com/news /jerry-seinfeld-says-political-correctness-is-hurting-comedy/.

13 Molly Ball, "The Agony of Frank Luntz," Atlantic, January 6, 2014.

14 Madeleine Morgenstern, "Bill Maher Defends Paula Deen After Firing: 'Do We Always Have to Make People Go Away?,'" Blaze.com, June 22, 2013, http://www.theblaze.com/stories/2013/06/22/bill-maher-defends -paula-deen-after-firing-do-we-always-have-to-make-people-go-away/.

15 See, e.g., George Will, "Donald Trump Is a Counterfeit Conservative," Washington Post, August 12, 2015.

16 For example, Julie Pace and Jill Colvin, "Trump Rivals Decry His Call for Registering US Muslims," Associated Press, November 20, 2015, http://news.yahoo.com/trump-carson-ratchet-heated-rhetoric-muslims -145349296--election.html#.

17 Dan Balz, "All Politics Are Local? Think Again," Washington Post, April 18, 2015.

18 Meredith Blake, "Jon Stewart Wonders 'What Is Wrong' With Same-Sex Marriage Opponents," Los Angeles Times, June 30, 2015.

19 Harry Potter author J. K. Rowling's description of Voldemort in Jeff Jensen, "Fire Storm," Entertainment Weekly, September 7, 2000, http:// www.accio-quote.org/articles/2000/0900-ew-jensen.htm.

20 Evelyn Beatrice Hall, The Friends of Voltaire (London: Smith, Elder & Co., 1906), p. 199.

21 Ryan J. Reilly, "Justice Alito: 'The Constitution Says Nothing About a Right to Same-Sex Marriage,'" Huffington Post, June 26, 2015, http:// www.huffingtonpost.com/2015/06/26/alito-dissent-gay-marriage_n _7671560.html.

22 Joseph Epstein, "The Unassailable Virtue of Victims," Weekly Standard, May 18, 2015, p. 25.

23  Richard Hofstadter, "The Paranoid Style in American Politics," *Harper's Magazine*, November 1964, pp. 77–86.

24  Tami Luhby, "Elizabeth Warren Is Worth Millions," CNN Money, January 8, 2015, http://money.cnn.com/2015/01/08/news/economy /elizabeth-warren-wealth/index.html.

25  For example, U.S. companies that move overseas, Warren asserted, "renounce their American citizenship and turn their backs on this country simply to boost their profits." See Sen. Elizabeth Warren, "Enough Is Enough: The President's Latest Wall Street Nominee," *Huffington Post*, November 19, 2014, http://www.huffingtonpost.com /elizabeth-warren/presidents-wall-street-nominee_b_6188324.html.

26  Saul D. Alinsky, *Rules for Radicals* (New York: Random House, 1971).

27  Hofstadter, "The Paranoid Style," p. 85.

28  Jake Tapper, "VP Biden Says Republicans Are 'Going to Put Y'all Back in Chains,'" ABC News, August 14, 2012, http://abcnews.go.com /blogs/politics/2012/08/vp-biden-says-republicans-are-going-to-put -yall-back-in-chains/.

29  Hofstadter, "The Paranoid Style," pp. 85.

30  Ibid., pp. 84–85.

31  See, e.g., Tom Nichols, "The New Totalitarians Are Here," *TheFederalist.com*, July 6, 2015, http://thefederalist.com/2015/07/06/the -new-totalitarians-are-here/. See also Jonah Goldberg, *Liberal Fascism: The Secret History of the American Left, From Mussolini to the Politics of Meaning* (New York: Doubleday, 2007).

32  See, e.g., Valerie Tarico, "Right-Wing Christianity Teaches Bigotry: The Ugly Roots of Indiana's New Anti-Gay Law," *Salon.com*, April 4, 2015, http://www.salon.com/2015/04/04/right_wing_christianity _teaches_bigotry_the_ugly_roots_of_indianas_new_anti_gay_law _partner/.

33  Frank Bruni, "Bigotry, the Bible, and the Lessons of Indiana," *New York Times*, April 3, 2015.

34  Kerry Pickett, "Hillary on Abortion: 'Deep-Seated Cultural Codes, Religious Beliefs and Structural Biases Have to Be Changed,'" *Daily Caller*, April 23, 2015, http://dailycaller.com/2015/04/23/hillary-on -abortion-deep-seated-cultural-codes-religious-beliefs-and-structural -biases-have-to-be-changed/.

35  See Valerie Richardson, "Video Puts Muslim Bakeries, Florists in Gay Rights Spotlight," *Washington Times*, April 5, 2015; Kelsey Harkness, "Bakers Facing $135K Fine Over Wedding Cake for Same-Sex Couple Speak Out," *Daily Signal*, April 27, 2015, http://

dailysignal.com/2015/04/27/exclusive-bakers-facing-135k-fine-over-wedding-cake-for-same-sex-couple-speak-out/; and Zack Ford, "This Baker Refused to Bake an Anti-Gay Cake. Here's Why That's Not Discrimination," *Think Progress,* April 6, 2015, http://thinkprogress.org/lgbt/2015/04/06/3643178/colorado-bakery-wins-against/.

36  Indeed, on September 2, 2015, a court clerk in Kentucky was jailed for not issuing a marriage license to a gay couple. See Alan Blinder and Tamar Lewin, "Clerk in Kentucky Chooses Jail over Deal on Same-Sex Marriage," *New York Times,* September 3, 2015.

37  Pickett, "Hillary on Abortion."

38  Michael W. Chapman, "Huckabee: 'We Are Moving Rapidly Toward the Criminalization of Christianity,'" CNS News, April 28, 2015, http://www.cnsnews.com/blog/michael-w-chapman/huckabee-we-are-moving-rapidly-toward-criminalization-christianity.

39  This is already happening in the controversies over crosses and Christmas crèches in public spaces. See e.g., *Lynch v. Donnelly,* 465 U.S. 668 (1984).

40  Steve Doughty, "Millionaire Gay Fathers to Sue the Church of England for Not Allowing Them to Get Married in the Church," *Daily Mail,* August 2, 2013.

41  Much of this section appeared in a *Washington Times* opinion column by the author on May 5, 2014, used here with permission from *The Washington Times.*

42  Andy Campbell, "6-Year-Old Suspended for Pointing Fingers in the Shape of a Gun," *Huffington Post,* March 6, 2015, http://www.huffingtonpost.com/2015/03/06/6-year-old-fingers-shape-of-gun-suspended_n_6813864.html.

43  "Boy, 6, Suspended for Playing with Imaginary Bow and Arrow," *ABC13.com,* November 5, 2015, http://abc13.com/education/boy-6-suspended-over-imaginary-bow-and-arrow/1069386/.

44  Alexandra Petri, "Pop-Tart 'Gun' Suspension: Seriously, Folks?," *Washington Post,* March 5, 2013.

45  WBTW News, "NC High School Students Charged in Water Balloon Prank, Parents Outraged," video, posted May 17, 2013, http://wbtw.com/2013/05/18/nc-high-school-students-charged-in-water-balloon-prank-parents-outraged/.

46  Alexandra Klausner, "Sober Student, 17, Is Suspended from High School and Stripped of Volleyball Captaincy Because She Drove Her Drunk Friend Home from a Party," *Daily Mail,* October 14, 2013.

47  Donna St. George, "Md. Officials: Letting 'Free Range' Kids Walk or Play Alone Is Not Neglect," *Washington Post,* June 11, 2015.

48  Matt Schiavenza, "The *Rolling Stone* Retraction," *Atlantic,* April 5, 2015.

49  Regarding allegations against the Duke lacrosse team, see Evie Salomon, "60 Minutes Investigates: The Duke Rape Case," *60 Minutes: Overtime,* April 12 2015, http://www.cbsnews.com/news/60-minutes-investigates -the-duke-rape-case/; and regarding the Kamilah Willingham/Brandon Winston case, see Emily Yoffe, "How *The Hunting Ground* Blurs the Truth," *Slate.com,* June 1 2015, http://www.slate.com/articles/news _and_politics/doublex/2015/06/the_hunting_ground_a_closer_look _at_the_influential_documentary_reveals.html.

50  See, e.g., Advancement Project, Youth United for Change, & the Education Law Center, "Introduction," *Zero Tolerance in Philadelphia,* January 2011, p. 2, http://thenotebook.org/sites/default/files/YUC -report.pdf.

51  "Sean Penn: Ted Cruz Is Mentally Ill and Should Be Committed (CNN Interview with Piers Morgan)," transcript posted by Ian Schwartz at *RealClearPolitics.com,* October 29, 2013, accessed August 6, 2015, http://www.realclearpolitics.com/video/2013/10/29/sean_penn_ted _cruz_has_mental_health_problems_and_should_be_committed.html.

52  Sergio Bichao, "Catholic Teacher Who Was Suspended After Anti-Gay Comment Firestorm Returns to Job," *MyCentralJersey.com,* April 13, 2015, at http://www.mycentraljersey.com/story/news/local/somerset -county/2015/04/10/patricia-jannuzzi-gets-job-back-immaculata-high -school/25587809/.

53  Cavan Sieczkowski, "Azealia Banks Talks 'Fat White Americans,' Kanye West and Race in Playboy Interview," *Huffington Post,* March 17, 2015, http://www.huffingtonpost.com/2015/03/17/azealia-banks-playboy_n _6885026.html.

54  Doug Heye, "The Left's Limited Outrage at Hitler Comparisons," *U.S. News & World Report,* October 6, 2011, http://www.usnews.com /opinion/blogs/doug-heye/2011/10/06/celebs-should-avoid-the-hitler -president-comparison-be-it-bush-or-obama.

55  Janeane Garofalo, "Should California Delay Recall Vote?" CNN *Crossfire,* August 18, 2003, accessed August 6, 2015, http://www.cnn .com/TRANSCRIPTS/0308/18/cf.00.html.

56  John Fund, "Totalitarian Troubadour," *National Review,* January 29, 2014.

57  David Brooks, *Bobos in Paradise: The New Upper Class and How They Got There* (New York: Simon & Schuster, 2000), pp. 10–11.

58  Charles A. Murray, *Coming Apart: The State of White America, 1960–2010* (New York: Crown Forum, 2012), p. 16.

59  Robert B. Reich, *The Work of Nations: Preparing Ourselves for 21st-Century Capitalism* (New York: Alfred A. Knopf, 1991), p. 219.

60  Murray, *Coming Apart*, pp. 18–20.

61  According to Murray, "The centile score is based on the sum of standardized scores for zip code's percentage of adults with college education and its median family income, weighted by population." Ibid., pp. 78, 88, 315.

62  Jerry Hirsch, "Elon Musk's Growing Empire Is Fueled by $4.9 Billion in Government Subsidies," *Los Angeles Times*, May 30, 2015.

63  Jacob Bogage, "Marking Cultural Shift, Corporations Express Support for Landmark Decision, *Washington Post,* June 27, 2015, p. A11.

64  PR Newswire, "Global Food Companies Unite on Climate Action," news release, October 1, 2015, http://www.prnewswire.com/news-releases/global-food-companies-unite-on-climate-action-300152700.html.

65  See, e.g., Jesse Solomon, "Wall Street Donors Dump Democrats," CNN Money, November 3, 2014, http://money.cnn.com/2014/11/03/investing/election-donations-wall-street-republicans/.

66  Paul Blumenthal and Aaron Bycoffe, "Here Are the Top Super PAC Mega-Donors in 2014 Elections," *Huffington Post*, October 31, 2014, http://www.huffingtonpost.com/2014/10/31/super-pac-donors-2014_n_6084988.html.

67  For campaign contribution totals in 2008 and 2012, see Federal Election Commission, annual report for Presidential Campaign Finance, accessed August 6, 2015, http://fec.gov/disclosurep/pnational.do; see also "2012 Presidential Campaign Finance Explorer," *Washington Post*, December 7, 2012, http://www.washingtonpost.com/wp-srv/special/politics/campaign-finance/.

68  Richard Larsen, "This Is Why We Should Fear George Soros, Not the Koch Brothers," *Western Journalism*, April 10, 2014, http://www.westernjournalism.com/koch-brothers-george-soros-fear/.

69  *Politico.com*, "2014 House Election Results," December 17, 2014, accessed August 6, 2015, http://www.politico.com/2014-election/results/map/house/#.VW9r-1_D_cs.

70  Jeffery M. Jones, "Liberal Self-Identification Edges Up to New High in 2013," *Gallup.com,* January 10, 2014, http://www.gallup.com/poll/166787/liberal-self-identification-edges-new-high-2013.aspx.

71  Ibid.

72  Ibid.

73  John Hinderaker, "Defunding the Left, One Union at a Time,"

*Powerline.com,* September 14, 2013, http://www.powerlineblog.com /archives/2013/09/defunding-the-left-one-union-at-a-time.php.

74 "Top Organization Contributors," *OpenSecrets.com,* March 9, 2015, accessed August 6, 2015, https://www.opensecrets.org/orgs/list.php.

75 Susan Berry, "GAO Confirms: Planned Parenthood and Other Groups Use Taxpayer Funds to Promote Abortions," *Breitbart.com,* March 25, 2015, http://www.breitbart.com/big-government/2015/03/25/gao -confirms-planned-parenthood-and-other-groups-use-taxpayer-funds -to-promote-abortions/.

76 Bruce Walker, "Republicans Look at Defunding the Left," *New American,* April 3, 2011, http://www.thenewamerican.com/usnews /congress/item/2334-republicans-look-at-defunding-the-left.

77 Carl Hulse, "House Votes to Ban Federal Funds for ACORN," *New York Times,* September 17, 2009; see also Sharon Theimer and Pete Yost, "Did ACORN Get Too Big for Its Own Good?" NBC News, September 20, 2009, http://www.nbcnews.com/id/32925682/ns /politics-more_politics/#.VXC021_D_ct.

78 U.S. House of Representatives Committee on Oversight and Government Reform, "Follow the Money: ACORN, SEIU, and their Political Allies," *Staff Report,* 111th Cong., 2nd Sess., February 18, 2010, http://oversight.house.gov/wp-content/uploads/2012/01/20100218 followthemoneyacornseiuandtheirpoliticalallies.pdf.

79 Michael B. Farrell, "ACORN Scandal, How Much Federal Funding Does it Get?" *Christian Science Monitor,* September 19, 2009, http:// www.csmonitor.com/USA/2009/0919/p02s13-usgn.html; see also California Attorney General's Office, "Report of the Attorney General on the Activities of ACORN in California," April 1, 2010, http://ag.ca .gov/cms_attachments/press/pdfs/n1888_acorn_report.pdf.

80 Pew Research Center, "How Journalists See Journalists in 2004," *State of the News Media,* March 15, 2004.

81 Sahil Kapur, "'Nuclear Option' Helps Obama Reshape the Courts for a Generation," *Talking Points Memo,* December 18, 2014, http://talking pointsmemo.com/dc/senate-nuclear-option-seals-obama-judicial-legacy.

82 Percentages of total justices are based on calculations using each circuit court's listing of current sitting judges on their individual websites on June 11, 2015.

83 John Schwartz, "'Liberal' Reputation Precedes Ninth Circuit Court," *New York Times,* April 24, 2010, http://www.nytimes.com/2010/04/25 /us/25sfninth.html?_r=0.

84 Neil Gross explores the liberal voting preferences and liberal self-identification of academics in *Why Are Professors Liberal and Why Do Conservatives Care?* (Cambridge, MA: Harvard University Press, 2013).

85 John K. Delaney, "The Last Thing America Needs? A Left-Wing Version of the Tea Party," *Washington Post*, May 28, 2015.

86 Holly Yeager, "Think Tank's Criticism of Elizabeth Warren's Populist Policies Leads to Democratic Feud," *Washington Post*, December 5, 2013.

87 Ibid.

88 Ibid.

## CHAPTER FIVE

1 "Hillary Clinton's Greatest Hits," Seattlepi Slideshow, slide 7 of 15, *Seattle Post-Intelligencer,* April 12, 2015.

2 Sarah Westwood, "New Documents Show Justice Dept. Linked to IRS Scandal," *Washington Examiner*, July 8, 2015.

3 Chris Safran, "Judicial Watch: Lois Lerner, DOJ Officials, and FBI Met to Plan Criminal Charges for Obama Opponents," *Washington Free Beacon*, July 7, 2015, http://freebeacon.com/issues/judicial-watch-lois-lerner-doj-officials-and-fbi-met-to-plan-criminal-charges-for-obama-opponents/.

4 Eliana Johnson, "Conservative Group Uncovers New Roots of the IRS Scandal," *National Review,* May 19, 2015.

5 Richard Samuelson, "Tenured Partisans," *National Review,* July 21, 2014.

6 In late October 2015, a resolution was introduced into the House Oversight and Government Reform Committee to begin proceedings to impeach IRS Commissioner John Koskinen. See Committee on Oversight and Government Reform, "Resolution Introduced to Impeach IRS Commissioner," press release, October 27, 2015, https://oversight.house.gov/release/resolution-introduced-impeach-irs-commissioner/.

7 See, e.g., John A. Andrew, *Power to Destroy: The Political Uses of the IRS From Kennedy to Nixon* (New York: Ivan R. Dee, 2002); see also Alan Farnham, "IRS Has Long History of Political Dirty Tricks," ABC News, May 15, 2003, http://abcnews.go.com/Business/irs-irs-long-history-dirty-tricks/story?id=19177178.

8 Michael Scherer, "New IRS Scandal Echoes a Long History of Political Harassment," *Time,* May 14, 2013, http://swampland.time.com/2013/05/14/anger-over-irs-audits-of-conservatives-anchored-in-long-history-of-abuse/.

9 Kevin Liptak, "Secret Service Chief Knew about Jason Chaffetz Leak Earlier than Initially Reported," CNN, October 2, 2015, http://www.cnn.com/2015/10/02/politics/jason-chaffetz-secret-service-director-joe-clancy/index.html.

10 Samuelson, "Tenured Partisans."

11 David French, "Wisconsin's Shame: 'I Thought It Was a Home Invasion,'" *National Review,* May 4, 2015.

12 Ibid.

13 Steven Verburg, "State Supreme Court Halts John Doe Probe Looming over Scott Walker's Presidential Bid," *LaCrosse Tribune*, July 16, 2015.

14 Alliance Defending Freedom, "Govt Tells Christian Ministers: Perform Same-Sex Weddings or Face Jail, Fines," press release, October 18, 2014, http://www.adfmedia.org/News/PRDetail/9364.

15 Fred Jackson, "Houston's Lesbian Mayor Changing Tune on Pastors' Sermon Subpoenas," *One News Now*, October 16, 2014, http://onenewsnow.com/culture/2014/10/16/houstons-lesbian-mayor-changing-tune-on-pastors-sermon-subpoenas.

16 Barbara Boland, "'Sweet Cakes' Owner Defiant in Face of $135,000 Fine for Refusing to Bake Gay Wedding Cake: 'Get Ready to Take a Stand,'" *Washington Examiner*, July 3, 2015, http://www.washingtonexaminer.com/sweetcakes-owner-defiant-in-face-of-135000-fine-for-refusing-to-bake-gay-wedding-cake-get-ready-to-take-a-stand/article/2567584; see also Hans von Spakovsky and Katrina Trinko, "Sorry, Slate: Oregon Did Put a 'Gag Order' on Those Christian Bakers," *Daily Signal*, July 6, 2015, http://dailysignal.com/2015/07/06/sorry-slate-oregon-did-put-a-gag-order-on-those-christian-bakers/.

17 Ryan Anderson, "ENDA Threatens Fundamental Civil Liberties," Heritage Foundation *Backgrounder* no. 2857, November 1, 2013, p. 7, http://www.heritage.org/research/reports/2013/11/enda-threatens-fundamental-civil-liberties, discussing *Good News Employee Association et al. v. Joyce M. Hicks*.

18 Richard D. Ackerman, "Ninth Circuit Declares Right of Government to Censor the Terms 'Natural Family,' 'Marriage' and 'Family Values,'" *Christian News Wire*, March 7, 2007, http://www.christiannewswire.com/news/634712410.html.

19 Todd Starnes, "Former SEALs Chaplain Could Be Kicked Out of Navy for Christian Beliefs," *FoxNews.com,* March 9, 2015, http://www.foxnews.com/opinion/2015/03/09/former-seals-chaplain-could-be-kicked-out-navy-for-christian-beliefs.html.

20 Austin Ruse, "Gays Want Navy Chaplain Fired, Congress Responds," *Breitbart.com*, March 31, 2015, http://www.breitbart.com/big-govern ment/2015/03/31/gays-want-naval-chaplain-fired-congress-responds/.

21 On September 3, 2015, the U.S. Navy granted a religious accommodation to Modder. See Andrew Tilghman, "Navy Spares Controversial Chaplain Accused of Misconduct," *Military Times*, September 4, 2015.

22 Yuval Levin, "The Church and the Left," *National Review*, April 3, 2015.

23 Robert Barnes and Scott Clement, "Poll: Gay-Marriage Support at Record High," *Washington Post,* April 23, 2015.

24 A gay couple, the State of Washington, and the ACLU are suing the owner of Arlene's Flowers for declining to make floral arrangements for the couple's wedding. See Sara Schilling, "Attorneys Argue Motions in Arlene's Flowers Discrimination Lawsuit," *Tri-City Herald,* December 5, 2014.

25 "Family Research Council Statement on Governor Mike Pence's Proposed Change to the Religious Freedom Restoration Act," *PRNewswire*, Reuters, March 31, 2015.

26 Molly Young, "Sweet Cakes by Melissa Violated Same-Sex Couple's Civil Rights When It Refused to Make Wedding Cake, State Finds," *Oregonian*, January 17, 2014, http://www.oregonlive.com/business /index.ssf/2014/01/sweet_cakes_by_melissa_investigation_wraps_up_as _state_finds_evidence_that_bakery_violated_civil_rights_for_refusing _to_make_same-sex_wedding_cake.html#incart_m-rpt-2.

27 Valerie Richardson, "University of Delaware Spurns House Democrat's Probe into Climate Change Professor," *Washington Times*, March 18, 2015.

28 Ibid.

29 Mark Hemingway, "Senator: Use RICO Laws to Prosecute Global Warming Skeptics," *Weekly Standard* (blog), June 2, 2015, http://m .weeklystandard.com/blogs/sen-whitehouse-d-ri-suggests-using-rico -laws-global-warming-skeptics_963007.html.

30 Michael Bastasch, "Scientists Ask Obama to Prosecute Global Warming Skeptics," *Daily Caller,* September 17, 2015, http://dailycaller.com/2015 /09/17/scientists-ask-obama-to-prosecute-global-warming-skeptics/.

31 See, e.g., Larry Bell, "Climategate Star Michael Mann Courts Legal Disaster," *Forbes,* September 18, 2012, www.forbes.com/sites/larrybell /2012/09/18/climategate-star-michael-mann-courts-legal-disaster/; see also John R. Lott, "The Next Climate-gate?" *FoxNews.com,* February 10, 2010, http://www.foxnews.com/opinion/2010/02/09/john-lott-joseph -daleo-climate-change-noaa-james-hansen.html.

32  Chris Mooney, "Exxon Investigated over Climate Change Research,"
    *Washington Times*, November 5, 2015, p. A1.

33  Sara Malm, "UN Planning an 'International Tribunal for Climate Justice'
    Which Would Allow Nations to Take Developed Countries to Court,"
    *Daily Mail* (UK), November 2, 2015, http://www.dailymail.co.uk
    /news/article-3300366/UN-planning-international-tribunal-climate
    -justice-allow-nations-developed-countries-court.html.

34  Thomas Sowell, "The New Inquisition," *Real Clear Politics,* April 14,
    2015, http://www.realclearpolitics.com/articles/2015/04/14/the_new
    _inquisition__126253.html.

35  Suzanne Goldenberg, "Work of Prominent Climate Change Denier
    Was Funded by Energy Industry," *Guardian*, February 21, 2015.

36  For a good overview of these debates, see Matthew Spalding, ed.,
    *The Heritage Guide to the Constitution*, Fully Revised Second Edition
    (Washington, DC: Regnery Publishing, 2014).

37  Harold Meyerson, "Uniting a House Divided," *Washington Post*,
    October 1, 2015, p. A23.

38  CNN Transcript, "Obama on Super Tuesday: 'Our Time Has Come,'"
    *Washington Post*, February 6, 2008, http://www.washingtonpost.com
    /wp-dyn/content/article/2008/02/06/AR2008020600199.html.

39  CBS News, "Obama on Executive Actions: 'I've Got a Pen and I've Got
    a Phone,'" *CBSNews.com*, January 14, 2014, http://washington.cbslocal
    .com/2014/01/14/obama-on-executive-actions-ive-got-a-pen-and-ive
    -got-a-phone/.

40  For a breakdown of these actions, see Elizabeth H. Slattery and Andrew
    Kloster, "An Executive Unbound: The Obama Administration's
    Unilateral Actions," Heritage Foundation *Legal Memorandum* no. 108,
    February 12, 2014, http://www.heritage.org/research/reports/2014/02
    /an-executive-unbound-the-obama-administrations-unilateral-actions.

41  Matt Wolking, "22 Times President Obama Said He Couldn't Ignore
    or Create His Own Immigration Law," Office of the Speaker of the
    House John Boehner, November 19, 2014, http://www.speaker.gov
    /general/22-times-president-obama-said-he-couldn-t-ignore-or-create
    -his-own-immigration-law#sthash.CsMBC6Bb.dpuf.

42  Ariane de Vogue, "Federal Appeals Court Sides with Texas Against
    Obama on Immigration," CNN, May 27, 2015, http://www.cnn
    .com/2015/05/26/politics/obama-immigration-texas-federal-appeals
    -court/index.html.

43  Ibid.

44  Ibid.

45  Matt Ford, "A Ruling Against the Obama Administration on Immi-
    gration," *Atlantic,* November 10, 2015, http://www.theatlantic.com
    /politics/archive/2015/11/fifth-circuit-obama-immigration/415077/.
46  Slattery and Kloster, "An Executive Unbound."
47  Ibid.
48  *Burwell v. Hobby Lobby Stores, Inc.,* 573 U.S.13-354 (2014); see also Adam
    Liptak, "Supreme Court Rejects Contraceptives Mandate for Some
    Corporations," *New York Times,* June 30, 2014.
49  See Becket Fund, "Court Rules Against Little Sisters of the Poor:
    Government to Force Nuns to Violate Faith or Pay Massive IRS
    Penalties," press release, July 14, 2015, http://www.becketfund.org
    /tenth-circuit-rules-against-little-sisters-hhs-mandate/; see also "Sonia
    Sotomayor Grants ObamaCare Contraception Stay," editorial, *Investor's
    Business Daily,* January 2, 2014, http://articles.latimes.com/2013/dec/31
    /nation/la-na-obamacare-nuns-20140101.
50  Becket Fund, "Little Sisters of the Poor Appeal to the Supreme Court,"
    press release, July 23, 2015, http://www.becketfund.org/littlesisters
    -scotus-appeal/.
51  Associated Press, "Appeals Court Upholds Injunction Halting
    Contraception Mandate at Colleges in 3 States," September 17, 2015,
    http://www.foxnews.com/us/2015/09/17/appeals-court-upholds
    -injunction-halting-contraception-mandate-at-colleges-in-3/.
52  See White House Office of the Press Secretary, "Executive Order—
    Further Amendments to Executive Order 11478, Equal Employment
    Opportunity in the Federal Government, and Executive Order 11246,
    Equal Employment Opportunity," press release, July 21, 2014, https://
    www.whitehouse.gov/the-press-office/2014/07/21/executive-order
    -further-amendments-executive-order-11478-equal-employmen.
53  Slattery and Kloster, "An Executive Unbound."
54  Much of this argument on executive authority is taken directly, with
    permission, from an article published previously by this author. See Kim
    R. Holmes, "How the United States Government Lost Its Liberalism,"
    *Public Discourse,* Witherspoon Institute, June 19, 2014, http://www
    .thepublicdiscourse.com/2014/06/13343/. The Heritage Foundation
    republished the piece, with permission, on July 16, 2014, http://www
    .heritage.org/research/commentary/2014/7/how-the-united-states
    -government-lost-its-liberalism.
55  478 U.S. 714, 733 (1986).
56  On September 27, 2002, Congress passed the 2003 Foreign Relations

Authorization Act, which stated that U.S. citizens born in Jerusalem would be recorded as "born in Israel" for passport purposes. However, the Department of State refused to do so for Menachem Zivotofsky, who was born in Jerusalem on October 17, 2002. The family sued the State Department, but the court ruled in *Zivotofsky v. Kerry*, 576 U.S. _ (2015) that the president has authority over foreign relations, including what appears on a passport.

57 Article II, Section 3 of the U.S. Constitution.

58 "In 1972, after President Nixon in a signing statement indicated that a provision in a bill submitted to him did not 'represent the policies of this Administration' and was 'without binding force or effect,' a federal district court held that no executive statement, even by a President, 'denying efficacy to the legislation could have either validity or effect.' DaCosta v. Nixon." Library of Congress Law Library, "Presidential Signing Statements: Overview," https://www.loc.gov/law/help/state ments.php.

59 *Clinton v. City of New York* (1998), No. 97-1374, 985 F. Supp. 168, affirmed.

60 Duaa Eldeib, "Feds: Palatine District Discriminated Against Transgender Student by Barring Her from Girls' Locker Room," *Chicago Tribune*, November 3, 2015, http://www.chicagotribune.com/news/ct-trans gender-student-federal-ruling-met-20151102-story.html.

61 See, e.g., "Cooper v. Aaron," Heritage Foundation, "Rule of Law: Judicial Activism" web page, accessed July 23, 2015, http://www.heri tage.org/initiatives/rule-of-law/judicial-activism/cases/cooper-v-aaron.

62 For an excellent discussion of these and other cases, see Spalding, *The Heritage Guide to the Constitution*.

63 433 U.S. 425 (1977).

64 See, e.g., note 7 in Justice Rehnquist's opinion for the majority in *United States v. Morrison*, 169 F.3d 820 (2000).

65 See, e.g., "Judicial Activism," Heritage Foundation website, accessed November 20, 2015, http://www.heritage.org/initiatives/rule-of-law /judicial-activism.

66 Elizabeth Slattery, "How Obama Is Remaking Federal Courts in One Chart," *Daily Signal*, October 22, 2013, http://dailysignal.com/2013 /10/22/how-obama-is-remaking-federal-courts-in-one-chart/.

67 In his dissent on *Obergefell v. Hodges,* Justice Roberts wrote: "Supporters of same-sex marriage have achieved considerable success persuading their fellow citizens—through the democratic process—to adopt their view. That ends today. Five lawyers have closed the debate and enacted their

own vision of marriage as a matter of constitutional law. Stealing this issue from the people will for many cast a cloud over same-sex marriage, making a dramatic social change that much more difficult to accept." The ruling, he said, "has nothing to do with the Constitution." Mark Berman, "How Each Supreme Court Justice Came Down on Same-Sex Marriage," *Washington Post,* June 26, 2015.

68 See David Bernstein, "Justice Kennedy's Opinion in the Gay Marriage Case May Upend Fifty-Plus Years of Settled Equal Protection and Due Process Jurisprudence," *Washington Post*, June 26, 2015.

69 John C. Eastman, "Just the Facts, Ma'am: Rebutting the False 'Inevitability' Narrative," *Public Discourse*, Witherspoon Institute, April 20, 2015, http://www.thepublicdiscourse.com/2015/04/14865/.

70 For an exhaustive analysis of hate speech practices around the world, see Alex Brown, *Hate Speech Law: A Philosophical Examination* (New York: Taylor and Francis, 2015), location 618–27. Kindle edition.

71 Southern Poverty Law Center, "Extremist Files," accessed June 25, 2015, http://www.splcenter.org/get-informed/intelligence-files/groups.

72 Holmes did walk back his statement a few years later. See Trevor Timm, "It's Time to Stop Using the 'Fire in a Crowded Theater' Quote," *Atlantic*, November 2, 2012, http://www.theatlantic.com/national /archive/2012/11/its-time-to-stop-using-the-fire-in-a-crowded-theater -quote/264449/.

73 See Brown, *Hate Speech Law*, location 617–18.

74 U.S. Department of Commerce, National Telecommunications & Information Administration. "The Role of Telecommunications in Hate Crimes," report to Congress, December 1993, http://www.ntia.doc .gov/legacy/reports/1993/TelecomHateCrimes1993.pdf.

75 William Safire, "Essay: The Paranoid Style," *New York Times,* April 27, 1995.

76 Chon A. Noriega and Francisco Javier Iribarren, "Hate Speech on Commercial Talk Radio: Preliminary Report on a Pilot Study," *Latino Policy & Issues Brief,* UCLA Chicano Studies Research Center, no. 22, February 2009, http://www.chicano.ucla.edu/files/PB22_000.pdf.

77 Adi Robertson, "Supreme Court Says Intent Matters in Facebook Threat Case," *Verge*, June 1, 2015, http://www.theverge.com/2015 /6/1/8697919/supreme-court-facebook-threat-elonis.

78 Jeremy Waldron, *The Harm in Hate Speech* (Cambridge, MA: Harvard University Press, 2012), pp. 106-43; see also Anthony Lewis, *Gideon's Trumpet* (New York: Vintage Books, 1964).

79 Waldron, *The Harm in Hate Speech,* p. 15.

80 John Locke, "Letter Concerning Toleration" (1689), trans. by William

Popple, *Constitution Society.org*, http://www.constitution.org/jl/tolerati.
htm.

81 BBC News, "Swedish Anti-Gay Pastor Acquitted," November 29, 2005,
http://news.bbc.co.uk/2/hi/europe/4477502.stm.

82 John Malcolm, "Defining the Problem and Scope of Over-criminalization and Over-federalization," Heritage Foundation *Congressional
Testimony*, June 14, 2013, http://www.heritage.org/research/testimony
/2013/06/defining-the-problem-and-scope-of-overcriminalization
-and-overfederalization; see also Karen Stealey, "On Thin Ice," National
Federation of Independent Business, October 1, 2004, accessed August
18, 2015, http://www.nfib.com/article/on-thin-ice-53435/.

83 Malcolm, "Defining the Problem."

84 John Malcolm, "Over-Criminalization Undermines Respect for Legal
System," *Washington Times*, December 11, 2013; see also Evan Bernick,
Paul Larkin, and Jordan Richardson, "Is Congress Addressing Our Over-
criminalization Problem? Reviewing the Progress of the Overcriminalization Task Force," Heritage Foundation *Legal Memorandum* no. 131,
August 12, 2014, http://www.heritage.org/research/reports/2014/08/is
-congress-addressing-our-overcriminalization-problem-reviewing-the
-progress-of-the-overcriminalization-task-force.

85 Malcolm, "Defining the Problem."

86 Ibid.

## CHAPTER SIX

1 See Michael Paulson, "College and Evangelicals Collide on Bias Policy,"
*New York Times,* June 9, 2014.

2 Noelle Hedges-Goettl, "Pronouns a Right, Not a Preference," *Oberlin
Review*, April 3, 2015, http://oberlinreview.org/7855/opinions/pro
nouns-a-right-not-a-preference.

3 "College Prof Makes Students Recite Anti-American Pledge of
Allegiance," *Fox News,* December 8, 2014, http://www.foxnews.com
/us/2014/12/08/college-prof-makes-students-recite-anti-american
-pledge-allegiance/; see also Caleb Bonham, "Professor Distributed
'New Pledge' to Racist America That Excludes Rights for 'Black,
Homosexuals,'" *CampusReform.org,* December 8, 2014, http://www
.campusreform.org/?ID=6116.

4 Anthony T. Kronman, *Education's End: Why Our Colleges and Universities
Have Given Up on the Meaning of Life* (New Haven, CT: Yale University
Press, 2007), p. 163.

5 American Council of Trustees and Alumni and the Connecticut Center

for Survey Research & Analysis, "Politics in the Classroom: A Survey of Students at the Top 50 Colleges & Universities, October–November 2004," November 28, 2007, http://www.goacta.org/publications /politics_in_the_classroom.

6 Foundation for Individual Rights in Education, "Spotlight on Speech Codes 2015," report, December 13, 2014, http://www.thefire.org /new-report-u-s-colleges-violate-students-free-speech-rights/; see also Greg Lukianoff, "Free Speech on Campus: The 10 Worst Offenders of 2014," *Huffington Post*, February 20, 2015, http://www .huffingtonpost.com/greg-lukianoff/10-worst-for-free-speech_b _6769564.html.

7 Yoel Inbar and Joris Lammers, "Political Diversity in Social and Personality Psychology," *Perspectives on Psychological Science,* vol. 20, no. 10 (2012), p. 1, http://yoelinbar.net/papers/political_diversity.pdf.

8 See, for example, Allan David Bloom, *The Closing of the American Mind: How Higher Education Has Failed Democracy and Impoverished the Souls of Today's Students* (New York: Simon and Schuster, 1987); Karl Zinsmeister, "Case Closed," *American Enterprise*, January/February 2005, pp. 42–45; and Gary A. Tobin et al., *The Uncivil University: Intolerance on College Campuses,* rev. ed. (Lanham, MD: Lexington Books, 2009). For an opposing viewpoint, see Lawrence W. Levine, *The Opening of the American Mind: Canons, Culture, and History* (Boston: Beacon Press, 1996).

9 Andy Kiersz and Hunter Walker, "These Charts Show the Political Bias of Workers in Each Profession," *BusinessInsider.com*, November 3, 2014, http://www.businessinsider.com/charts-show-the-political-bias-of-each -profession-2014-11?op=1.

10 Kathryn Watson, "Ivy League Professors, Staff Donate More than $2 Million in 2014—Mostly to Dems," *Watchdog.org*, December 5, 2014, https://watchdog.org/185892/ivy-league-donate-political/.

11 Suzy Lee Weiss, "I Was Recruited by the Thought Police," *Pittsburgh Post-Gazette*, March 8, 2015.

12 Dave Urbanski, "Classic Tip Encouraging Hard Work Now Considered a Racial Microaggression by College," *Blaze*, June 27, 2015, http:// www.theblaze.com/stories/2015/06/27/classic-tip-encouraging-hard -work-now-considered-a-racial-microaggression-by-college/; see also Derald W. Sue, *Microaggressions in Everyday Life: Race, Gender, and Sexual Orientation* (Hoboken, NJ: Wiley, 2010).

13 American Association of University Professors, Committee A, "On

Trigger Warnings," *Reports and Publications*, August 2014, http://www
.aaup.org/report/trigger-warnings.

14 Heather Mac Donald, "The Microaggression Farce," *City Journal*
(Autumn 2014), pp. 1–12.

15 Ibid.

16 Ibid.

17 Office of the President, Smith College, "Messages in Response to
Grand Jury Decisions," *Speeches,* December 5, 2014, http://www.smith
.edu/president/speeches-writings/grand-jury-decisions.

18 Maxim Lott, "College President Sorry for Saying 'All Lives Matter,' "
Fox News, December 10, 2014, http://www.foxnews.com/us/2014
/12/10/college-president-sorry-for-saying-all-lives-matter/.

19 Office of the President, Smith College, "Messages."

20 Eugene Volokh, "Marquette University Tells Employees: 'Opposition to
Same-Sex Marriage' Could Be 'Unlawful Harassment,' " *Washington Post*,
December 17, 2014.

21 Conor Friedersdorf, "Stripping a Professor of Tenure Over a Blog Post,"
*Atlantic,* February 10, 2015.

22 See Catharine A. MacKinnon and Andrea Dworkin, eds., *In Harm's
Way*: *The Pornography Civil Rights Hearings* (Cambridge, MA: Harvard
University Press, 1997); Catharine A. MacKinnon, *Only Words*
(Cambridge, MA: Harvard University Press, 1993); and Andrea
Dworkin, *Pornography*: *Men Possessing Women* (New York: Perigee Books,
1981); see also Wendy Kaminer, "The Progressive Ideas Behind the Lack
of Free Speech on Campus," *Washington Post*, February 20, 2015.

23 Weiss, "I Was Recruited by the Thought Police."

24 Ibid.

25 Ibid.

26 Mike Vilensky, "CUNY: Don't Address Students as 'Mr.' or 'Ms.,' "
*Wall Street Journal*, January 26, 2015.

27 Alexandra Desanctis, "At Johns Hopkins University, Effort to Ban
Chick-fil-A From Campus Meets Resistance," *College Fix,* July 9, 2015,
http://www.thecollegefix.com/post/23266/.

28 Aamer Madhani and Roger Yu, "Missouri Controversy Highlights
Academia's Free Speech Struggle," *USA Today,* November 13, 2015.

29 Todd J. Zywicki, "Meet the Mid-Level Bureaucrats Who Impose
Speech Codes on America's Universities," commentary, John William
Pope Center for Higher Education Policy, February 4, 2015, http://
www.popecenter.org/commentaries/article.html?id=3140.

30 Devorah Goldman, "The Closing of the Campus Mind," *Weekly Standard*, April 6, 2015.

31 Ibid.

32 Ibid.

33 Pacific Justice Institute, "SF Bay Area School Permits Queer Straight Alliance to Bully Students," press release, February 5, 2015, http://www.pacificjustice.org/press-releases/sf-bay-area-school-permits-queer-straight-alliance-to-bully-students.

34 David French, "The Persecution of Gordon College," *National Review*, January 26, 2015.

35 Ibid.

36 Patricia Williams, "Anti-Intellectualism Is Taking Over the US," *Guardian*, May 18, 2012.

37 Brittany Corona, "Concerns Grow About Common Core High School Standards," *Daily Signal*, March 12, 2015, http://dailysignal.com/2015/03/12/concerns-grow-about-common-core-high-school-standards/.

38 See, e.g., Home School Legal Defense Association, "Does the Common Core Have a Philosophical Bias?," *Common Core Issues*, accessed March 24, 2015, http://www.hslda.org/commoncore/topic4.aspx; and Jeff Bryant, "It's Not Just Wing-Nuts! Slate Gets Liberal Opposition to the Common Core All Wrong," *Salon.com*, Apr 24, 2014, http://www.salon.com/2014/04/24/its_not_just_wing_nuts_slate_gets_liberal_opposition_to_the_common_core_all_wrong/.

39 Ben Velderman, "Teacher: I Helped Write Common Core to Combat White Privilege," *Progressives Today*, May 21, 2014, http://www.progressivestoday.com/teacher-i-helped-write-common-core-to-combat-white-privilege/.

40 Stanley Kurtz, "Let's Embrace Competition in Advanced-Placement Testing," *Washington Post*, February 27, 2015.

41 Laura Kipnis, "My Title IX Inquisition," *Chronicle Review*, May 29, 2015, http://chronicle.com/article/My-Title-IX-Inquisition/230489.

42 Alex Kane, "The Year Ahead in Academic Boycotts of Israel," *Mondoweiss.net* (blog), January 6, 2015, http://mondoweiss.net/2015/01/academic-boycotts-israel.

43 Rupert Darwall, "Science as McCarthyism," *National Review Online*, May 15, 2014.

44 Ibid.

45 Ibid.

46 Editors, "Global Warming With the Lid Off," *Wall Street Journal*, November 24, 2009.

47 See, e.g., Larry Bell, "ClimateGate Star Michael Mann Courts Legal Disaster," *Forbes.com*, September 18. 2012, www.forbes.com /sites/larrybell/2012/09/18/climategate-star-michael-mann-courts-legal -disaster.

48 Editors, "Climate Science and Candor," *Wall Street Journal,* November 24, 2009.

49 Ibid.

50 Christopher Booker, "Polar Bear Expert Barred by Global Warmists," *Telegraph*, June 27, 2009.

51 Eric Owens, "US College Professor Demands Imprisonment for Climate Change Deniers," *Daily Caller*, March 17, 2014, http://dailycaller.com /2014/03/17/u-s-college-professor-demands-imprisonment-for-climate -change-deniers/.

52 Fuhai Hong and Xiaojian Zhao, "Information Manipulation and Climate Agreements," *American Journal of Agricultural Economics*, February 24, 2014, http://ajae.oxfordjournals.org/content/early/2014/02/24/ajae.aau001 .abstract.

53 Michael Gerson, for example, has accused climate skeptics of conspiracy-mongering. In some cases it may be true, but what about the charge of "climate change deniers"? Is that not conspiracy-mongering as well? Science is not an article of faith but a place where skepticism should be welcomed, not shunned as if it were apostasy. A refusal to recognize the difference leads climate change supporters to treat their opponents as the equivalent of an end-times cult. See Michael Gerson, "Americans' Aversion to Science Carries a High Price," *Washington Post,* May 12, 2014.

54 David Auerbach, "The Curious Case of Mencius Moldbug," *Slate.com*, June 10, 2015, http://www.slate.com/articles/technology/bitwise/2015 /06/curtis_yarvin_booted_from_strange_loop_it_s_a_big_big_problem .single.html.

55 Ibid.

56 Wency Leung, "Study Links Low Intelligence with Right Wing Beliefs," *Globe and Mail*, February 3, 2012.

57 As cited in ibid.

58 For a survey of how the behavioral sciences are abused for political purposes, see Andrew Ferguson, "Making It All Up: The Behavioral Sciences Scandal," *Weekly Standard*, October 19, 2015, p. 18,

59 Terrence McCoy, "Declaring War Against Thy Neighbor over a House and a Shared Driveway," *Washington Post,* June 8, 2015.

60 Ibid.

61 Donna Brazile, "Why 'All Lives Matter' Misses the Point," CNN, July 22, 2015, http://www.cnn.com/2015/07/22/opinions/brazile-black-lives-matter-slogan/index.html.

62 See Charles Murray, *Coming Apart: The State of White America, 1960–2010* (New York: Crown Forum, 2012); and Robert D. Putnam, *Bowling Alone: The Collapse and Revival of American Community* (New York: Simon & Schuster, 2000).

63 Maeve Duggan, "Online Harassment," Pew Research Center, October 22, 2014, accessed July 29, 2015, http://www.pewinternet.org/2014/10/22/online-harassment/.

64 Cathy Young, "The Social Media Shaming of Pax Dickson," *Real Clear Politics*, July 8, 2015, http://www.realclearpolitics.com/articles/2015/07/08/social_media_shaming_mob_strikes_again_127292.html.

65 Ibid; see also Jon Ronson, *So You've Been Publicly Shamed* (New York: Riverhead Books, 2015).

## CHAPTER SEVEN

1 Immanuel Kant, *An Answer to the Question: What Is Enlightenment?* ed. H. S. Reiss, trans. H. B. Nisbet (New York: Cambridge University Press, 2010), p. 54.

2 Anthony Pagden, *The Enlightenment: And Why It Still Matters* (New York: Random House, 2013), location 312. Kindle edition.

3 Biographical information from *Encyclopædia Britannica Online*, accessed July 31, 2015, http://www.britannica.com/.

4 Joseph Dorman, *Arguing the World: The New York Intellectuals in Their Own Words* (New York: Free Press, 2000), location 1825. Kindle edition.

5 For more on this issue, see John Earl Haynes, Harvey Klehr, and Alexander Vassiliev, *Spies: The Rise and Fall of the KGB in America* (New Haven, CT: Yale University Press, 2009); House Committee on Un-American Activities, "The Communist 'Peace' Offensive: A Campaign to Disarm and Defeat the United States," H. R. rep., 51st Congress, 1st Sess., April 1, 1951, https://archive.org/stream/reportoncommunisoounit#page/n3/mode/2up; and Stephen Koch, *Double Lives: Spies and Writers in the Secret Soviet War of Ideas Against the West* (New York: Free Press, 1994).

6 For a history of the public intellectuals in the 1950s, see Dorman, *Arguing*

*the World*. For a discussion of the decline of the intellectual, see Russell Jacoby, *The Last Intellectuals: American Culture in the Age of Academe* (New York: Basic Books, 2000).

7 Kevin R. Kosar, "The Quasi Government: Hybrid Organizations with Both Government and Private Sector Legal Characteristics," Congressional Research Service *Report for Congress* no. RL30533, June 22, 2011, http://fas.org/sgp/crs/misc/RL30533.pdf.

8 National Science Foundation, National Center for Science and Engineering Statistics, "Table 1. Higher Education R&D Expenditures, by Source of Funds and R&D Field: FYs 1953–2013," *Higher Education Research and Development Survey, Fiscal Year 2013*, accessed March 11, 2015, http://ncsesdata.nsf.gov/herd/2013/html/HERD2013_DST_01.html; see also Association of American Universities, "AAU Data & Policy Brief," Policy Brief, February 2015, accessed August 4, 2015, http://www.aau.edu/WorkArea/DownloadAsset.aspx?id=15974.

9 National Science Foundation, National Center for Science and Engineering Statistics, "Table 18. Higher Education R&D Expenditures, Ranked by All R&D Expenditures, by Source of Funds: FY 2013," *Higher Education Research and Development Survey, Fiscal Year 2013*, accessed March 11, 2015, http://ncsesdata.nsf.gov/datatables/herd/2013/html/HERD2013_DST_18.html.

10 Association of American Universities, "University Research: The Role of Federal Funding," Policy Brief, January 2011, http://www.aau.edu/WorkArea/DownloadAsset.aspx?id=11588.

11 Ibid.

12 For all data, see the following tables at National Science Foundation, National Center for Science and Engineering Statistics, *Higher Education Research and Development Surveys*: "Federally Financed Higher Education R&D Expenditures, Financed by the Department of Health and Human Services, Ranked by HHS R&D expenditures, by R&D field: FY 2012," http://ncsesdata.nsf.gov/herd/2012/html/HERD2012_DST_59.html; "Federally Financed Higher Education R&D Expenditures, Financed by the National Science Foundation, Ranked by NSF R&D expenditures, by R&D field FY 2012," http://ncsesdata.nsf.gov/herd/2012/html/HERD2012_DST_61.html; "Federally Financed Higher Education R&D Expenditures, Financed by the Department of Defense, ranked by DOD R&D expenditures, by R&D field: FY 2012," http://ncsesdata.nsf.gov/herd/2012/html/HERD2012_DST_57.html; and "Federally Financed Higher Education R&D Expenditures, Financed by the

Department of Energy, Ranked by DOE R&D Expenditures, by R&D Field: FY 2012," http://ncsesdata.nsf.gov/herd/2012/html/HERD2012 _DST_58.html (all accessed January 4, 2015).

13 National Science Foundation, National Center for Science and Engineering Statistics, "Federally Financed Higher Education R&D Expenditures, by Federal Agency and R&D field, FY 2012," *Higher Education Research and Development Survey,* accessed August 4, 2015, http://ncsesdata.nsf.gov/herd/2012/html/HERD2012_DST_03.html.

14 U.S. Government Accountability Office, "Federally Funded Research Centers: Agency Reviews of Employee Compensation and Center Performance," report no. GAO-14-593, August 11, 2014, http://www .gao.gov/products/GAO-14-593.

15 Ibid.

16 The Affordable Care Act became law in March 2010. See Glenn Kessler, "Did Jonathan Gruber Earn 'Almost $400,000' From the Obama Administration?" *Washington Post,* November 14, 2014.

17 Richard Muller, "Global Warming Bombshell," *MIT Technology Review,* October 15, 2004, http://www.technologyreview.com/news/403256 /global-warming-bombshell/.

18 Michael E. Mann, "Curriculum Vitae," posted on Pennsylvania State University website, accessed August 9, 2015, http://www.meteo.psu .edu/holocene/public_html/Mann/about/cv.php.

19 Joakim Kasper Oestergaard Balle, "About Patriot & PAC-3," *Aerospace Defense & Intelligence Report 2014, Aeroweb,* December 22, 2014, https:// www.bga-aeroweb.com/Defense/Patriot-PAC-3.html.

20 Larry Bell, "ClimateGate Star Michael Mann Courts Legal Disaster," *Forbes.com,* September 18, 2012, www.forbes.com/sites/larrybell/2012 /09/18/climategate-star-michael-mann-courts-legal-disaster/.

21 Ibid. According to the article in *Forbes*, CRU director Philip Jones wrote to colleagues: "I've just completed Mike's *Nature* [journal] trick . . . to hide the decline [in global temperatures]."

22 See, for example, the discussion that follows on Harvard professor Steven Wofsy, a member of the National Academy of Sciences who also serves on the Scientific Advisory Board of a company that manufactures high-precision gas analyzers used in the climate field.

23 Steve Cohen, "Columbia University's Earth Institute: An Academic Institution for the 21st Century," *Huffington Post,* August 12, 2013, http://www.huffingtonpost.com/steven-cohen/columbia-universitys -eart_b_3743197.html.

24 "[T]he Earth Institute draws upon the scientific rigor and academic leadership for which [Columbia] University is known to create an inter-disciplinary community dedicated to cutting-edge research. The Earth Institute is grounded in the hundreds of research projects that involve over 850 scientists, students and postdoctoral fellows across more than 30 Columbia-based research centers and programs." See Earth Institute, "Research: the Foundation of the Earth Institute," accessed November 20, 2015, http://www.earth.columbia.edu/articles/view/1788.

25 For example, a news release in 2011 on Jeffrey Sachs's extending his stay as director of the Institute reads: "Sachs is uniquely positioned on the world stage to lead the research, teaching and policy advocacy work of the Earth Institute." Earth Institute, Columbia University, "Jeffrey Sachs Extends Term as Director of Earth Institute," news release, April 28, 2011, accessed November 20, 2015, http://earth.columbia.edu/articles/view/2803.

26 Earth Institute, Columbia University, "James Hansen to Lead New Program on Climate Science and Policy," press release, September 5, 2013, http://earth.columbia.edu/articles/view/3117.

27 Steve Cohen, "Columbia University's Earth Institute: An Academic Institution for the 21st Century," *Huffington Post,* August 12, 2013, http://www.huffingtonpost.com/steven-cohen/columbia-universitys -eart_b_3743197.html.

28 Earth Institute, Columbia University, "A Successful Year for Sustainable Development," *Annual Donor Report 2010,* http://www.earth.columbia. edu/sitefiles/file/get_involved/donorreport/2010/A%20Successful%20 Year%20for%20Sustainable%20Development.pdf and "Partnerships for Sustainable Development," *Annual Donor Report 2015,* http://issuu.com /earthinstitute/docs/ei_pdf_hq_pgs/26?e=4098028/6665148.

29 See Steven C. Wofsy, "Curriculum Vita 2013," Harvard University School of Engineering and Applied Sciences, accessed August 4, 2015, http://atmos.seas.harvard.edu/people/faculty/scw/cv.SW.pdf.

30 Calculations based on various years' data at: National Science Foundation, "Award Summary: By Top Institutions," http://dellweb .bfa.nsf.gov/Top50Inst2/default.asp and Harvard University Office of Technology Development, "All Funding Sources: Steven Wofsy," https://www.collectiveip.com/technology-transfer/harvard-university /grants?fgi=Steven+Wofsy (both accessed August 5, 2015).

31 Harvard University John A. Paulson School of Engineering and Applied Sciences, "Steven C. Wofsy Awarded Roger Revelle Medal," news

release, July 19, 2012, http://www.seas.harvard.edu/news/2012/07
/steven-c-wofsy-awarded-roger-revelle-medal.

32 For more information, see Harvard University, "Imaging the Chemistry
of the Global Atmosphere," press release, *Phys.org*, December 16, 2014,
http://phys.org/news/2014-12-imaging-chemistry-global-atmosphere
.html; and "NASA's Earth-Observing Satellites to Study Climate
Change," *Northern Voices Online*, December 2, 2014, http://nvonews
.com/nasas-earth-observing-satellites-study-climate-change/.

33 For example, on August 9, 2015, NASA's "Climate" homepage at
http://climate.nasa.gov/ featured pieces on sea levels, California's
drought, and longer and more frequent fire seasons, as well as tabs
showing rising temperatures and levels of carbon dioxide, and decreasing
levels of Arctic and land ice.

34 For example, the summary of the IPCC's Fifth Assessment Report states:
"Continued emission of greenhouse gases will cause further warming
and long-lasting changes in all components of the climate system,
*increasing the likelihood of severe, pervasive and irreversible impacts for people
and ecosystems.* Limiting climate change would require substantial and
sustained reductions in greenhouse gas emissions which, together with
adaptation, can limit climate change risks." See Intergovernmental Panel
on Climate Change, *Climate Change 2014 Synthesis Report*, November 1,
2014, http://ipcc.ch/pdf/assessment-report/ar5/wg1/WG1AR5_ALL
_FINAL.pdf. Emphasis added.

35 Picarro "Pioneering Greenhouse Gas Scientist and Harvard Professor,
Steven Wofsy, Joins Picarro's Scientific Advisory Board," press release,
*Picarro.com*, October 27, 2010, http://www.picarro.com/about/media
_center/press_releases/20101027.

36 Joel Kotkin, *The New Class Conflict* (Candor, NY: Telos Press
Publishing, 2014).

37 Noam Chomsky called the liberal intellectuals who supported the
Kennedy and Johnson administrations' war in Vietnam the "new
Mandarins." Noam Chomsky, *American Power and the New Mandarins*
(New York: Random House, 1969), p. 24. Today's mandarins are quite
different—people of the left using the state not only for personal gain but
to enhance the power base of a class of people of which Chomsky is a part.

38 Richard Hofstadter, *Anti-Intellectualism in American Life* (Toronto: Knopf
Doubleday Publishing Group, 1966), p. 430. Kindle edition.

39 Ibid., p. 200.

40 Quoted in Dorman, *Arguing the World*, location 2568–570.

## CHAPTER EIGHT

1 By ideology I mean a logical system of ideas and ideals aimed at political action.

2 This concept of radical and moderate Enlightenment traditions is taken from historian Jonathan Israel. See Jonathan I. Israel, *Enlightenment Contested: Philosophy, Modernity, and the Emancipation of Man 1670–1752* (Oxford: Oxford University Press, 2006).

3 Ibid., p. 412.

4 Ibid., p. 867.

5 Thomas Hobbes, *Leviathan* (Harmondsworth, England: Penguin, 1986), p. 89.

6 Siep Stuurman, *François Poulain de la Barre and the Invention of Modern Equality* (Cambridge, MA: Harvard University Press, 2004).

7 David Hume, *Enquiries Concerning the Human Understanding and Concerning the Principles of Morals: Reprinted from the Posthumous Edition of 1777*, ed. L. A. Selby-Bigge, 2nd ed. (Oxford: Clarendon Press, 1963), p. 155, available at http://oll.libertyfund.org/titles/hume-enquiries-concerning-the-human-understanding-and-concerning-the-principles-of-morals.

8 Israel, *Enlightenment Contested*, p. 547.

9 John Locke, *Two Treatises of Government* (London: Everyman Paperback, 1993).

10 For example, Locke wrote: "All mankind . . . being all equal and independent, no one ought to harm another in his life, health, liberty or possessions" (Chapter II, Section 4), and "Man . . . hath by nature a power . . . to preserve his property, that is, his life, liberty and estate" (Chapter VII, Section 87). John Locke, *Second Treatise of Government* (Indianapolis, IN: Hackett Publishing Company, 1980). In a previous essay in 1681, Locke wrote, "The necessity of pursuing happiness is the foundation of liberty," and "the highest perfection of intellectual nature lies in a careful and constant pursuit of true and solid happiness." John Locke, *An Essay Concerning Human Understanding,* ed. Peter H. Nidditch (Oxford: Clarendon Press, 1974), Book 2, Chapter 21, Section 51.

11 Dan Edelstein, *The Terror of Natural Right: Republicanism, the Cult of Nature, and the French Revolution* (Chicago: University of Chicago Press, 2009).

12 Susan Dunn, *Sister Revolutions: French Lightning, American Light* (New York: Faber and Faber, 1999).

13 Clinton Rossiter, ed., *The Federalist Papers* (New York: New American Library, 1961), p. 81.

14 Alexis de Tocqueville, *Democracy in America* (New York: Alfred A. Knopf, 1945), p. 308.

15 Ibid., pp. 305–306.

16 Thomas Jefferson, "Letter to William Short, January 3, 1793," in *Jefferson: Writings,* ed. Merrill D. Peterson (New York: Library of America, 1984), location 16238. Kindle edition.

17 Thomas Jefferson, "Your Prophecy and Mine," in Peterson, *Jefferson,* location 24096.

18 Thomas Jefferson, "Autobiography," in Peterson, *Jefferson,* location 1482.

19 Carl L. Becker, *The Heavenly City of the Eighteenth-Century Philosophers,* 2nd ed. (New Haven, CT: Yale Nota Bene Publication, 2003), p. xiii. First published by Yale University Press (New Haven, CT) in 1932.

20 Ibid., p. 39.

21 "I openly confess, the suggestion of David Hume was the very thing, which many years ago first interrupted my dogmatic slumber, and gave my investigations in the field of speculative philosophy quite a new direction." Immanuel Kant, *Prolegomena to Any Future Metaphysics and the Letter to Marcus Herz* (Indianapolis, IN: Hackett Publishing, 2001), p. 5.

22 For Kant's views of the perfect state, see Immanuel Kant, *Critique of Pure Reason,* trans. Norman Kemp Smith, unabridged ed. (New York: St. Martin's Press, 1965), p. 312.

23 Jacques Barzun, *From Dawn to Decadence, 1500 to the Present: 500 Years of Western Cultural Life* (New York: HarperCollins, 2001).

## CHAPTER NINE

1 Jonathan V. Last, "You Will Be Assimilated," *Weekly Standard,* June 22, 2015.

2 Ronald C. Den Otter, *In Defense of Plural Marriage* (Oxford: Oxford University Press, 2015).

3 Margo Kaplan, "Pedophilia: A Disorder, Not a Crime," *New York Times,* October 5, 2014. In this respect, we should remember that mental disorders are often only temporary way stations on the road to public acceptance. What used to be called gender dysphoria has now become known as transgender rights.

4 Alexa Tsoulis-Reay, "What It's Like to Date a Horse," *New York* magazine, November 20, 2014.

5 Alexa Tsoulis-Reay, "What It's Like to Date Your Dad," *New York* magazine, January 15, 2015.

6 Olga Khazan, "Multiple Lovers, Without Jealousy," *Atlantic,* July 21, 2014.

7 Lindsey Bever, "Children of Same-Sex Couples Are Happier and Healthier Than Peers, Research Shows," *Washington Post*, July 7, 2014.

8 A list of LGBT-friendly publishing houses compiled by the pro-gay rights group Lambda Literary that includes St. Martins, Penguin Random House, University of Chicago Press, and even Simon and Schuster Children can be found at http://www.lambdaliterary.org/resources/publishers/ (accessed June 27, 2015).

9 David Millward, "Florida Man Demands Right to Wed Computer," *Telegraph*, May 7, 2014.

10 Piper Kerman, *Orange Is the New Black: My Year in a Women's Prison* (New York: Spiegel and Grau, 2010).

11 Actually this has been tried. On the TV series *Big Love*, Mormon polygamy was featured to give the plural marriage theme a socially conservative veneer.

12 See, e.g., Colleen C. Hoff et al., "Relationship Characteristics and Motivations Behind Agreements Among Gay Male Couples: Differences by Agreement Type and Couple Serostatus," *AIDS Care*, July 22, 2010, http://www.ncbi.nlm.nih.gov/pmc/articles/PMC2906147/.

13 Stephen Ohlemacher, "Conservatives Warn IRS Could Target Gay Marriage Opponents," *The Big Story*, Associated Press, July 16, 2015.

14 Kim Palmer, "Ohio High Court Advises Judges Not to Refuse to Perform Gay Marriages," Associated Press, August 11, 2015, http://www.reuters.com/article/2015/08/11/us-usa-gaymarriage-ohio-idUSKCN0QF2CZ20150811. See also Mark Hemingway, "Ohio Judges Can't Choose Not to Marry Couples," *Weekly Standard* (blog), August 11, 2015, p. 1.

15 Anthony Berteaux, "An Open Letter to Jerry Seinfeld From a 'Politically Correct' College Student," *Huffington Post*, June 9, 2015, http://www.huffingtonpost.com/anthony-berteaux/jerry-seinfeld-politcally-correct-college-student_b_7540878.html.

16 Ibid.

17 See, for example, T. W. Adorno, et al., *The Authoritarian Personality* (New York: Harper & Brothers, 1950).

18 Jordan Weissmann, "The Beautiful Closing Paragraph of Justice Kennedy's Gay Marriage Ruling," *Slate.com*, June 26, 2015, http://www.slate.com/blogs/the_slatest/2015/06/26/supreme_court_legalizes_gay_marriage_here_is_the_beautiful_last_paragraph.html.

19 See James Suroweicki, *The Wisdom of Crowds: Why the Many Are Smarter Than the Few and How Collective Wisdom Shapes Business, Economies, Societies and Nations* (Boston: Little, Brown, 2004).

20  Last, "You Will Be Assimilated."

21  Sherif Girgis, Robert P. George, and Ryan T. Anderson, *What Is Marriage?* (New York: Encounter Books, 2012).

22  Hilton Kramer and Roger Kimball, eds., *The Betrayal of Liberalism: How the Disciples of Freedom and Equality Helped Foster the Illiberal Politics of Coercion and Control* (Chicago: Ivan R. Dee, 1999), pp. 41–42.

23  *Tabula rasa* is a Latin phrase often translated as "blank slate."

24  Jacques Barzun, *From Dawn to Decadence: 500 Years of Western Cultural Life* (New York: HarperCollins, 2001).

25  Erich Fromm, *Escape from Freedom* (New York: Avon Books, 1965), p. 261.

26  Ibid., p. 289.

27  Herbert Marcuse, *Eros and Civilization: A Philosophical Inquiry into Freud,* New Ed ed. (Boston: Beacon Press, 1974).

28  Kramer and Kimball, *Betrayal of Liberalism,* p. 14.

29  For example: "Currently, just 19% say they can trust the government always or most of the time, among the lowest levels in the past half-century. . . . Yet at the same time, most Americans have a lengthy to-do list for this object of their frustration: Majorities want the federal government to have a major role in addressing issues ranging from terrorism and disaster response to education and the environment." Pew Research Center, "Beyond Distrust: How Americans View Their Government," *U.S. Politics & Policy,* November 23, 2015, http://www.people-press .org/2014/11/13/public-trust-in-government/. A poll of millennials in 2012 found: "A majority (59%) said that the government should do more to solve problems, while 37% said the government is doing too many things better left to businesses and individuals." Pew Research Center, "Young Voters Supported Obama Less, But May Have Mattered More," *U.S. Politics and Policy,* November 26, 2012, http://www.people -press.org/2012/11/26/young-voters-supported-obama-less-but-may -have-mattered-more/.

30  For a broader discussion of the necessity of these institutions, see Kim R. Holmes, *Rebound: Getting America Back to Great* (Lanham, MD: Rowman & Littlefield, 2013).

31  Joel B. Pollak, "Scalia Blasts Obamacare Ruling: 'Words Have No Meaning,'" *Breitbart.com,* June 25, 2015, http://www.breitbart.com /big-government/2015/06/25/scalia-blasts-obamacare-ruling-words -have-no-meaning/.

32  Bloom, *Closing of the American Mind,* p. 205.

33 Lawrence W. Levine, *The Opening of the American Mind: Canons, Culture, and History* (Boston: Beacon Press, 1996).

34 Thomas Jefferson, "Thomas Jefferson to Dr. Benjamin Rush, Monticello, September 23, 1800," in Barbara B. Oberg, ed., *The Papers of Thomas Jefferson*, Vol. 32 (Princeton, NJ: Princeton University Press, 2005), p. 168.

## CONCLUSION

1 Kevin Jones, "Gay-Rights Advocate Wants to Win Religious-Liberty Fight Within Three Years," *National Catholic Register,* July 30, 2015.

2 Lucy McCalmont, "Dem Senator Defends the Koch Brothers," *Politico.com*, April 10, 2014, http://www.politico.com/story/2014/04/dem-senator-defends-the-koch-bros-105570.html.

3 Max Fisher, "From Gamergate to Cecil the Lion: Internet Mob Justice Is Out of Control," *Vox.com*, July 30, 2015, http://www.vox.com/2015/7/30/9074865/cecil-lion-palmer-mob-justice.

4 Brendan Bordelon, "Gay Journalist Andrew Sullivan 'Disgusted' By Gay Rights 'Fanaticism' After Mozilla CEO Resigns," *Daily Caller*, April 4, 2014, http://dailycaller.com/2014/04/04/andrew-sullivan-disgusted-by-gay-rights-fanaticism-mozilla/.

5 Conor Friedersdorf, "Should Mom-and-Pops That Forego Gay Weddings Be Destroyed?," *Atlantic,* April 3, 2015, http://www.theatlantic.com/politics/archive/2015/04/should-businesses-that-quietly-oppose-gay-marriage-be-destroyed/389489/.

6 See Catherine Rampell, "Free Speech Is Flunking Out on Campus," *Washington Post*, October 23, 2015, p. A21; and Geoffrey R. Stone and Will Creeley, "Restoring Free Speech on Campus," *Washington Post*, September 27, 2015, p. A23.

7 Some progressives favored eugenics, for example, but so too did some conservatives at the time. It was more a sign of the times than a peculiar worldview of progressivism.

8 Julie Deardorff, "Woman Seeks Pardon in Gift to First Lady," *Chicago Tribune*, October 27, 2000.

# SELECT BIBLIOGRAPHY

Adorno, T. W., Else Frenkel-Brunswik, Daniel J. Levinson, and R. Nevitt Sanford. *The Authoritarian Personality*. New York: Harper & Brothers, 1950.

Alinsky, Saul D. *Rules for Radicals*. New York: Random House, 1971.

American Association of University Professors, Committee A. "On Trigger Warnings." *Reports and Publications*, August 2014.

American Council of Trustees and Alumni and the Connecticut Center for Survey Research & Analysis. "Politics in the Classroom: A Survey of Students at the Top 50 Colleges & Universities, October–November 2004." *Report*, November 28, 2007.

Anderson, Ryan T. "ENDA Threatens Fundamental Civil Liberties." Heritage Foundation *Backgrounder*, no. 2857, November 1, 2013.

———. *Truth Overruled: The Future of Marriage and Religious Freedom*. Washington, DC: Regnery Publishing, 2015.

Andrew, John A. *Power to Destroy: The Political Uses of the IRS From Kennedy to Nixon*. New York: Ivan R. Dee, 2002.

Arneson, Richard. "Rawls, Responsibility, and Distributive Justice." Faculty Paper, University of California, San Diego, April 1997.

Aronowitz, Stanley. *The Death and Rebirth of American Radicalism*. New York: Routledge, 1996.

Association of American Universities. "AAU Data & Policy Brief." *Policy Brief*, February 2015.

———. "University Research: The Role of Federal Funding." *Policy Brief*, January 2011.

Attkisson, Sharyl. *Stonewalled: My Fight for Truth Against the Forces of Obstruction, Intimidation, and Harassment in Obama's Washington*. New York: Harper, 2014.

Barzun, Jacques. *From Dawn to Decadence, 1500 to the Present: 500 Years of Western Cultural Life*. New York: HarperCollins, 2001.

Becker, Carl L. *The Heavenly City of the Eighteenth-Century Philosophers*. 2nd ed. New Haven, CT: Yale Nota Bene Publication, 2003. First published 1932 by Yale University Press.

Bell, Daniel. "Communitarianism." In *The Stanford Encyclopedia of Philosophy*, edited by Edward N. Zalta. Stanford, CA: Metaphysics Research Lab, Fall 2013.

Bernick, Evan, Paul Larkin, and Jordan Richardson. "Is Congress Addressing Our Overcriminalization Problem? Reviewing the Progress of the Over-criminalization Task Force." Heritage Foundation *Legal Memorandum*, no. 131, August 12, 2014.

Bernstein, David E. *Lawless: The Obama Administration's Unprecedented Assault on the Constitution and the Rule of Law*. New York: Encounter Books, 2015.

Billias, George Athan, and Gerald N. Grob. *Interpretations of American History: Since 1877*. 6th ed. New York: Simon & Schuster, 2010.

Bloom, Allan David. *The Closing of the American Mind: How Higher Education Has Failed Democracy and Impoverished the Souls of Today's Students*. New York: Simon & Schuster, 1987.

Bourne, Randolph Silliman. *The Radical Will: Selected Writings, 1911–1918*. Edited by Olaf Hansen. Berkeley, CA: University of California Press, 1992.

Broadie, Alexander. *The Scottish Enlightenment*. Edinburgh: Birlinn Ltd., 2012.

Brooks, Arthur. *The Conservative Heart: How to Build a Fairer, Happier, and More Prosperous America*. New York: Harper Collins, 2015.

Brooks, David. *Bobos in Paradise: The New Upper Class and How They Got There*. New York: Simon & Schuster, 2000.

Brown, Alex. *Hate Speech Law: A Philosophical Examination*. New York: Taylor and Francis, 2015.

Calhoun, John C. "A Disquisition on Government" (1849). Published posthumously in 1851 by Walker & James (Charleston, SC). http://www.constitution.org/jcc/disq_gov.htm.

———. "The 'Positive Good' of Slavery." *Speech in the U.S. Senate* (1837). http://www.stolaf.edu/people/fitz/COURSES/calhoun.html.

Carson, D. A. *The Intolerance of Tolerance*. Grand Rapids, MI: William B. Eerdmans, 2012.

Chomsky, Noam. *American Power and the New Mandarins*. New York: Random House, 1969.

Cohen, Robert. *Freedom's Orator: Mario Savio and the Radical Legacy of the 1960s*. New York: Oxford University Press, 2009.

Conquest, Robert. *Reflections on a Ravaged Century*. New York: Norton, 2000.

Constant, Benjamin. *Principles of Politics Applicable to All Representative Governments*. In *Constant: Political Writings*. Translated and edited by Biancamaria Fontana. Cambridge: Cambridge University Press, 1988. First published in Paris, 1815.

Couvares, Francis G., ed. *Interpretations of American History: Patterns and Perspectives*. 7th ed. New York: Simon & Schuster, 2000.

Croly, Herbert David. *Progressive Democracy*. New York: MacMillan Company, 1915.

———. *The Promise of American Life*. Los Angeles: Library of Alexandria, 2012.

Cudd, Ann. "Contractarianism." In *The Stanford Encyclopedia of Philosophy*, edited by Edward N. Zalta. Stanford, CA: Metaphysics Research Lab, Winter 2013. http://plato.stanford.edu/entries/contractarianism/.

DeMint, Jim. *Falling in Love with America Again*. New York: Center Street, 2014.

Den Otter, Ronald C. *In Defense of Plural Marriage*. Oxford: Oxford University Press, 2015.

Derrida, Jacques. *Of Spirit: Heidegger and the Question*. Translated by Geoffrey Bennington and Rachel Bowlby. Chicago: University of Chicago Press, 1989.

Dewey, John. *Democracy and Education: An Introduction to the Philosophy of Education*. New York: The Macmillan Company, 1916.

Doherty, Brian. *Radicals for Capitalism: A Freewheeling History of the Modern American Libertarian Movement*. New York: PublicAffairs, 2009.

Dorman, Joseph. *Arguing the World: The New York Intellectuals in Their Own Words*. New York: Free Press, 2000.

Downs, Donald Alexander. *Restoring Free Speech and Liberty on Campus*. Oakland, CA: Independent Institute, 2005.

Dunn, Susan. *Sister Revolutions: French Lightning, American Light*. New York: Faber and Faber, 1999.

Durham, Martin. *White Rage: The Extreme Right and American Politics*. London: Routledge, 2007.

Dworkin, Andrea. *Pornography: Men Possessing Women*. New York: Perigee Books, 1981.

Dworkin, Ronald. *Taking Rights Seriously*. Cambridge, MA: Harvard University Press, 1977.

Edelstein, Dan. *The Terror of Natural Right: Republicanism, the Cult of Nature, and the French Revolution*. Chicago: University of Chicago Press, 2009.

Ekirch, Arthur A., Jr. *The Decline of American Liberalism*. Oakland, CA: Independent Institute, 2009.

Ellis, John M. *Literature Lost: Social Agendas and the Corruption of the Humanities*. New Haven, CT: Yale University Press, 1997.

Ellis, Richard. *The Dark Side of the Left: Illiberal Egalitarianism in America*. Lawrence, KS: University Press of Kansas, 1998.

Epstein, Richard Allen. *The Classical Liberal Constitution: The Uncertain Quest for Limited Government*. Cambridge, MA: Harvard University Press, 2014.

Ernst, Carl W., ed. *Islamophobia in America: The Anatomy of Intolerance*. New York: Palgrave Macmillan, 2013.

Evans, M. Stanton. *The Theme Is Freedom: Religion, Politics, and the American Tradition*. Washington, DC: Regnery Publishing, 1996.

Farber, Daniel A., and Suzanna Sherry. *Beyond All Reason: The Radical Assault on Truth in American Law*. New York: Oxford University Press, 1997.

Fawcett, Edmund. *Liberalism: The Life of an Idea*. Princeton, NJ: Princeton University Press, 2014.

Fish, Stanley. *Doing What Comes Naturally: Change, Rhetoric, and the Practice of Theory in Literary and Legal Studies*. Durham, NC: Duke University Press, 1989.

Florida, Richard. *The Rise of the Creative Class*. New York: Basic Books, 2002.

Flynn, Daniel J. *A Conservative History of the American Left*. New York: Crown Forum, 2008.

Fontana, Biancamaria, ed. *Constant: Political Writings*. Cambridge: Cambridge University Press, 1988.

Ford, Paul Leicester, ed. *The Works of Thomas Jefferson*. Federal ed. New York: Knickerbocker Press, 1904–1905.

Foucault, Michel. *The Archaeology of Knowledge and the Discourse on Language*. Translated by A. M. Sheridan Smith. New York: Pantheon Books, 1972.

———. *The Order of Things: An Archaeology of the Human Sciences*. New York: Pantheon Books, 1970.

Foundation for Individual Rights in Education. "Spotlight on Speech Codes 2015." Report, December 13, 2014.

Friedrich, Rainer. "The Enlightenment Gone Mad (I): The Dismal Discourse of Postmodernism's Grand Narratives." *Arion, a Journal of Humanities and the Classics* 19, no. 3 (2012): 31–78.

Fromm, Erich. *Escape From Freedom.* New York: Avon Books, 1965.

Gairdner, William D. *The Book of Absolutes: A Critique of Relativism and a Defence of Universals.* Montreal: McGill-Queen's University Press, 2008.

Gauthier, David. *Morals By Agreement.* Oxford: Oxford University Press, 1986.

George, John, and Laird M. Wilcox. *American Extremists: Militias, Supremacists, Klansmen, Communists and Others.* Amherst, NY: Prometheus Books, 1996.

George, Robert P. *Conscience and Its Enemies: Confronting the Dogmas of Liberal Secularism.* Wilmington, DE: Intercollegiate Studies Institute, 2013.

Girgis, Sherif, Robert P. George, and Ryan T. Anderson. *What Is Marriage?* New York: Encounter Books, 2012.

Goldberg, Jonah. *Liberal Fascism: The Secret History of the American Left, From Mussolini to the Politics of Meaning.* New York: Doubleday, 2007.

Gosse, Van. *Rethinking the New Left: An Interpretative History.* New York: Palgrave Macmillan, 2005.

Gross, Neil. *Why Are Professors Liberal and Why Do Conservatives Care?* Cambridge, MA: Harvard University Press, 2013.

Guiora, Amos N. *Tolerating Intolerance: The Price of Protecting Extremism.* New York: Oxford University Press, 2014.

Guizot, François. *History of the Origins of Representative Government in Europe.* Translated by Andrew R. Scoble. London: Henry G. Bohn, 1861.

Hall, Evelyn Beatrice. *The Friends of Voltaire.* London: Smith, Elder & Co., 1906.

Hall, Jamie Bryan. "The Research on Same-Sex Parenting: 'No Differences,' No More." Heritage Foundation *Issue Brief*, no. 4393, April 23, 2015.

Ham, Mary Katharine. *End of Discussion: How the Left's Outrage Industry Shuts Down Debate, Manipulates Voters, and Makes America Less Free (and Fun).* New York: Crown Forum, 2015.

Hartz, Louis. *The Liberal Tradition in America: An Interpretation of American Political Thought Since the Revolution.* Orlando, FL: Harcourt, Inc., 1991.

Haynes, John Earl, Harvey Klehr, and Alexander Vassiliev. *Spies: The Rise and Fall of the KGB in America.* New Haven, CT: Yale University Press, 2009.

Hicks, Stephen R. C. *Explaining Postmodernism: Skepticism and Socialism From Rousseau to Foucault.* Tempe, AZ: Scholargy Publishing, 2004.

Himmelfarb, Gertrude. *The Roads to Modernity: The British, French, and American Enlightenments*. New York: Vintage Books, 2005.

Hobbes, Thomas. *Leviathan*. Harmondsworth, England: Penguin, 1986.

Hofstadter, Richard. *The American Political Tradition and the Men Who Made It*. New York: Vintage, 2011.

———. *Anti-Intellectualism in American Life*. Toronto: Knopf Doubleday Publishing Group, 1966.

———. "The Paranoid Style in American Politics," *Harper's Magazine*, November 1964.

Holmes, Kim R. *Rebound: Getting America Back to Great*. Lanham, MD: Rowman & Littlefield, 2013.

———. "How the United States Government Lost Its Liberalism," *Public Discourse*, Witherspoon Institute, June 19, 2014.

Holmes, Stephen. *The Anatomy of Antiliberalism*. Cambridge, MA: Harvard University Press, 1996.

———. *Passions and Constraint: On the Theory of Liberal Democracy*. Chicago: University of Chicago Press, 1995.

Hong, Fuhai, and Xiaojian Zhao. "Information Manipulation and Climate Agreements." *American Journal of Agricultural Economics* 93, no. 3 (2014): 851–61.

Horkheimer, Max, and Theodor W. Adorno. *Dialectic of Enlightenment: Philosophical Fragments*. Stanford, CA: Stanford University Press, 2002.

Horowitz, David. *The Black Book of the American Left: The Collected Conservative Writings of David Horowitz*. New York: Encounter Books, 2013.

Hume, David. *Enquiries Concerning the Human Understanding and Concerning the Principles of Morals: Reprinted Posthumously From the Edition of 1777*. 2nd ed. Edited by L. A. Selby-Bigge. Oxford: Clarendon Press, 1963.

Hunt, Lester H. *Nietzsche and the Origin of Virtue*. New York: Routledge, 2002.

Inbar, Yoel, and Joris Lammers. "Political Diversity in Social and Personality Psychology." *Perspectives on Psychological Science*, 20, no. 10 (2012): 1.

Intergovernmental Panel on Climate Change. *Climate Change 2014 Synthesis Report*, November 1, 2014.

Israel, Jonathan I. *Enlightenment Contested: Philosophy, Modernity, and the Emancipation of Man, 1670–1752*. Oxford: Oxford University Press, 2006.

Jacoby, Russell. *The Last Intellectuals: American Culture in the Age of Academe*. New York: Basic Books, 2000.

Jameson, Fredric. *Postmodernism, Or, the Cultural Logic of Late Capitalism*. Durham, NC: Duke University Press, 1991.

Jefferson, Thomas. *Jefferson: Writings*. Edited by Merrill D. Peterson. New York: Library of America, 1984.

*Judicial Yellow Book*. New York: Leadership Directories, Inc., Winter 2015.

Kant, Immanuel. *An Answer to the Question: What Is Enlightenment?* Edited by H. S. Reiss. Translated by H. B. Nisbet. New York: Cambridge University Press, 2010.

———. *Critique of Pure Reason*. Translated by Norman Kemp Smith. Unabridged ed. New York: St. Martin's Press, 1965.

———. *Groundwork of the Metaphysics of Morals*. Radford, VA: Wilder Publications, 2008.

———. *On the Metaphysics of Morals and Ethics*. Radford, VA: Wilder Publications, 2008.

———. *Prolegomena to Any Future Metaphysics: and the Letter to Marcus Herz*. Indianapolis, IN: Hackett Publishing, 2001.

Katz, William Loren. *Eyewitness: The Negro in American History*. New York: Pitman Publishing Corp., 1967.

Kazin, Michael. *American Dreamers: How the Left Changed a Nation*. New York: Vintage Books, 2012.

Kelly, Mark G. E. "Foucault Against Marxism: Althusser Beyond Althusser." In *(Mis)readings of Marx in Continental Philosophy*, edited by Jernej Habjan and Jessica Whyte. Basingstoke (UK): Palgrave Macmillan, 2014.

Kerman, Piper. *Orange Is the New Black: My Year in a Women's Prison*. New York: Spiegel and Grau, 2010.

Koch, Stephen. *Double Lives: Spies and Writers in the Secret Soviet War of Ideas Against the West*. New York: Free Press, 1994.

Kok-Chor, Tan. *Toleration, Diversity, and Global Justice*. University Park, PA: Pennsylvania State University Press, 2000.

Kosar, Kevin R. "The Quasi Government: Hybrid Organizations with Both Government and Private Sector Legal Characteristics." Congressional Research Service, *CRS Report for Congress*, no. RL30533, June 22, 2011.

Kotkin, Joel. *The New Class Conflict*. Candor, NY: Telos Press Publishing, 2014.

Kramer, Hilton, and Roger Kimball, eds. *The Betrayal of Liberalism: How the Disciples of Freedom and Equality Helped Foster the Illiberal Politics of Coercion and Control*. Chicago: Ivan R. Dee, 1999.

Kronman, Anthony T. *Education's End: Why Our Colleges and Universities Have Given Up on the Meaning of Life*. New Haven, CT: Yale University Press, 2007.

Kurland, Philip B., and Ralph Lerner. "Popular Basis of Political Authority."

In Philip B. Kurland and Ralph Lerner, eds., *The Founders' Constitution.* Vol. 1. Chicago: University of Chicago Press, 1985.

Kymlicka, Will. *Contemporary Political Philosophy: An Introduction.* Oxford: Clarendon Press, 1990.

———. *Multicultural Citizenship: A Liberal Theory of Minority Rights.* Oxford: Oxford University Press, 1995.

Lawlor, Leonard. "Jacques Derrida." In *The Stanford Encyclopedia of Philosophy,* edited by Edward N. Zalta. Stanford, CA: Metaphysics Research Lab, Spring 2014. http://plato.stanford.edu/archives/spr2014/entries /derrida/.

Levin, Mark. *Plunder and Deceit: Big Government's Exploitation of Young People and the Future.* New York: Simon & Schuster, 2015.

Levine, Lawrence W. *The Opening of the American Mind: Canons, Culture, and History.* Boston: Beacon Press, 1996.

Lewis, Anthony. *Gideon's Trumpet.* New York: Vintage Books, 1964.

Linden, A. A. M. van der. *A Revolt Against Liberalism: American Radical Historians, 1959–1976.* Atlanta, GA: Rodopi, 1996.

Lindgren, James. "Measuring Diversity: Law Faculties in 1997 and 2013." *Northwestern Law & Econ Research Paper,* no. 15-07, March 20, 2015.

Livingston, James. *The World Turned Inside Out: American Thought and Culture at the End of the 20th Century.* Lanham, MD: Rowman & Littlefield, 2010.

Locke, John. *An Essay Concerning Human Understanding.* Edited by Peter H. Nidditch. Oxford: Clarendon Press, 1974.

———. "Letter Concerning Toleration." Translated by William Popple 1689. Constitution Society.org. http://www.constitution.org/jl /tolerati.htm.

———. *Second Treatise of Government.* Indianapolis, IN: Hackett Publishing Company, 1980.

———. *Two Treatises of Government.* London: Everyman Paperback, 1993.

Londregan, John. "Same-Sex Parenting: Unpacking the Social Science." Witherspoon Institute, February 24, 2015.

Lukes, Steven. *Individualism.* Colchester: European Consortium for Political Research Press, 1973.

Lukianoff, Greg. *Freedom From Speech.* New York: Encounter Books, 2014.

———. *Unlearning Liberty: Campus Censorship and the End of American Debate.* New York: Encounter Books, 2012.

Lynd, Staughton. *Intellectual Origins of American Radicalism.* Cambridge: Cambridge University Press, 2009.

Lyotard, Jean-François. *The Postmodern Condition: A Report on Knowledge.* Translated by Geoffrey Bennington and Brian Massumi. Minneapolis,

MN: University of Minnesota Press, 1984. First published by Minuit, Paris, 1979.

Mac Donald, Heather. "The Microaggression Farce." *City Journal*, Autumn 2014.

MacKinnon, Catharine A. *Only Words*. Cambridge, MA: Harvard University Press, 1993.

MacKinnon, Catharine A., and Andrea Dworkin, eds. *In Harm's Way: The Pornography Civil Rights Hearings*. Cambridge, MA: Harvard University Press, 1997.

Malcolm, John. "Defining the Problem and Scope of Over-criminalization and Over-federalization." Heritage Foundation *Congressional Testimony*, June 14, 2013.

Manent, Pierre. *An Intellectual History of Liberalism*. Reprint ed. Princeton, NJ: Princeton University Press, 1996.

Marcuse, Herbert. *Eros and Civilization: A Philosophical Inquiry Into Freud*. New Ed ed. Boston: Beacon Press, 1974.

Marsden, George M. *The Twilight of the American Enlightenment: The 1950s and the Crisis of Liberal Belief*. New York: Basic Books, 2014.

Matusow, Allen J. *The Unraveling of America: A History of Liberalism in the 1960s*. Athens, GA: University of Georgia Press, 2009.

Mill, John Stuart. *On Liberty*. Edited by Alburey Castell. Northbrook, IL: AHM Publishing Corporation, 1947.

Mulloy, D. J. *American Extremism: History, Politics and the Militia Movement*. New York: Routledge, 2008.

Murray, Charles A. *By the People: Rebuilding Liberty Without Permission*. New York: Crown Forum, 2015.

————. *Coming Apart: The State of White America, 1960–2010*. New York: Crown Forum, 2012.

National Science Foundation. "Budget Internet Information Systems: Award Summary: By Top Institutions." http://dellweb.bfa.nst.gov/Top50Inst2/default.asp.

————. National Center for Science and Engineering Statistics. Higher Education Research and Development Surveys, various tables online, as cited.

Nock, Albert Jay. *The Myth of a Guilty Nation*. Auburn, AL: Ludwig von Mises Institute, 2011.

Novack, George. "American Intellectuals and the Crisis." *New International*, February 1936 and June 1936.

Novak, Michael. *The Universal Hunger for Liberty: Why the Clash of Civilizations Is Not Inevitable*. New York: Basic Books, 2004.

Nozick, Robert. *Anarchy, State, and Utopia*. New York: Basic Books, 2013.

Nussbaum, Martha C. "The Future of Feminist Liberalism." *Proceedings and Addresses of the American Philosophical Association*, November 2000.

———. *The New Religious Intolerance: Overcoming the Politics of Fear in an Anxious Age*. Cambridge, MA: Belknap Press, 2013.

Oberg, Barbara B., ed. *The Papers of Thomas Jefferson*. Vol. 32. Princeton, NJ: Princeton University Press, 2005.

Okin, Susan M. *Justice, Gender, and the Family*. New York: Basic Books, 1989.

Ortega y Gasset, Jose. *The Revolt of the Masses*. New York: W. W. Norton & Company, 1960.

Pagden, Anthony. *The Enlightenment: And Why It Still Matters*. New York: Random House, 2013.

Pew Research Center. "America's Changing Religious Landscape." *Report*, May 12, 2015. http://www.pewforum.org/2015/05/12/americas -changing-religious-landscape/.

———. "Beyond Distrust: How Americans View Their Government." *U.S. Politics & Policy*. November 23, 2015. http://www.people-press .org/2014/11/13/public-trust-in-government/.

———. "How Journalists See Journalists in 2004." *State of the News Media*. March 15, 2004. http://www.people-press.org/2004/05/23/iv-values -and-the-press/.

———. "Young Voters Supported Obama Less, But May Have Mattered More." *U.S. Politics & Policy*, November 26, 2012. http://www.people -press.org/2012/11/26/young-voters-supported-obama-less-but-may -have-mattered-more.

Powers, Kirsten. *The Silencing: How the Left Is Killing Free Speech*. Washington, DC: Regnery Publishing, 2015.

Putnam, Robert D. *Bowling Alone: The Collapse and Revival of American Community*. New York: Simon & Schuster, 2000.

Rawls, John. *A Theory of Justice*. Oxford: Clarendon Press, 1971.

Read, Jason. Review of *Marx Through Post-Structuralism: Lyotard, Derrida, Foucault, Deleuze*, by Simon Choat. *Notre Dame Philosophical Reviews: An Electronic Journal*, November 5, 2010.

Reed, Lawrence W., ed. *Excuse Me, Professor: Challenging the Myths of Progressivism*. Washington, DC: Regnery Publishing, 2015.

Reich, Robert B. *The Work of Nations: Preparing Ourselves for 21st-Century Capitalism*. New York: Alfred A. Knopf, 1991.

Reidy, David A. "John Rawls." *IVR Encyclopedia* (March 10, 2008): 30–31. http://ssrn.com/abstract=1069953.

Rhodes, Henry A. "Nativist and Racist Movements in the U.S. and Their Aftermath." In *Racism and Nativism in American Political Culture*. Yale-New Haven Teachers' Institute Curriculum Unit 94.04.05, IV (1994).

Ricci, David M. *The Tragedy of Political Science: Politics, Scholarship, and Democracy*. New Haven, CT: Yale University Press, 1984.

Rockwell, Llewellyn H., Jr. *Against the State: An AnarchoCapitalist Manifesto*. Auburn, AL: LewRockwell.com, 2014.

Ronson, Jon. *So You've Been Publicly Shamed*. New York: Riverhead Books, 2015.

Rorty, Richard. *Contingency, Irony, and Solidarity*. Cambridge: Cambridge University Press, 1989.

———. *Philosophy and the Mirror of Nature*. Princeton, NJ: Princeton University Press, 1979.

Rossiter, Clinton, ed. *The Federalist Papers*. New York: New American Library, 1961.

Rothbard, Murray N. *The Betrayal of the American Right*. Edited by Thomas E. Woods. Auburn, AL: Ludwig von Mises Institute, 2007.

Rudolph, Frederick. *The American College and University: A History*. Athens, GA: University of Georgia Press, 1990.

Ryan, Alan. *The Making of Modern Liberalism*. Princeton, NJ: Princeton University Press, 2012.

Sandel, Michael J. *Liberalism and the Limits of Justice*. Cambridge: Cambridge University Press, 1982.

Sanger, Margaret. *Woman and the New Race*. New York: Brentano, 1920.

Scruton, Roger. *Fools, Frauds, and Firebrands: Thinkers of the New Left*. London: Bloomsbury Continuum, 2015.

Sekulow, Jay. *Undemocratic: How Unelected, Unaccountable Bureaucrats Are Stealing Your Liberty and Freedom*. New York: Howard Books, 2015.

Sen, Amartya. *The Idea of Justice*. Cambridge, MA: Belknap Press, 2009.

Shone, Steve J. *American Anarchism*. Chicago: Haymarket Books, 2014.

Siegel, Frederick F. *The Revolt Against the Masses: How Liberalism Has Undermined the Middle Class*. New York: Encounter Books, 2013.

Skinner, Quentin, ed. *The Return of Grand Theory in the Human Sciences*. New York: Cambridge University Press, 1985.

Slattery, Elizabeth H., and Andrew Kloster. "An Executive Unbound: The Obama Administration's Unilateral Actions." Heritage Foundation *Legal Memorandum*, no. 108, February 12, 2014.

Sokal, Alan D., and Jean Bricmont. *Fashionable Nonsense: Postmodern Intellectuals' Abuse of Science*. New York: Picador USA, 1998.

Sorin, Gerald. *Irving Howe: A Life of Passionate Dissent*. New York: New York University Press, 2005.

Spalding, Matthew, ed. *The Heritage Guide to the Constitution*. 2nd ed. Washington, DC: Regnery Publishing, 2014.

Stern, Fritz Richard. *The Failure of Illiberalism: Essays on the Political Culture of Modern Germany*. New York: Columbia University Press, 1992.

Strauss, Leo. *Liberalism Ancient and Modern*. Chicago: University of Chicago Press, 1995.

———. *Natural Right and History*. Chicago: University of Chicago Press, 1999.

———. *On Tyranny*. New York: Free Press, 1991.

———. "Political Philosophy and the Crisis of Our Time." In *The Post-Behavioral Era*, edited by George Graham and George Carey. New York: David McKay, 1972.

———. "Relativism." In *Relativism and the Study of Man*, edited by Helmut Schoeck and James W. Wiggins. Princeton, NJ: Van Nostrand, 1961.

Strauss, Leo, and Joseph Cropsey. *The History of Political Philosophy*. Chicago: University of Chicago Press, 2012.

Stuurman, Siep. *François Poulain de la Barre and the Invention of Modern Equality*. Cambridge, MA: Harvard University Press, 2004.

Sue, Derald W. *Microaggressions in Everyday Life: Race, Gender, and Sexual Orientation*. Hoboken, NJ: Wiley, 2010.

Sunstein, Cass R. *Law and Happiness*. Chicago: University of Chicago Press, 2010.

Suroweicki, James. *The Wisdom of Crowds: Why the Many Are Smarter Than the Few and How Collective Wisdom Shapes Business, Economies, Societies and Nations*. Boston: Little, Brown, 2004.

Talman, J. L. *The Origins of Totalitarian Democracy*. New York: W.W. Norton & Company Inc., 1970.

Tobin, Gary A., Aryeh Kaufmann Weinberg, and Jenna Ferer. *The Uncivil University: Intolerance on College Campuses*. Revised ed. Lanham, MD: Lexington Books, 2009.

Tocqueville, Alexis de. *Democracy in America*. New York: Alfred A. Knopf, 1945.

Tyson, Lois. *Critical Theory Today: A User-Friendly Guide*. New York: Routledge, 2006.

Urofsky, Melvin I., and Paul Finkelman. "Abrams v. United States (1919)." In *Documents of American Constitutional and Legal History*. 3rd ed. New York: Oxford University Press, 2008.

U.S. Department of Commerce, National Telecommunications & Information Administration. "The Role of Telecommunications in Hate Crimes," *Report to Congress*, December 1993.

U.S. Government Accountability Office. "Federally Funded Research Centers: Agency Reviews of Employee Compensation and Center Performance." *Report*. GAO-14-593, August 11, 2014.

U.S. House of Representatives. Committee on Oversight and Government Reform. "Follow the Money: ACORN, SEIU, and Their Political Allies." *Staff Report*, 111th Cong., 2nd Sess., February 18, 2010.

———. House Committee on Un-American Activities. "The Communist 'Peace' Offensive: A Campaign to Disarm and Defeat the United States." *House Report*, 51st Cong., 1st Sess., April 1, 1951.

Vaughan, Leslie J. *Randolph Bourne and the Politics of Cultural Radicalism.* Lawrence, KS: University Press of Kansas, 1997.

Vujadinovic, Dragica. "Ronald Dworkin–Theory of Justice." *European Scientific Journal* 8, no. 2 (February 2012): 7–8.

Waldron, Jeremy. *The Harm in Hate Speech*. Cambridge, MA: Harvard University Press, 2012.

Walzer, Michael. *Spheres of Justice: A Defense of Pluralism and Equality.* New York: Basic Books, 1983.

Williams, Walter E. *American Contempt for Liberty*. Stanford, CA: Hoover Institution Press, 2015.

Windschuttle, Keith. *The Killing of History: How Literary Critics and Social Theorists Are Murdering Our Past*. New York: Encounter Books, 2000.

Zakaria, Fareed. "The Rise of Illiberal Democracies." *Foreign Affairs*, November/December 1997.

Zalta, Edward N., ed. *The Stanford Encyclopedia of Philosophy*. Stanford, CA: Metaphysics Research Lab, Spring 2014.

# INDEX